THE RISE AND FALL OF THE ANCIENT WORLDS

THE RISE AND FALL

OF THE ANCIENT WORLDS

Herbert Wender

Philosophical Library
New York

Copyright, 1976, by Philosophical Library, Inc.,
15 East 40 Street, New York, N. Y. 10016
All rights reserved

Library of Congress Catalog Card No. 75-39330
SBN 8022-2178-5

Manufactured in the United States of America

To
My Wife
Sybil

"Worlds on worlds are rolling ever
  From creation to decay
Like the bubbles on a river
  Sparkling, bursting, borne away."

Sir Walter Scott

CONTENTS

CHAPTER		PAGE
I	Prehistoric Man	1
II	Egypt—The Land of the Nile	9
III	Mesopotamians—The People of the Two Rivers	22
IV	Phoenicians, Hebrews, Persians, et al.	37
V	The Civilization of India	57
VI	The Chinese—Their Notable Achievements	77
VII	The Greeks	107
	1. Their Political History	107
	2. Their Customs and their Cultural Contributions	130
VIII	The Roman World	172
	1. From its Beginning to its Pinnacle	172
	2. Pax Romana and Prosperity	199
	3. Roman Culture from its Prime to its Decline	209
	4. Religious Faith Replaces Decadent Imperial Power	243
Bibliography		287
Index		291

PREFACE

This is a brief but comprehensive account of ancient history which the author hopes can be used as the first volume in college survey courses on the development of civilization; and owing to the book's many facts of human interest and amusing anecdotes it may also have a popular appeal to the general reader.

Each chapter contains descriptions of the ancient political, economic, social, religious, intellectual and artistic customs and institutions. There is an account of every important nation's contribution to civilization.

In relating the numerous events and achievements of the peoples that flourished in antiquity I always had in mind the temper and comfort of the reader, and so wherever possible preferred the piquant to the vapid and the racy to the pedestrian facts in the style and manner of narration.

H.W.

THE RISE AND FALL OF THE ANCIENT WORLDS

CHAPTER I

Prehistoric Man

About two million years ago human beings looked and lived like their cousin, the ape. But man was destined to have a more interesting and complex career in this world than that of his wild, simian relative who was just another animal. Man would become a superanimal, the supreme primate and finally, a sport or mutant—the progenitor of a new species. So he left home, which was the trees, where he had been living for a long time and where he had learned to use his front limbs to swing from the branches and to grope and scratch and throw. This momentous step may have have been a random or fortuitous move or it may have been a necessary ploy in the struggle for existence; it was the genesis or the creation of man. On the ground he began to stand in an upright position and to walk on two feet, which freed his hands with the opposable thumb, enabling him to use tools and weapons and protect his head. Manual dexterity stimulated the brain while the protection of the head allowed the brain to grow, to improve its function of memory and to become more imaginative and ingenious. A unique voice box enabled man to talk and this combined with his natural propensity to imitate and with an excellent memory, made it possible to accumulate and transmit knowledge to his fellow men and his progeny. Thus over a period of many thousands of years man evolved from the beast to the savage, to the barbarian, always impelled by the instinct of self-preservation—prevail or perish.

In the earliest stage of human culture, the eolithic, the basic needs of man—food and sex—were provided by nature freely and indiscriminately. The economy was collectional; i.e., people would eat what they could find—fruits, nuts, roots, eggs and small animals.

There was no industry, no invention because all tools or sticks and stones were discovered and were not man-made. Men lived and moved about in rude packs or small herds; mating was spontaneous and informal, since marriage as an institution was yet unknown.

During the Stone Age man's intelligence continued to grow and develop. In handling and playing with the tools he invented ways of improving on nature's implements and weapons. He would scrape, shape, chip, sharpen, and polish the stones, or put handles on them, or employ any artificial device to render them more effective in hunting, fishing and fighting. He began to make and use fire, to domesticate plants and animals, to spin and weave cloth, make pottery out of clay, construct huts or dwellings, and to travel by boat, and later by wheeled cart.

It was early in the Stone Age that simple, rudimentary religious beliefs appeared and then men learned how to draw and paint pictures. Tribes and clans were organized during the hunting stage while the family seems to have been established with the coming of agriculture. All these innovations and steps toward civilization evolved over a very long period of time; the Stone Age lasted more than a half million years.

Unlike the animals, early man became aware of his environment and manifested a reverential fear for the forces and phenomena of nature, but he could not understand or explain what he observed. There was something mysterious about them; they must therefore be controlled by supernatural powers. Today science can give us fairly convincing explanations for light and darkness, storms and floods, birth, growth, and death, but in those days of man's childhood and innocence natural happenings excited fear, wonder, and curiosity and a belief that awesome spirits rule the world. What they feared they revered. Religion thus began.

Most people no doubt were as contented as the cows they had tamed so long as they had simple food and good health, but when food became scarce or hard to obtain and when storms, earthquakes, drought, sickness, plagues, and wars decimated the population they would become perplexed and mystified. And if they could not help themselves they would implore the aid of the world governnent; i.e., the almighty spirits of the universe. They begged the gods to please drive away the evil cause of their misery and restore health and prosperity. The petitioners gladly paid the gods in advance for these expected favors. They offered as gifts some of their best animals, tools or weapons, and if that was not adequate they would even sacrifice human beings in order to propitiate the gods and bring an end to their adversities and disasters. Prayers and sacrifices were accompanied by ritual and ceremonies. For fear that the gods might not understand their words alone the petitioners sometimes would act out in pantomime the objective they requested. For example, if they had been suffering from a long drought they would simulate the falling of rain on their crops or go into the fields with open umbrellas.

To promote fertility of the soil primitives have been known to resort to quaint suggestive magic. For example, peasants and their wives would copulate publicly in a rice field to influence the gods of vegetation, and in Africa a shaman removed the genitals from the dead body of a virile young man, cooked them, ground them into a powder and then sprinkled them over the planted seeds. If it were more meat and hides they wanted, a congregation of herdsmen or hunters would dress themselves in animal skins and imitate the habits and activities of the cows, bears and wolves.

Since the spirits controlled all the forces of nature it behooved man to be in the good graces of the supernatural. Communications between the people and the deities were generally conveyed by adroit middle men who were conversant with the nature and character of the divinities. These officials came to be known as priests and were often the elite in their societies because of their superior intelligence and expertise in spirituality and the occult. They devised the magic formulas and incantations that were indispensable in effecting a rapport between men and the gods.

In the beginning men were animists believing that all nature was alive, that every object was possessed of a ghost or spirit either good or evil. In time these spirits became anthropomorphic, that is, they were personified; they assumed human form and attributes, they would walk over the earth, talk to people and could be both benevolent and malicious. The number of deities increased as the people's interests increased and the kind of gods they created varied with environment, experience, occupations and concerns. Eventually the number of gods became overwhelming and the priests were forced to break them down, organize and arrange them in categories with major and minor deities in each class. During the hunting stage the moon was regarded as the lord of the sky but when farming became man's leading occupation the sun god and the earth mother became more important than the moon, In early Egypt, when agriculture and the flooding of the Nile were basic and vital they sought the good graces of the god of the Nile by throwing a beautiful virgin into the River once a year. Through this annual sacrifice, the people hoped to bring fertility to the soil and prosperity to the nation.

Prehistoric man believed in some sort of immortality—that when a person dies his soul separates from the body and survives. These spirits could curse, destroy and ruin people and property if they were not propitiated. A chieftain once instructed his slave to take a verbal message to one of these departed souls and then to expedite its delivery he cut off the slave's head. Rapid transit to the hereafter and prompt communication with the dead was thus available to anyone who possessed slaves and political power.

Women were natural nurses and the first healers of the sick in history. And being the first farmers and therefore most familiar with plant life, they tried to cure the invalid by administering concoctions of all sorts of herbs and roots. These female family doctors could drive away minor demons and thus cure the patients in some cases but when the demon was more formidable and stubborn they had to summon the shaman, a highly trained medicine man who employed magic and incantations to expel the malevolent spirit which had entered the patient's body. Wearing an animal skin and a terrifying mask he would endeavor to scare off the demon by grimaces, strange howls, noises, dances, clapping his hands, biting, pinching, kicking or sipping the tormentive spirit through a straw. They might also resort to fumigation, voodooism or appeasement to rid the body of the diabolical spirit. If during the exorcism the soul rather than the demon departed from the body and the patient died, the shaman would try to blow the soul back through the mouth, the ear or the anus. Among some tribes when a child became ill the father rather than the patient was given the medicine or treatment and the child generally recovered.

Primitive man liked to watch fires that occasionally were started by lightning, volcanic eruptions and by friction of wood or stone. The burning, colorful flame fascinated but it also frightened him and so he began to worship the marvelous spirits or the god of fire, and then some dexterous individual invented a method of making fire artificially by rubbing dry sticks together and before long they learned how to keep it going and to relight it. Now they could conquer the dark, keep away marauding beasts, warm themselves, bake pottery, cook their food, and later fuse and refine metals.

Clothing too was introduced in the Stone Age to serve the purpose of protection and adornment. In the cold climates as they began to lose their old shaggy coat of hair, furs and wool would keep men warm and in the temperate and torrid zones only the most sensitive parts of the body were covered. The genitals and sometimes the breasts of females could thus be protected when people walked through the jungles, the brush and the brambles. Possibly the astute priestly law makers perceived that by covering the sex organs they could deter immoderate attention, reduce copulation, and thus excessive procreation; or perhaps a fig leaf might induce a greater regard for one of life's hidden mysteries.

Cannibalism has been practiced at one time or another among all primitive nations. In some parts of the world human meat was bought and sold as articles of food and sometimes the victims, preferably females, were fattened like pigs, to inflate their value in the butcher shops. These precious human carcasses, considered to be exceptionally delectable, were then served to important guests at elaborate banquets. The savage custom of slaughtering and eating human beings may have arisen either when there was a dearth of meat or a plethora of people. The problem of overpopulation was sometimes mitigated by infanticide or by the consumption of surplus infants. Human blood was also considered a delicacy and was imbibed with meat or vegetables, as a kind of sauce, and sometimes it was drunk as a medicine or at religious rites, since it was thought to possess spiritual efficacy. Horses were eaten when first domesticated but like criminals and prisoners of war they were later found to be more suitable and beneficial as beasts of burden than as victuals.

Primitive art was realistic and was generally actuated by religious and utilitarian interests—to promote economic prosperity by pictorial prayer. Depicting wounded deer and buffalo was intended to apprise the gods of the people's wants—a successful hunt, plenty of meat, hide and bone. A colorful painting of just animals without the hunter's weapons may have been a cunning artifice to entice live, edible animals to the scene. Primitive art not only displayed technical skill but possessed some aesthetic sense as exemplified by the fine carvings, engravings and decorations on tools, weapons and ornaments. Early man was concerned about the beauty of pottery, statuary, graves, and he created music, song and dance, and both men and women painted their faces and bodies to enhance their charm.

A very basic prehistoric unit was the family, a social institution that served the purposes of care and education of the young, provided for the division of labor, and met other vital needs. The human infant required several years of a mother's care and protection and sufficient schooling to absorb the traditional customs and beliefs. Another reason for the rise of the family was biological. Among most of the lower animals the female craves a mate only at particular periods but the human female desires to be loved at all seasons of the year and therefore a more durable mating arrangement was necessary. Marriage probably became most popular in the New or High Stone Age when agriculture was introduced, when a number of plants and animals became domesticated and many men and women found that they could obtain so much more food and other necessaries if they added farming to their customary economic pursuits. They now ceased roaming around so much, and settled down on the land.

But the introduction of agriculture brought many new tasks and occupations which necessitated a new social organization and a division of labor between the sexes. A man would therefore make an agreement with his prospective spouse. He was to continue to engage in the old, more heroic and savage enterprises of hunting, fishing and fighting, which required him to go away for a while. The woman, on the other hand, would be obliged to do most of the homework, that is, plant the seeds, till the soil, harvest the crops, look after the children, and the flocks and herds, make pottery, cook and clean, make the clothing, keep the house in repair, and attend to a few other domestic chores. In return, as compensation, he promised to be her husband and protect her and their family, to bring home the bacon and keep the wolf from the door. Under this patriarchal system, the wives promised complete fidelity but the husband might enjoy unbridled promiscuity.

A wife thus became a profitable slave, an indispensable domestic servant, and her primary function in life was to produce and rear offspring. Since the husband adopted a proprietary attitude toward his spouse adultery became a capital crime, akin to stealing. He also wanted to make certain that his land and animals would be inherited by his own legitimate children and so extra-marital intimacies by his wife, which might lead to illicit childbirth, were forbidden. Divorce too was uncommon for it meant the loss of serviceable wealth and productive capital.

Monogamy was the prevailing type of marriage in prehistoric times, but when the number of females became excessive, as often happened, a man might add a few concubines to his household. An overworked spouse sometimes helped her husband procure one or more additional wives in order to lighten her burden. This would lessen her chores, augment the supply of labor and increase the wealth of the family. Polygamy would also obviate the need for adultery, wife swapping and other sexual irregularities.

Greater skill in methods of production resulted in the accumulation of an economic surplus which in turn led to trade or bartering and the emergence of individual differences and class distinction among the members of society. Before the advent of agriculture land and animals belonged to nobody, though weapons, boats and tools were probably the property of a clan or group of kinsmen. However, with the growth of an agrarian society individual enterprising farmers began to take possession of plots of fertile land as well as flocks and herds of animals, and thus there was introduced the concept of private property. As the demand for labor increased, especially on the farms, the employment of slaves was started, thus relieving the women and children who had been bearing the burden of much of this arduous work. Prisoners of war had been customarily butchered and eaten or just slaughtered and discarded but with the need for more labor on the farms it became more profitable to enslave the captured enemy warriors. Thus cannibalism declined and the supply of farm products increased as a result of the spread of the practice of slavery. Defaulting debtors and incurable criminals were also enslaved in many places. The introduction of forced labor was then considered social and economic progress.

Distinct classes now came into existence, namely, priests, nobles, farmers, artisans and slaves. The most capable and intelligent, that is, the priests and nobles, rose to the top and became masters of the group. During the hunting stage strong men and great hunters had generally been the chieftains, though the priests were also very influential, but as farming became the most prevalent occupation, the priests took over completely because of their reputed supernatural power over the flocks and fields. It was about this time too that groups and tribes began to engage in organized warfare, fighting as nations do today, for wealth, power and prestige.

After a successful war the chieftain generally became the head of a government to protect the individual, the family, the clan and the tribe or tribes. He could maintain his power with an armed force or he could have the priests announce his descent from one of the important gods, usually the sun god. That would fortify his position and assure him of the people's loyalty and devotion.

About 6000 years ago in some parts of the world metal began to replace stone as the basic substance from which implements were produced. The first metal found to be useful was copper, then tin was added to the copper and so bronze became most prevalent. By 1500 B.C. iron was discovered to be harder and more durable than bronze and it has been the basic metal ever since. Finally, some clever fellows invented a way of writing and we thus entered the age of literate history when men began to leave written records of what they did, said and thought. Writing helps people's memory enormously and so their descendants can profit from past experience and thereby gain more knowledge and wisdom. This was the beginning of the road to greater progress and civilization. At first ideas were conveyed in writing by signs or pictograms but eventually this was supplanted by the alphabet or characters representing sounds. The discovery of metal and the invention of writing became prerequisites for the advancement of the human race from barbarism to civilization.

CHAPTER II

Egypt—The Land of the Nile

The first peoples to advance from barbarism to civilization were the Egyptians in northeast Africa and the Sumerians who lived in the southwestern part of Asia in the little country called Iraq today. About 6000 years ago these people learned how to make their tools, weapons and implements out of metal, which was superior to stone, bone and wood; they learned how to write and record their experiences, and they began to live in cities rather than in small rural villages. Other cultural innovations that helped them emerge from barbarism were the concept of time, resulting in the invention of the calendar, and the development of the arts of irrigation and navigation. The rest of the world remained illiterate and unenlightened.

Why did civilization begin where it did and not elsewhere? It was because nature scatters its favors indiscriminately over the world and some areas are more fortunate than others. Egypt and Sumeria were provided with the indispensable requirements for cultural growth—a great amount of environmental advantage and a large number of talented individuals. Environmental advantages included a favorable geographic location, desirable topographic features, necessary natural resources, a temperate climate and fertile soil; but equally important was an ample supply of persons who were intelligent, curious, imaginative, inventive and educated.

Today Egypt is an attractive place to visit because of its antiquity but in ancient times it was an excellent place to live in because it had such an abundance of food and the people could thrive and be happy. Prosperity depended on the behavior of the Nile River, which comes down from the hills of Ethiopia and overflows its banks at the beginning of the summer. For four months it floods the Egyptian valley basin and then subsides—returning slowly to the normal level by the end of the year. When the water recedes it leaves behind deposits of rich black silt containing valuable chemicals that enables the soil to produce three crops of food a year. Since most of Egypt gets very little rainfall it has been imperative to build reservoirs in order to save some of this most precious commodity for dry rainless days and to construct an elaborate system of irrigation, with trenches and canals to carry the water to all parts of the land. The beneficent River also served as a convenient highway for trade and travel, and so they correctly called Egypt the Land of the Nile. A healthful climate too, was a factor in fostering energy and enterprise. In the winter the weather was moderate and in the summer, even though it might get extremely hot, the air was always dry and the nights were always cool.

Nature also provided the people with the required raw material to make clothing and shelter, the need for which, thanks to the climate, was not very great. Flax was skillfully woven into linen and was almost universally used for wearing apparel. There was an abundance of clay and stone but hardly any wood suitable for building purposes, so their humble homes were made out of mud, brick and reeds of which they had a plentiful amount. The wealthy used stone and brick and lived in splendid mansions and villas.

The Egyptians belonged to the Mediterranean Hamitic-speaking branch of the white race; they had short bodies and long heads, slightly aquiline noses, and straight black hair; their skin was white at birth but after exposure to the sun it turned to a reddish brown. There were foreign strains, particularly that of the Semites who moved in from Western Asia and that of the Negroes who came up from the south, but both minorities were in due time culturally and biologically absorbed by the more numerous Egyptians.

The basic economic activity was farming and the chief agricultural products were wheat, barley, vegetables, dates, olives, flax, cotton, and the papyrus reed, from which a kind of paper was made. They raised most of the common animals—cows, sheep, goats, pigs, ducks, geese and chickens. Horses were used mostly in the army and oxen and donkeys were generally the beasts of burden. Farmland belonged to the king, priests, and nobles while the mass of the people who toiled in the fields were regimented and exploited ruthlessly by their masters. The employers hired club-carrying supervisors to induce diligence. At times the government allowed the peasants to gain possession of a little land and become independent farmers but during most of Egyptian history the rural laborer worked for the landlords, the aristocrats.

The Egyptians displayed a high degree of technical skill and craftsmanship, producing articles of excellent quality, such as pottery, glass, textiles, metal objects, vases, jewelry and furniture. They built many boats and ships and conducted considerable commerce with neighboring Africans and west Asians and the islands of the eastern Mediterranean. As early as 2000 B.C., they built a Suez Canal, though it later fell into disuse and became filled with sand.

Trade was carried on mostly by barter though there is evidence to show that for larger transactions they sometimes used gold and silver rings as money. Egyptian merchants were familiar with bookkeeping and accounting, orders, receipts, contracts and wills. They had regular postal service though roads were few and bad. They imported raw materials, exported finished products and sometimes set up high tariffs to protect their industries.

All phases of economic life were generally controlled and regulated by the state. In crises and wartime, during the imperial period, especially industry, commerce and agriculture were nationalized. All forms of production were directed by royal officials and the state could conscript workers to serve in war industries, and during peace time on the great engineering projects undertaken by the government. Collectivism prevailed.

Social differentiation was based on occupation and economic status. There were seven classes. Highest in rank, of course, was the royal family, then came the priests, the nobles, the soldiers, the middle class including scribes, merchants, artisans, and farmers, then the serfs, and finally the slaves. It was possible to pass from one class to another, and social prestige based on occupation, varied from time to time in Egyptian history. Artisans, for example, were mostly members of the free middle class but they usually worked in the shops that belonged to the king, the temples and the nobles and economically were not much better off than the peasants. However, some craftsmen occasionally could undertake manufacturing or trading and if successful would lift themselves into a higher rank.

In Egypt, as elsewhere, families related to one another formed clans and lived in small villages, and after a while the villages would unite into larger units that were based on territorial rather than kinship grouping. Gradually through this process of consolidation there evolved the Egyptian state sometime before 4000 B.C. It comprised all Egyptians and a few non-nationals too. Although some physical force was necessary, the chief inducement for union was the urgent need for agricultural and commercial group cooperation.

At the head of the government was a king, referred to as the Pharaoh. The people were taught to believe that their ruler was the offspring of an earthly mother and a spiritual father—Ra, the sun god. Being an incarnation of divinity, he could make no mistake and his power was unlimited. He was high priest and head of the state, religious leader, commander of the military, chief justice, and the executive of the administration of the various branches of the government. Of course, these powers were nearly all delegated to numerous officials, the most important of whom was the vizier or prime minister. Agriculture, industry and commerce were strictly regulated by the state, for all land, wealth, and people belonged to the Pharaoh and were at his disposal.

Omnipotence of the monarch did not always prevail, for at times the provincial governors would revive decentralization and occasionally the royal officials would reduce the Pharaoh's sovereignty. Internal dissension would sometimes weaken the kingdom and this would be followed by invasions. At one time they were attacked by their kinsmen, the Lybians, and by the Nubian Negroes from the south— ancestors of the modern Sudanese. Most of the invaders were forced back, though many were absorbed by the Egyptians. The Pharaoh's army then conquered Nubia, made it a dependency, and set up forts on the Nile to prevent the immigration of the black colonials. During the period from July to November when most of the land was flooded and the water of the Nile was high, farming was impossible and navigation was made easy and so the Egyptians would engage in predatory activity. Their military would call on their neighbors for an unfriendly visit, returning with cargoes of valuables, booty and slaves.

Peace, prosperity and good government lasted for a few hundred years and then came times of trouble. Nobles began seeking power, then the masses flared up in revolt resulting in confusion, anarchy and the establishment of feudalism. Then came invasion again. In about 1750 B.C. a Semitic-speaking, militaristic people, called Hyksos, moved in from the east. Using new effective methods of fighting with horses and chariots they defeated the Egyptians, then plundered and exploited the people. After a few years, however, the Hyksos adopted the culture of the vanquished, while the Egyptians learned much about the science of war from their conquerors. A highly improved military machine was developed and under the leadership of Ahmose I they carried on a patriotic war of liberation, and around 1600 B.C. overthrew the foreign despots and regained their independence.

The Egyptians now became imperialistic themselves, expanding to the south and east. Then like modern powers, they saw the need to protect their gains and defend their new empire against envious and aggressive rivals and so they established military outposts and buffer states. It was also considered more profitable and more convenient to own the valuable metals and other commodities they had to buy from their neighbors. During the reign of Thutmose III in the 15th century B.C., the Egyptians conquered Syria, Phoenicia and Palestine. Material prosperity was at its height and boasting of a powerful army and navy, they did a thriving foreign commerce in gold, ivory, ebony, black slaves and ostrich feathers.

The Egyptian empire flourished until the middle of the 12th century B.C., then it collapsed. Thereafter, Egypt was subjugated again and again by various foreign armies and was ruled by a long line of aliens—Libyans, Sudanese, Assyrians, Persians, Greeks, Romans, Arabs, Turks, French and British. They had been an independent nation for about 2500 years; they were ruled by foreign conquerors about 3000 years. Not until 1923 did the Egyptians finally regain their freedom. By this time they were probably somewhat of an ethnic admixture.

The people of civilized Egypt, like their prehistoric ancestors, believed that life was full of mystery and that supernatural or spiritual beings controlled all physical phenomena and all human experiences. Every aspect of life was affected by the gods and so religion was extremely important.

Before Egypt was unified each locality had its own set of gods but with the establishment of the National state more universal divinities, suitable for all, were created. The gods dwelt in sacred abodes in heaven, on earth, in the ocean, sun, moon and stars, but also in the bodies of certain animals, such as the cat, hawk, beetle, jackal, bull, ram, crocodile, and ibis. These were symbols of the deities and thus objects of reverence. When these holy animals died they were embalmed and carefully buried in their own special cemeteries. When a cat died it was customary for all the persons in the house to shave their eyebrows and when a dog died they would shave the entire body, from head to foot. Sometimes beautiful women were offered in coitus to the goat and bull; this was considered an honor. The goat and the bull were especially sacred to Egyptians as symbolic of the sexual creative powers. The bull also was particularly venerated as the incarnation of Osiris, one of the superior national gods.

There were thousands of deities but the most important was Ra, lofty and mighty spirit of the sun, the omnipotent creator and ruler of the universe. His representative in Egypt was the earthly but theocratic Pharaoh whose duty was to promote the welfare of the state. Closer and more familiar with the common people and their mundane problems was Osiris, the god of the Nile, or the god of water. Associated with Osiris was his sister and wife, Isis, the earth goddess who was worshipped with great love and devotion because of her contribution to agriculture. They told of how she, by virtue of a miracle, conceived a divine son, and how the baby was nursed in a stable. He was given the name Horus and was proclaimed God of the Sun and the Son of God. Isis was referred to as the Mother of God.

One day Osiris was brutally murdered by his wicked, diabolical brother Seth, who cut the victim's body into many pieces and scattered them over the land. His saddened widow went out in search of the pieces, found them and reassembled the parts, and brought her divine brother back to life again. Subsequently, when Horus grew up he avenged his father's death by slaying the wicked Seth. Since Osiris had triumphed over death through the love and warmth of Isis and good had prevailed over evil, then it behooved the people to have unbounded faith in this divine trio. His experience in dying and being resurrected had given Osiris the power and faculty to raise everyone from death to life. The Egyptians were very much concerned about life after death and so sought passionately the secret formula for escaping eternal death.

During one of his visits to the nether world Osiris became judge of the dead and he promulgated rules and requirements for the attainment of salvation and immortality. First of all the person's corpse must be preserved and, like Osiris, who was the first mummy, the body must be embalmed and dried and buried in a tomb or grave. The deceased would in due time appear before the judge, who gave the person a soul-testing examination. The applicant would have to testify that he had not committed any of 42 deadly sins, which included murder, treason, blasphemy, stealing, lying, adultery, exploiting the poor or taking milk from a baby.

After delivering himself of the numerous vices that he had shunned he proceeded to recite the many requisite virtuous deeds; such as, giving bread to the hungry, water to the thirsty, clothing to the naked and a boat to ferry someone across the river. After these declarations the candidate for heaven was given an old fashioned lie test whereby his heart was weighed in balance against a feather, the symbol of truth. Osiris would decide the fate of the dead man—whether his soul was to be resurrected to live forever in eternal happiness and heavenly bliss with all the physical delights and pleasures or should remain forever in a dark tomb, perpetually hungry and thirsty and tortured by hideous crocodiles. The Book of the Dead was a collection of prayers, charms, and formulas designed to aid the soul to secure eternal reward. A copy of this valuable scroll was placed in the tomb for the deceased to consult and study in preparation for judgment day when he would appear before Osiris for his ultimate comprehensive examination. The book was written by clever and mercenary priests who guaranteed its efficacy. These godly agents conducted a lucrative business selling this publication as well as sundry superstitious amulets, charms and talismans. And yet the priests did bring comfort, consolation and hope to the sick, the poor, the bereaved and the unhappy. They were a privileged group—exempt from forced labor, military service, and taxation. Rich, intelligent, educated and prestigious, they imparted their learning and skill to their sons and elite youth of the country. To preserve their health and cleanliness the priests were circumcised, they shaved their entire body every three days and washed themselves in cold water every day.

Every person was said to have a double, called the Ka, who survived the death of an individual and would remain in the grave with the corpse so long as he had food and creature comforts. He was therefore provided with ample food, clothing, a lavatory, weapons, salacious stories, and even joke books. In women's graves they left toilet sets, mirrors, combs and cosmetics. Sometimes a man's wives and slaves were also interred in the tomb to serve their master. After a while the women began to find this custom of being buried alive somewhat annoying and discriminatory and so the priests decided to substitute paintings or statuettes for live beings, and during an economic slump pictures of edible objects might be used in place of real food. And when the burial reforms brought no protest from the *ka* the more humane and less extravagant practices were continued.

The desire for immortality and heavenly reward eventually became an obsession with the Egyptians and resulted in a bonanza for the priests. Taking advantage of the people's fear, superstition and gullibility, the cunning priests dispensed with the difficult requirements of good deeds and clear conscience. Thereafter they demanded of candidates for the afterlife only to purchase magical charms, amulets and guide books. Thus by reducing the price of admission to heaven the crafty priests who manufactured and sold all the sacred aids, increased the number of clients and became immensely wealthy and powerful.

As the relationship between religion and morality disappeared the Egyptian empire began to decay, with widespread corruption in the government and fraudulence and venality in the priesthood. In 1375 B.C. a reforming Pharoah, named Ikhnaton, came to power. He was a poet, an idealist, a revolutionary heretic, and an advocate of monotheism. Ikhnation reduced the number of divinities to one, proclaiming Aton as the only god, a universal deity, the creator, righteous, gentle, peaceful, benevolent. This enlightened Pharoah ruled for a few years, but when he died the old time religion was restored—polytheism, idolatry, superstition, and an avaricious priesthood. Faith in and devotion to many gods continued until the Arabs subjugated the Egyptians in the 7th century A.D. and converted them to Mohammedanism.

Architects in ancient Egypt wanted their buildings to symbolize strength, stability, grandeur, and permanence. Preoccupied with religion they had a penchant for tombs and temples. One of the largest structures ever built was the pyramid of Khufu— 481 feet high and 775 feet long at its base. It covers thirteen acres, a solid mass of masonry containing 2,300,000 limestone blocks, each of which weighs about two and a half tons. It took about thirty years and the work of 100,000 men to construct this royal mausoleum. The temples too were gigantic, the famous one at Karnak, 1300 feet long, being one of the largest religious edifices ever constructed. An important feature of the temple was the rows of huge columns, an important Egyptian architectural innovation. Construction workers used flint and copper tools, levers, ropes, ramps and stone rollers.

Sculpturing and painting were supplementary arts—their function being to embellish the tombs and temples which were veritable art museums. The Great Sphinx was put up in front of a pyramid and is a figure of a lion with a human head. It is a colossal statue conveying the impression of the strength and majesty of the Pharaoh. Sculptors made many smaller statues and busts of kings, queens, and other important persons. There were also exquisite carvings, bas-reliefs for wall decorations and on the columns. The statues were also huge—some as high as seventy to ninety feet. They were often colored—the men a reddish brown and the women white or yellow. Most portrait paintings made the figures appear rigid and stereotyped, unemotional, and looking straight ahead. Artists usually depicted the head and legs in profile but shoulders and eyes in front view because it might anger the gods to show an incomplete image of the body, especially of important people. However, pictures of common people were often painted or carved in profile engaged in every day tasks and particularly vivid and realistic was the portrayal of animals. In the minor arts the Egyptians also exhibited great skill and imagination. They worked with metal, wood, glass, terra cotta, alabaster, and semi-precious stones to make elegant amulets, jewelry, figurines, vases, and architectural decorations.

The Egyptians were among the first people to learn how to write and were the first to use a kind of alphabet—single symbols for individual sounds. The ability to write enabled them to accumulate and record knowledge and transmit it to their descendants. At first they cut hieroglyphics on stone, then they introduced a sort of script, using pen and ink to write by hand on papyrus, which was a substance resembling paper. Men who were able to master this difficult art were called scribes and were employed mostly by the government to draw up legal papers and documents, keep records and accounts and perform other civil service jobs requiring literacy. They took the census, examined income tax returns and assisted in the regulation of the nation's economy. Some scribes were talented writers—imaginative, romantic and philosophical. They composed poetry, love songs, hymns, books of devotion, fables, proverbs, ghost stories, and tales of travel and adventure. There were also treatises on medicine and other scientific subjects, as well as philosophical bits in the form of dialogues and wise maxims urging moral idealism.

Education was available to selected sons of the wealthy and middle class. These boys learned how to read and write, were given some instruction in manners and morals and were trained to take over the jobs and offices of the scribes in the Pharaoh's bureaucracy.

Science was important in ancient Egypt only when it was applied in solving economic and technological problems. Egyptians were seldom preoccupied with theoretical ideas and possessed very little intellectual curiosity about scientific law and natural philosophy. A calendar was devised so that the people would know exactly when to cultivate, when to harvest their crops, and the dates of their holy days. This solar calendar, with certain modifications, is still used in the world today. Mathematics was rather highly developed and was extensively utilized in building, surveying, engineering and in commerce. They were familiar with addition, subtraction and division, the decimal system, but they had no symbol for zero and had a little trouble with multiplication and common fractions when the numerator was more than one. They used the abacus, the sun dial, water clock, the inclined plane, they were good mechanics, engineers, and metallurgists, and they made paper and glass. Their mathematicians computed the area of a circle by giving pi the value of 3.16 and measured the area of squares, cubes, and the volume of pyramids, cylinders and hemispheres.

The Egyptians were the founders of the science of medicine, for they were the first to ascribe the cause of disease to physical factors; however, religion and magic usually accompanied its practice. In fact, charms and incantations were often more indispensable than the remedies prescribed. Disease was still popularly regarded as a possession of an evil spirit and the doctor was also a priest. He sought to drive the demon from the body of his patient by petition, by chanting curses, and by magic and solemn ceremonies. The occult, esoteric treatment was followed by a physical prescription, either a cathartic or an emetic. The patient could force the malevolent demon to leave the body either through the oral egress by swallowing repulsive emetics or through the anal egress by taking a strong laxative. Purgatives included olive oil, castor oil, and salts of the various metals, while popular vomit inducers were blood of a bat or lizard, dung of the crocodile, womb of a cat, semen and testicles of a donkey, genitals of a female dog, fly-specks scraped from a wall, moisture from a pig's ear, putrid meat, urine of a chaste woman, and excreta of men and various animals. Enemas and suppositories were used frequently for purges and for contraception.

Egyptians believed that excessive eating often caused disease and so the doctors recommended fasting occasionally and cleansing the alimentary canal every few days. Head surgeons still resorted to the prehistoric practice of boring or scraping a hole in the head to relieve pressure on the brain to ventilate it and give the confined evil spirit an opportunity to escape. General practitioners helped to heal the poor and served as glorified cosmeticians for the affluent. Health conscious, Egyptians collected pure rainwater, disposed of sewage through copper pipes and practiced circumcision of males. Hundreds of medicaments, including salt as a disinfectant were prescribed and people collected as many as their medicine chests could hold. The first doctor was also the first really known historical person. He lived in Egypt around 3000 B.C. and his name was Imhotep—a genius and a sage, the first physician, artist, engineer and architect. He was so versatile and talented that the Egyptians worshiped him as the god of knowledge.

Although there were no policemen and very few soldiers in Egypt, life was safe, property was secure, law and order prevailed. This ideal condition was probably due to the conservative nature of the people and the psychological discipline produced by the Pharaoh's divine prestige. In the courts justice and equality before the law were the pretended ideal and aim but class distinction obtained, litigants were privileged and unprivileged, and Egyptian judges were neither devoid of bias nor immune to influence. Their civil code was fairly developed but criminal laws were not quite so civilized. Torture was practiced to extract information and magic was used to determine the innocence or guilt of an accused person. Frequent punishments were cutting off one's nose, ears, hands, tongue, toiling in the mines, beating with a stick on the soles of the feet or on the buttocks. Among the crimes punishable by death were murder, perjury, stealing from a temple. Extreme penalties included beheading, strangling, impaling, burning at the stake, or converting the living victim into a mummy by dehydration and embalming. A person of high rank convicted of a capital crime was given the option of public execution or suicide.

Women in Egypt generally occupied a favored position—being complete mistresses in the house, enjoying full rights to own and bequeath property, to engage in business, to drink and dine in public, and to walk safely in the city streets. Women, as elsewhere, were considered to exist primarily to be wives and mothers but at least two women became queens who ruled in their own right like female Pharaohs. There was considerable liberty and equality in sexual matters and young ladies would often take the initiative in courtship, address amorous poems and love letters to men, caress them, beg them for dates, and make formal proposals for marriage. Egyptian girls apparently mature very early, for at ten they were considered nubile. Marital relations were generally happy and wholesome, and though divorce was allowable it never became very prevalent. Incest was not considered immoral and was practiced by the Pharaohs, and in the later centuries of Egyptian history by non-royalty as well. By marrying his sister the king or aristocrat would preserve the purity of regal or elite blood and also he would be assured that his property would not be inherited by a stranger or an in-law.

The Egyptian women tried to make themselves as attractive as possible. They used rouge, lipstick, perfume, eye make-up, nail polish, and hair pins; they bobbed their hair or wore wigs. Men shaved their faces but on occasion bedecked their heads with wigs instead of hats. Both men and women in the early centuries wore just a little white skirt covering them from the navel to the knee, but later in history, as the people became more wealthy and refined, they began to clothe the upper parts of their bodies too and donned capes and robes. They were fond of jewelry and both men and women adorned themselves with rings, bracelets, beads and earrings. Egyptians both as spectators and participants enjoyed various games and contests, dancing, singing and instrumental music.

For 2500 years Egypt stood out as a leader among the nations of the world and then in the 12th century B. C. it began to decline. An internal struggle for power set in between the Pharaohs, who insisted on maintaining centralization of government, and the priests and nobles who favored a decentralized or feudal system of political control. In this conflict the priests emerged as victors and henceforth dominated the government and the people. The political ascendancy of the priesthood led to the secularization and commercialization of religion, to increased superstition and to preoccupation with life after death. Surrounded by enormous wealth and power and unable to resist the temptation, the amoral ecclesiastical hierarchy became corrupt and degenerate.

With a natural aversion to change, the pious conservative leaders neglected to keep up with progress in the technology of industry and shipping and in the military arts. Egypt worshipped tradition and the past; economic and cultural innovation was taboo and she had to give way to new nations that were more inventive and enterprising, and more proficient in the arts of war. The Egyptians lost their Asiatic provinces and then their own country, their pride and their glory. They were subdued and ruled successively by invading Libyans, Sudanese, and Assyrians, and in 525 B.C. the Persians conquered and annexed the entire land. There were three intervals of freedom between the tenth and fourth centuries B.C. and then Alexander the Great made Egypt a possession of the Greeks. The Romans and other imperialists took their turn in ruling over the territory through the centuries although the former great ancient nation was not destroyed; it was permitted to exist but it was no longer in the vanguard of civilization, no longer a factor in international affairs and no longer independent. Not until the 20th century did Egypt become a sovereign state again, poor and insignificant in the present world, but rich in its cultural heritage and in its historical contributions to mankind.

CHAPTER III

Mesopotamians—The People of the Two Rivers

About the same time that Egypt rose from barbarism to civilization the Sumerians grew into an equally advanced nation in Western Asia. They lived in what is now known as Iraq, historically called Mesopotamia, a word that means the land between the two rivers—the Tigris and the Euphrates. The Sumerians were not the aborigenes of Mesopotamia but they were the first settlers in that region about whom we have considerable and significant information.

A short, stocky, dark-haired people, evidently Caucasian, they spoke a unique language that differed from the Aryan, Semitic and Hamitic tongues, and they took a fancy for the uncommon tonsorial custom of shaving their heads as well as their faces. They were the first people in Western Asia to learn how to write, to smelt and work with metal and to use the wagon-wheel in transportation. The Elamites, a kindred warlike nation, who conquered the Sumerians at one time and later were subjugated by them, were also familiar with writing, metallurgy and the wheel. But it was evidently the Sumerians who pioneered and introduced the inventions as well as other customs and ideas to the surrounding world. Of obscure origin, these people sometime before the 40th century B.C. came down from the northeast and moved into Mesopotamia. They overwhelmed the stone age natives living there and began to build up the land, ushering in and inculcating their arts of civilization. After a few centuries the Sumerians developed a high level of culture with flourishing cities and well organized city-state governments.

Like the Nile, the Tigris and Euphrates rivers overflowed every Spring and deposited silt and mud which enriched the soil with a copious supply of plant food. Consequently agriculture became the principal means of gaining a livelihood, and the most profitable farm products were grains, dates, figs, grapes, apples, pomegranates, cattle and sheep. Irrigation was necessary because of a long, dry season and so they built canals, dikes, and basins to conserve and distribute water to fertilize the fields. Most of the Sumerians were farmers but the land was owned by the rulers, the priests and the nobles. Labor was performed by slaves and tenant farmers or sharecroppers. All agricultural activity was controlled by the state, who fixed rents, regulated plowing, seeding and harvesting and provided for farm relief. They were the first people to cultivate their land by animal-driven plows and at least one of their mechanical implements was almost modern; it plowed the earth and dropped seeds in the soil at the same time. The Babylonians, successors to the Sumerians, introduced the earliest known recipe for making beer—2800 B.C.

Commerce and industry were also important economic pursuits. Donkey caravans or rafts on the rivers carried Mesopotamian exports of grain, woolen and leather goods, dried fish, cosmetics and fine bronze products in exchange for imports of linen, metals, lumber and limestone. The wheeled vehicle was probably introduced by the Sumerians in the 36th century, B.C. Around 1500 B.C. mules, horses and camels were added to the donkey as popular means of transportation. Like other nations Mesopotamians progressed from primitive barter to the use of copper and lead, then to precious metals by weight and finally to the coinage of money. There was more economic freedom in Mesopotamia than in Egypt but there were some strict commercial laws regulating business practices. All economic transactions involving purchase required a formal contract and witnesses and failure to comply was punishable by death. Laws also regulated land deeds, house leases, wills, promissory notes, interest on loans, and relations between debtor and creditor. Large factories were owned and operated either by priests or nobles and many small shops were managed by the artisans. Some laborers were free men and women working for wages, others were slaves who received no pay. The free skilled workers, which included surgeons as well as tailors, butchers and carpenters, were organized into guilds, controlled by the state. These guilds protected the workers, regulated their particular crafts, fixed wages with the sanction of the government, and trained new apprentices. Sometimes members of a guild would all live on one street or all organized laborers might work and reside in their own segregated part of town.

Mesopotamian society was dominated by the privileged few—the royal family, the priests, and the nobles. They possessed most of the land, the wealth and the power, they enjoyed leisure and luxuries. As the country became more urbanized the upper bourgeoisie—rich merchants, bankers, and more important bureaucrats were allowed to join the aristocracy. A lower class of freemen included shopkeepers, small farmers, sharecroppers, artisans, craftsmen, and wage workers. Unskilled slaves were quite numerous and cheap, were often branded like cattle and sometimes had to wear chains. Yet slaves in Mesopotamia, unlike other contemporaneous societies, enjoyed certain rights. A domestic slave was allowed to marry a free woman, acquire property and bequeath it to his wife and children who were recognized as free persons. Some slaves practiced trades, engaged in business and were permitted to buy their freedom. Slaves of wealthy masters were economically secure—being provided with food, clothing, shelter, and care when sick and old. Consequently poor freemen often sold themselves or their children into slavery. Yet every slave was legally a piece of property that could be disposed of in any way that the master chose, with one exception: he was not permitted to sell a female slave who had borne him a child.

The Mesopotamians lived in self-governing communities that united for defense purposes under the leadership of a king. This ruler generally was not considered a deity but he governed by divine right as an agent or representative of God. Some kings regarded themselves as direct descendants of the gods and the priests were always very influential advisers. Ultimate power rested in the monarch who was the arbiter of all matters, military, social and economic. Unlike the Pharaoh of Egypt the Mesopotamian king did not legally own all the land, but important projects, such as irrigation, the building of dikes and canals were supervised by the state.

Mesopotamia, having no natural boundaries was easily invaded by numerous peoples seeking plunder, land and new homes. There was a succession of conquerors beginning with the Sumerians, who arrived between the 50th and 40th centuries B.C. From time to time various wandering Semitic tribes emanating originally from Arabia invaded or filtered into the Fertile Crescent overrunning the land and becoming the dominant powers. They absorbed and assimilated the superior culture of the Sumerians and by the 20th century B.C. the latter had disappeared in the Semitic population. Of the many conquerors the most important were the Babylonians, named after Babylon, the city which they made their capital and which made them famous. After enjoying ascendancy for over 200 years the Babylonians were overpowered by the Kassites who were not very civilized but quite formidable fighters and innovators in warfare. They introduced the horse as an effective instrument in battle and so the chariot and cavalry henceforth became tremendous reinforcement to the traditional armies of foot soldiers. The Kassites ruled Mesopotamia for almost 500 years—till the 10th century, when the Assyrians supplanted them. After subduing and annexing Syria, Phoenicia, Israel and Egypt, the Assyrians subjugated Babylonia and thus controlled all the civilized garden spots of western Asia and northeast Africa.

The Assyrians were even more proficient than their predecessors in the art of warfare; they had the most efficient military system the world had ever seen. Their large standing army was equipped with the latest in iron weapons, with infantry, cavalry, battering rams, chariots, horse-drawn tanks or armored cars, military engineers, and intelligence service. The army pursued a policy of deliberate cruelty, mayhem and slaughter to terrorize their enemies. They inflicted inhuman torture on prisoners—gouging out eyes, tearing out tongues, cutting off ears, noses, sex organs; impaling them on sharp posts, skinning them alive, throwing them in furnaces. Beheading the wounded on the battlefield was a kind of competitive game and the soldiers were praised and rewarded in accordance with the number of heads they collected. Every ambitious soldier tried to get a head. Mutilated victims who had lost their eyes, ears, or limbs, or had been castrated were exhibited in cages for the edification of the still independent or recalcitrant cities. Children were tortured before their parents and pieces of human flesh were fed to dogs, swine and wolves. Incidentally, among the bloodthirsty Assyrian troops only the officers ate meat. Their victories were often followed by triumphant celebrations, including spectacular parades and elaborate feasts featured by excessive eating and drinking and a sort of public sharing of the spoils. Men, women and children of all classes participated in the revelry and becoming intoxicated on these occasions was considered a patriotic duty. Heads of important persons were hung from the trees in the royal garden and the inebriated king and his lords saluted and drank to their health.

Besides brutal military violence, the Assyrians practiced the policy of deporting or transplanting conquered peoples to discourage rebellion and facilitate assimilation. By their ruthless methods of force and fear they succeeded in unifying the vast empire under the rule of one king, though he did allow the subject nations to have provincial governments and some local cultural autonomy. Frequent administrative and military inspection facilitated by a good system of roads kept the imperial organization effectively cemented. But the splendor and glory, the plunder and tribute enjoyed by the Assyrian imperialists lasted only for a little over a hundred years. Constant war and continuous drain on Assyrian manpower weakened the military and emboldened the subject nations to rebel against their hateful and ferocious oppressors. Not only did the conquered countries join in a war of liberation but other nations fearing future assault and annexation by the Assyrians also took up arms against the scourge of the Middle East. In 612 B.C. the mighty Assyrian empire collapsed. Not only was hated Assyria overwhelmed, it was pillaged, sacked and annihilated. There is no Assyria today. The Fertile Crescent, or the arc-shaped land, between the Persian Gulf and the Mediterranean Sea, fell under the control of the Chaldeans, who like the earlier Babylonians, made the city of Babylon the royal capital.

Chaldean supremacy, however, did not last long, for these neo-Babylonians also became greedy for land and power and by pursuing a policy of imperialism and exploitation aroused the patriotism and animosity among their oppressed neighbors and engendered competition among equally strong and ambitious nations. Such a rival imperialistic power was Persia, who crushed the Chaldeans in 539 B.C. and thereby brought to an end the political history of Mesopotamia.

The Sumerian people as an ethnic entity had disappeared by the 20th century B.C. but the civilization which they had inaugurated continued to exist in the land of the Two Rivers. The basic customs and institutions were modified and enriched as they became mixed with the culture of the various conquerors. A very valuable contribution to this cultural blend was the Code of Hammurabi, the famous king of Babylonia, who ruled in the late 20th century. This Code was a compilation and elaboration of the laws under which the Sumerians and the Semites had lived for thousands of years.

The king sought to unify the empire by replacing the diverse local clan and tribal customs with a uniform code of national laws, to institute public instead of private protection, and to have justice administered not by the injured party or his kinsmen but by judges sitting in a court, their decisions guided by prescribed legal formula. The Hammurabi Code did not observe the principle of equality before the law and so the judges recognized class distinction and discrimination. Nobles were worth more than commoners therefore crimes against aristocrats were more severely punished than those against workers, slaves, or the middle class. Yet in some cases if a noble committed a crime he would be given a stiffer penalty than a plebeian would get for the same crime. Punishment of an offender was based on the principle of retaliation, that is; an eye for an eye, a tooth for a tooth, a limb for a limb, a life for a life. As the Babylonians grew older they amended the rude primitive penalties and made them more lenient by substituting the payment of damages for physical retribution. Capital crimes included such items as, murder, banditry, kidnapping, rape, incest, protecting a runaway slave, stealing from a temple or a palace, casting a spell on a person, or inflating the price of beer. If a son struck his father his hands were to be cut off; if a patient died or lost an eye as a result of an operation the surgeon's fingers would be cut off; if a nurse deliberately substituted one child for another her breasts were to be removed; if a house collapsed, and the owner was killed, the builder was to be put to death; and if it caused the death of the owner's son, a son of that builder must die. The death penalties, which included burning, impaling, drowning or mutilation, depended on whether it was intentional or accidental or the result of negligence.

In their early history the Babylonians regarded crimes as offenses against the gods, the judges were priests, and trials were conducted in a temple. Law and religion were closely related and they often resorted to trial by ordeal, that is, allowing the gods to decide on the innocence or guilt of the defendant. A man accused of practicing black magic or a woman charged with adultery was ordered to leap into a river and if after a certain length of time the person was still swimming he or she was innocent, but if that person had drowned he was guilty, and all his property was given to the accuser. Babylonian gods were evidently partial toward good swimmers.

During the reign of Hammurabi the courts became almost totally secularized and the judges were henceforth to be responsible to the government rather than to the gods. The country was also becoming more commercialized and the people were more interested than ever in material things and property rights. All business transactions were strictly regulated by the Code and judges were generally inclined to favor businessmen and their interests. Property was considered more valuable than human life and physical punishment was commuted to payment of money. Fines became a source of income for the state. Now eyes, teeth, limbs, and lives as well as all sorts of injuries had their price and they varied with the value of the victim—that is, his social rank. The eye or bone of a nobleman, a priest, or a rich man was more valuable than that of a shopkeeper, laborer or poor man, and reparations must be paid accordingly. Injury to a slave was redressed by paying damages to his master.

Babylonians possessed the right of appeal, the king being the supreme judge; but the individual did not have rights against the state and was never permitted to sue city hall. However, the government was generous sometimes. For example, if a brigand robbed a person and was not apprehended the governments of the city and of the province within whose jurisdiction the robbery was committed would reimburse the victim for whatever amount he had lost.

The women of Babylon were legally in a fairly favorable position, possessing the right to engage in business, own and deal in property, appear as witnesses and even learn to be scribes or professional writers. Yet if a husband could not pay his debt he was allowed to sell his wife in payment for it. Female commoners could walk about in public freely and safely but women of the upper classes were chaperoned by eunuchs and young male attendants.

Marriage was a legal contract arranged through negotiations between the two fathers and made binding by the presence of witnesses without benefit of clergy. The young man paid a sum of money to the bride and to her father while she contributed a dowry, usually some house furniture. In case of divorce she got back her furniture and all her property but he could not retrieve his monetary present. A husband was granted a divorce if his wife were guilty of adultery, were unable to bear children, were a careless housekeeper, or just incompatible. In fact, a man might cast off his spouse at will, while if she refused to cohabit with her husband the court was ordered to inquire into her physical deficiencies and shortcomings. If a man repudiated his wife and it was proved that her conduct was blameless she would keep the custody of the children and he must provide for them and for her. A wife was not allowed to divorce her husband but cruelty was ground for separation and if she had been a faithful spouse she was free to leave him. Monogamy was the rule among most men, though the wealthy Babylonians often procured secondary wives or concubines and equipped their households with well populated harems. A unique privilege enjoyed by the Mesopotamian women was the legally sanctioned custom that allowed a lonely wife whose husband was away on business or in a war for a long time, to live with another man for the duration. This accommodation was granted only to those wives who had no means of maintaining themselves and needed relief. Premarital sexual experience was not unlawful and young Babylonians were not averse to free love; so couples who were very fond of each other, would sometimes form unlicensed unions subject to nullification by either party. However, the female partner in such an arrangement had to apprise the public of her adulterated status that she was neither a virgin nor a legal spouse; and she was forced to wear a visible olive made of stone or clay as identification.

Religion was very important to the Mesopotamians because they believed that there was a divine spirit behind every event, that whatever happened did so by the will of a god. Most prominent among the gods were the supernatural powers that created and controlled the forces of nature—the sun, the moon, the wind, the rain, the rivers, fertility, and reproduction; these were all personified and worshipped. In addition there were minor individual town and country deities; in fact, there were about 65,000 distinct gods, each one represented by a physical image or idol. The large population in the national Sumerian-Babylonian pantheon was due to the practice of nationalizing many of the local divinities. Some of the major supernatural powers were Shamash, the sun god, Nannar, the moon god, and Marduk who rose from his local rank and file position as just the god of Babylon city, to become the leader of the nation's deities. It was Marduk who overcame a dragon or chaos and established an orderly universe, who created heaven and earth and then made man out of clay mixed with the blood of the dragon and his own blood. However, Marduk lost his supremacy when Babylon was temporarily replaced by Assyria as the dominant power in western Asia.

Other significant Babylonian deities were Tammuz, the god of vegetation and his consort, Ishtar, the goddess of love, beauty, procreation and prostitution. One day Tammuz, while out hunting, was killed by a wild boar and so like all deceased beings he descended to the dark gloomy underworld of Hades, the home of the dead. Ishtar lamented the loss of her beloved husband and resolved to restore him to life. Overcoming many obstacles and hurdles set up by her enemies in Hades, the great goddess of love finally succeeded in reviving her spouse, the lord of vegetation. After a while this extraordinary event became a yearly occurrence not only among the Babylonians but with slight variations and with different names for the divinities among other peoples in western Asia and Egypt. Tammuz would die every autumn and in the spring he would rise again. The annual death of Tammuz, which symbolized the death of vegetation, was accompanied by mourning and wailing and the shrill music of flutes. Hoping to assist Ishtar in her endeavor to revive Tammuz the people would chant dirges over an image of the dead god. During the absence of Ishtar, while she was in quest of her departed lover, plants ceased to grow, animals did not produce and there was no love in the land. But in due time came the resurrection of Tammuz, the reappearance of spring, and the rebirth of vegetation and soil fertility. These happy events were followed by riotous rejoicing featured by sacrifices, prayers, feasting and sexual license. The reunion of the sex goddess Ishtar and her lover Tammuz symbolized the rebirth of the mating season for man and animals, a renewal of the fertility of the soil, and a return of joyful days for the farmer and the family man.

Unlike the Egyptians, the Mesopotamians were vague about life beyond the grave, and their attitude toward life and death was fatalistic and gloomy. They had no conception about a real heaven or hell, believing that the souls of the departed lived in a world of darkness, in a land of no return. Yet the dead were buried with a great deal of care; they washed, bedecked and beautified the face and body of the deceased and even supplied the soul with a change of linen, as well as drink and articles of food.

The religion of the Mesopotamians was administered by the king, who was the chief steward of the major god and by the priests, who were the intellectuals that formulated the religious policies, devised the magic formulas, created the superstitions and who were the most influential class. The priests communicated with the gods to determine what they intended to do, and what they wanted the people to do. They examined the entrails of sacrificed chickens, especially the liver, to find out what the gods have in store for the country—whether there will be economic prosperity or a business slump. The red brown liver was considered to be a mystic organ—the seat of life, the residence of the soul and of the mind. In fact, the principles and methods of liver divination, as well as other methods of prophesying, were studied by the pupils in all Babylonian parochial schools. Priests taught that future happenings could be revealed by the behavior of birds, dogs or other animals, by the interpretation of dreams, or by observing the aspect and the movements of stars. Neither the king nor the people would ever undertake an important enterprise without first consulting an ecclesiastical forecaster for pertinent omens. Evil spirits, witches and demons infested the land, lurking in dark corners, bent on demonizing, possessing and bewitching innocent victims. In defense against these hostile, noxious and sometimes deadly beings the people would use magic charms and ceremonies, images of the gods, and impassioned prayers and incantations.

Since the government was a theocracy the king and the priests formulated their policies and promulgated their rules and regulations with the sanction of the gods. It was not only a crime to violate a law, it was a sin, and people were afraid of the divine powers. In Babylonia right was synonymous with rite and ethical conduct was strict adherence to ritual. Ceremonial practices accompanied by sacrifices, donations and contributions would attain the favor and grace of the gods. The priests and their temples were showered with so much money, land and gifts that many of them were converted into ecclesiastical capitalists who invested their wealth in farming, manufacturing, merchandising and money-lending. Priests became not only plutocrats, but were also the bureaucrats, the judges, the scribes and the lawyers.

The temples were not only houses of the gods, they were also kind of office buildings for the priestly businessmen—landowners, bankers and industrialists, and within the precincts of the temple there were workshops, stores, brothels, and other non-religious, lucrative establishments. A rather quaint ritual was the practice of sanctified prostitution whereby every woman, rich or poor, had to submit at least once in her life to sexual intercourse with a stranger at the Temple of Ishtar. The money she received from the man was turned over to a priest who blessed it and devoted it to the love and sex goddess. The sacred building was crowded with women waiting to observe the female sacrament. Beautiful and shapely girls were selected forthwith, they faithfully accepted the stranger's offer, and consummated their religious obligation, but the less attractive applicants had to wait there in some cases for years. This custom of hallowed harlotry with slight variations prevailed in many parts of western Asia. In some places women would prostitute themselves for hire only on certain festive days and then give all their earnings to the goddess Ishtar in order to win her favor. Virgin daughters were sometimes dedicated to the service of the goddess and also prepared for marriage financially and physiologically by engaging in prostitution for a time. In one place the women were given a choice on a certain festive day as a religious requirement of either having sexual intercourse with a stranger or having their heads shaved. In all cases the goddess Ishtar had to be appeased and the money collected was given to the priest as a sacrifice.

Being commercially inclined, the Mesopotamians were interested in the practical aspects of knowledge and therefore in the exact sciences. As early as 2500 B.C. they had already made conspicuous progress in the development of a complicated system of weights and measures. They learned how to add, subtract, multiply and divide, and even had a multiplication table. Their number system was based on both decimals and units of 60. The numeration used only three figures: sign for 1, repeated up to 9, a sign for 10, repeated up to 50; and a sign for 100. The circle was divided into 360 degrees, the clock into 12 hours, the hour into 60 minutes, the minute into 60 seconds, the year into 12 months, the month into 4 weeks and the weeks into 7 days. They invented the water clock and probably the sun dial, and used an awkward lunar calendar, based upon the cycles of the moon.

They devised tables showing squares, cubes, halves, quarters, and thirds, gave Pi the value of 3, understood arithmetic and geometric progressions, and were familiar with the circle, the triangle, the right triangle, the quadrangle, the hexagon, and other figures. The schools taught geometry, elementary algebra, which included lessons in the solution of quadratic equations, linear and cubic equations.

Priests in observing the mysterious phenomena in the heavens came to the conclusion that the rising and setting of the sun, the phases of the moon and the changing positions of the five great visible planets were manifestations of supernatural beings or divinities. Since there were seven major luminaries the number 7 became significant among the Mesopotamians. All movements of the celestial bodies, their conjunctions and eclipses, have a profound influence on the course of human affairs and affect the destiny of people and nations. The star gazers or astrologers could understand the occult behavior of the heavenly bodies and therefore could interpret their meaning, predict events, and foresee the future. Out of the superstitious gazing, recording and studying the data, they came across information useful to science. The Chaldean Babylonians were pioneers in this area of the pseudo-science of fortune telling which still exists in the western world. From the practice of reading horoscopes and making observations and prognostications there evolved the study of astronomy. The Babylonians learned to chart the stars and succeeded in making records of the rising and setting of the planet Venus, they fixed the position of various stars, and began to make scientific maps of the sky. They plotted the orbits of the sun and the moon, noted their conjunctions and eclipses, calculated the courses of the planets and distinguished the difference between a planet and a star, observing that the latter stays fixed while the former wanders about. The Babylonians also determined the dates of the winter and summer solstices and of the spring and autumnal equinoxes.

In the knowledge of medical science the Mesopotamians adhered to primitive principles and practices. They still believed that disease was caused by evil spirits and cures could be effected by expelling them from the body. Prayers, incantations and magic rites were generally used but in conjunction with drugs derived from minerals, vegetables and animals. Mouse meat was usually prescribed for a toothache because mice were believed to have the strongest teeth in the world.

There were hundreds of remedies and many of them were offensive to smell or taste, the purpose being to terrify and drive the demon out of the body. Ingredients in the medicines included raw meat, snake flesh, decayed food, oils and fat, onions, castor oil and human and animal urine and excrement. The doctors generally wanted to expel the demon from the body but sometimes they might try to imprison him by using the magic number—tying seven knots in a string. If the disgusting drugs and the magic formula failed to exorcise the malignant characters from the patient's body they might, as a last resort, try a kind of socialized medicine whereby the sick person would be carried out into the market place and any friendly Babylonian could come over and recommend his favorite remedy or therapy. The fees of surgeons and general practitioners were fixed by the national government and if the doctor's treatment or operation resulted in serious damage or injury the patient would be compensated commensurately.

The Mesopotamians wrote in the cuneiform way, that is, impressing wedge-shaped characters on soft wet clay tablets with a stylus pencil. When the tablets were filled they were dried and baked and then the composition was complete. Trained in a difficult and esoteric art, professional writers or scribes were very important people who held prestigious positions and utilized their talents in government, religion, commerce and law. The first writers were probably bookkeepers in the temple who needed inventory of their stock of goods to be sold, as well as bills, receipts, and records of loans and sales. Other writing consisted of hymns, religious rituals, magic incantations, royal inscriptions, legal codes, historic annals, dictionaries and grammars. Their imaginative literature inspired by religion, were poems relating the heroic and adventurous stories about Creation, the Fall of Man, the Great Flood, the Tower of Babel, and of a much afflicted character resembling the Biblical Job. Modified and improved versions of these legends appeared later in the Old Testament of the Hebrews.

Thousands of clay tablets have survived and provide modern historians with information about every aspect of Mesopotamian life. Outstanding among the collections was the royal library at Nineveh established by the great Assyrian emperor Assurbanipal. It contained over 22,000 clay tablets and gave European scholars their first sight of Sumerian, Babylonian and Assyrian literature.

Mesopotamian architecture was handicapped by the scarcity of stone; buildings were made mostly of bricks bound together by a kind of pitch. There were huge, imposing, luxurious palaces, temples and towers but they were not very durable because brick is a more perishable substance than stone. The walls were painted in vivid colors and embellished with glazed tiles, mosaics, and reliefs. It was the Mesopotamians who developed the dome, the vault, and the rounded arch, but they were not very adept in the use of columns. Dwellings were generally constructed around a court; those of the rich were built of brick, the homes of the poor were made of dried mud. Windows were rare for the people sought to exclude the heat in this part of the world. A very prevalent Mesopotamian edifice was the ziggurat, often a seven-storied terraced tower where one passed from one floor to another by means of an inclined ramp that wound around the structure. The ziggurat was primarily a religious building with a temple or shrine on top but it was also used as an observatory to study the stars. Surrounding the ziggurat were offices of the municipal government, schools and apartments for the priests, temple workshops, and warehouses where they stored manufactured goods and farm products. Huge public buildings and palaces were generally decorated with statues and bas reliefs as Mesopotamia abounded in skillful sculptors who carved animals and human forms in stone and clay. Particularly talented were the Assyrians, who portrayed very graphically and vigorously scenes of battles, torture, massacres, hunting, sailing, swimming as well as exotic and sometimes realistic figures of lions, bulls, horses, birds, grasshoppers and other animals. The Mesopotamians also produced many minor art objects, such as, jewelry, pottery and ornaments expertly cut out of stone, clay, wood and metal.

Under the rule of Nebuchadnezzar, the Chaldean king, Babylon became the most magnificent metropolis in the ancient world. The great king of Babylon, conqueror of Egypt, Syria, Phoenicia and Judea, was also a lavish builder of massive and ostentatious palaces and temples as well as grand arches, boulevards, highways, walls and reservoirs. For the pleasure of one of his favorite wives, Nebuchadnezzar built the famous Hanging Gardens, one of the "seven wonders of the world", tier on tier of gardens covered with a copious supply of top soil in which there grew a variety of beautiful flowers, plants and trees—a kind of Babylonian penthouse, seventy-five feet above the ground, far from the noisy traffic and the dusty streets. Babylon was a fabulously wealthy city with a flourishing commerce and unprecedented splendor but the empire became too vast and unwieldy and required a highly competent government and a powerful army to maintain political unity.

Nebuchadnezzar was followed by weak kings who allowed the priests to usurp the royal power. The military lost its appeal and the people began to prefer the pursuit of money and pleasure to the defense of their land. As a result the Chaldean Babylonian state crumbled, and in the year 539 B.C. the Mesopotamian world became a possession of the Persians who moved in under the leadership of Cyrus, a great military genius. Two hundred years later the Greeks took possession of Mesopotamia, and the Greeks were subsequently succeeded by the Romans. When the Romans retired, the Arabs and then the Turks ruled the area. The Turks in turn were conquered by the British and the French, and eventually by the Arabs, who are ethnically the closest to the ancient Mesopotamians, and who regained their independence after the First World War. The civilization of Mesopotamia was never destroyed; its customs and ideas were passed on to the succeeding conquerors, who adopted, modified and modernized the traditions of the Sumerians and Babylonians.

CHAPTER IV

Phoenicians, Hebrews, Persians, et al.

From the 19th to the 12th century B.C. a great military people, called the Hittites, occupied and ruled over Anatolia in what is now known as the Turkish republic. These folks were an Indo-European or Aryan-speaking people who not only dominated Asia Minor but also overran Syria, Phoenicia and Palestine and became a dangerous rival and foe of Egypt and Assyria. For a long time their military success was assured by their employment of the horse, the chariot and iron weapons, but their competitors, after a while, learned and used these more modern methods of warfare with even greater effect and overpowered them.

The Hittites spoke an Indo-European language though it seems that their original home was Turkestan. Egyptian sculptors depict them with round skulls, backward sloping foreheads and sharply aquiline noses. The curved or high-bridged nose often regarded as a characteristic anatomical trademark of the Hebrews was evidently a legacy of the Hittites, an Aryan folk. There seems to have been considerable miscegenation between the Hittites and the Semites. A more significant contribution of the Hittites was their working and smelting of iron, thereby helping western Asia to pass from the Bronze Age to the Age of Iron. They were the first people to make use of iron implements and to impart knowledge of their manufacture to the rest of the civilized world. They also mined silver, copper, and lead and engaged in many industries, as well as in foreign commerce and agriculture. The empire comprised a group of clans scattered over the land but acknowledging the authority of the king. The government, either national or local, enacted and enforced laws which controlled landholding and farming, fixed prices for essential commodities, and regulated wages and fees for services. Hittite laws were much influenced by the Mesopotamians but some of the penalties for serious crimes were more humane than those of the Hammurabi code. Capital punishment was indicated for a few crimes only; for example, witchcraft, stealing palace property and sexual intercourse with an animal. Mutilation was seldom employed and even murderers were only fined.

Most of the Hittite culture shows traces of Babylonian and Egyptian influence. In their religion there were numerous deities, local and national, male and female; a sun god and a mother goddess of fertility were among the most important. The Hittite language contained words that sound like Greek, Latin and English. They made use of both the cuneiform and hieroglyphic systems of writing and they wrote one line from left to right and the next from right to left. Hittite architecture was gross and ponderous but their sculpturing, although crude and rough, was interesting and was occasionally copied by the Assyrians. Most important perhaps was their role as a carrier of the culture of western Asia to the Aegean world and as diffusers of their metallurgical skill. As happened to most great powers, incessant and exhaustive warfare led to their downfall and disappearance as an independent nation.

The Hittite ascendancy in Anatolia or Asia Minor was replaced by the Phrygians who also aspired to dominate the Near East. Phrygian fame in history rests on legendary tales and religious mythology adopted and made popular by the Greeks and Romans. One story concerned the challenge of the Gordian knot that Alexander the Great would someday resolve and another describes the Phrygian king Midas's extraordinary power of turning into gold everything he touched. The Phrygians worshipped a deity known as Ma or Cybele, mother of the gods, who dwelt in the mountains and personified the reproductive energies of nature. Associated with the Mother Goddess was a handsome shepherd and god of vegetation named Attis, miraculously born of a virgin who conceived him by placing a pomegranate between her breasts. It was said that one day he was killed by a boar or according to another story he was compelled to emasculate himself in honor of the goddess Cybele and bled to death lying under a pine tree. The latter tale accounts for the practice of self-mutilation of the priests, who regularly castrated themselves as an initiation requirement for their service in the temple; while the story of the death of Attis by a wild hog explains why his devotees hated pigs and abstained from eating pork. It was also believed that after his death Attis changed into a pine tree. Each year this god of vegetation died and every spring he was reborn with the return of vernal sunshine, leaves, blossoms and trees in a general resurrection of nature. In a spring ceremony the pine tree was blessed and became a god and a festival was proclaimed with the blowing of trumpets. Then the worshippers stirred by the shrill, barbaric music of an orchestra consisting of cymbals, drums, horns and flutes, indulged in wild ecstatic dancing, and amidst the screaming and frenzied excitement some of the clergy pierced their bodies with knives and bespattered the sacred tree with their blood. During these sanguinary sacrifices a number of fanatic priests would emasculate themselves beside the sacred pine tree which had once been their beloved god Attis. The later mystery cults of Greece and Rome were derived from and influenced by the various legends and religious beliefs of the many peoples of western Asia.

Contemporaries of the Hittites and the Phrygians were the Lydians, also an Aryan folk who lived in Asia Minor. Lydia, too, became a first-class power and during the 7th and 6th centuries B.C. attained a high degree of civilization. It was regarded as an exceptionally affluent country with a high standard of living where monarchs wallowed in wealth and splendor. The proverbial phrase "rich as Croesus", is an evidential reference to the Lydian king's opulence and magnificence. A fortunate geographic location enabled the Lydian business men to control the trade routes on both land and water to the east and to the west. They had an abundance of sheep, and a great quantity of gold and silver, found with the sand in some of their streams, and which they traded for many articles of luxury.

The Lydians are best known in history for their introduction of metallic currency which seems to have appeared early in the eighth century B.C. although it was not very widely prevalent until about 700 B.C. Instead of using money made of weighed rings or metal bars, as was the prevailing custom, the Lydians mixed gold and silver, heated the mass of metal and hammered it all out into bean-shaped coins of various sizes, stamped with a definite value. The process of manufacture was of course a state monopoly. In 546 B.C. Lydian independence came to an end when King Croesus and his army succumbed to the conquering Persians. According to Herodotus, the Greek historian, the outcome of the crucial battle between the Persians and the Lydians was determined by the foul and offensive stench of the Persian camels which was so potent that the Lydian horses of the cavalry turned away and ran wildly from the battlefield. Another group of notorious invaders of the Middle East were the Scythians who contributed to the downfall of the famous Assyrian empire. For a time they occupied the land along the shores of the Black Sea and in the seventh century B.C. they conquered western Asia and penetrated Egypt. A strange and fierce race, half Mongol and half European, these ferocious fighters lived in wagons and rode wild horses bareback, drank the blood of their enemies and used their scalps as napkins. Girls, too, would mount horses, ride to battle, shoot and throw javelins and were as wild as their male companions. These female fighters had only left breasts because it was a Scythian custom for mothers to cauterize a female baby's right breast thereby arresting its growth and strengthening the right arm and shoulder. These military maidens were forbidden to violate their virginity until they had killed at least three of their enemies. Then they were allowed to get married and retire from the army. Like the Assyrians and many others the Scythians eventually were conquered by their neighbors and disappeared from history.

Phoenicians and Aramaeans were two small groups of Semites who, around the 15th century B.C., came out of the Arabian Desert and settled in modern Syria and Lebanon. The Aramaeans moved into the land east of the Lebanon Mountains while the Phoenicians occupied a narrow strip of territory about 150 miles long and 12 miles wide, between the mountains and the Mediterranean Sea. Both nations were conquered by the Babylonians and by the Egyptians but when these two great powers declined around the 12th century the small states had an opportunity to govern themselves. Their interests were primarily commercial though their soil was fairly fertile and agriculture was not shunned. The Aramaeans traded all over western

Asia and their language became so popular that it was used in many countries for over a thousand years as a medium of communication in international relations, in business and as a common tongue.

The Phoenicians, living on the shores of the Mediterranean, became fishermen and sailors and then skilled shipbuilders, commercial travelers and fearless navigators. They possessed fertile soil, fine natural harbors, plenty of timber and resin; manufactured a variety of commodities, such as, glassware, pottery, cloth, dyes and metal goods; bought and sold slaves, ivory and ostrich feathers; and were not averse to the occasional practice of raiding and piracy. Seeking markets and raw material they traded with the Mediterranean islands and with Greece, Italy, France, Spain and north Africa. In search of tin, the Phoenicians sailed as far as Britain and some historians believe they even circumnavigated the continent of Africa by way of the Red Sea. Some of their trading stations developed into cities like Marseilles and Cadiz and some into colonies, such as the famous Carthage. In nautical skill and knowledge of geography the Phoenicians surpassed all their contemporaries and their business methods were highly advanced. Underdeveloped nations, not yet sophisticated or adept in the art of making money, were envious of Phoenician economic success and so charged them with being greedy, crafty and deceptive, but when they themselves became worldly business men, they also became shrewd, wily and unethical.

The government of Phoenicia was a commercial oligarchy that ruled over a loose union of city-states and was more interested in making money than in fighting or conquering other lands. They did not seek political or ideological world power but were economic imperialists who would have liked to corner the market in all fields of business. Many of their customs and institutions were borrowed from the Babylonians and Egyptians and carried to the Greeks and other peoples they traded with. In the 8th century B.C. the independence of Phoenicia came to an end when the Assyrians took them over.

Phoenicians worshipped Ishtar the amorous deity of physical love, who required temple prostitution, ecstatic dancing, raucous music of flutes and drums, frenzied chest-beating, wailing of women, and bloody self-emasculation of priests. Their most terrible god was Moloch who required Phoenicians to offer living children as burnt sacrifices. Parents would have to attend the ceremony dressed as for a festival. The children were placed on the bronze hands of the huge idol from which they slid into the fiery furnace. The screaming of the victims was drowned out by the dancing and the piercing barbaric music of flutes and trumpets. Sometimes the ferocious Moloch would forgo human sacrifice and instead the priests were allowed to slash themselves and sprinkle their blood on the altar or they would cut off and offer to the deity a child's foreskin in lieu of his or her life, but the least painful sacrifice to induce the brutal divinity to be more humane, was the gift of a sum of money. The price of appeasement varied with circumstances or the gravity of the situation and in perilous times when the country was in alarming danger many little children were consumed in Moloch's oven.

The most important contribution of the Phoenicians was the alphabet, now found in the Near East and in all the nations of the Western World. They invented signs to represent 22 consonants or the sounds of the human voice, the use of alphabetic instead of pictographic writing. Being practical businessmen they naturally saw the need for a system of speed writing to take the place of the slow and cumbersome cuneiform or hieroglyphic method of engraving letters and records. The Phoenicians transmitted the alphabet to the Greeks who passed it on to the Romans and later to the Russians.

The Hebrews, a small group of Semitic-speaking people, made their first historical appearance about 4000 years ago in the ancient city of Ur in Sumeria. They had come out of the Arabian Desert and were wandering around from place to place in search of fertile soil and better living conditions. Sometime in the twentieth century B.C. the patriarch Abraham, their first great clan leader, guided them toward the west—to a land called Canaan. This place was near the Mediterranean Sea, a land of milk and honey where they would find wealth and happiness. To encourage and inspire confidence Abraham told the people of a covenant he had made with God whereby the land was promised to them on condition that they became and remained faithful followers of Yahweh or Jehovah and worshipped no other deity. Accordingly the Hebrews migrated into Canaan and lived and thrived there for many years. Then a famine swept the land and some of them moved to Egypt where the economy was favorable and immigrants were welcome. By this time the Hebrews had come to be known as Israelites, named for Abraham's grandson—Jacob Israel. The government of Egypt was hospitable and tolerant toward the Israelites, or the Defenders of God, for about 150 years but then with a change in administration a policy of persecution was adopted. The new Pharaoh undertook an elaborate program of public works and to complete the project he urgently needed an enormous amount of labor. So he enslaved his political predecessors and all non-Egyptian minorities including the Israelites. Suffering in their degradation as common slaves, the Hebrews longed for their freedom. In the thirteenth century B.C. their prayers were answered when a great new leader named Moses appeared, organized and freed them from the misery of bondage. The Israelites escaped from Egypt and for forty years they followed their inspired commander and prophet, moving over the Red Sea and wandering through the Sinai Desert on the way to the old homeland of their ancestors. During these years of slow arduous migration Moses instilled patriotism and religion among his followers, thus preparing and conditioning them for their great task ahead. He finally succeeded in creating a confederation, a cohesive union with a dedicated goal—to conquer the land of Canaan. And like Abraham, Moses too met with God and received a promise; then he apprised and warned the people that an indispensable requirement for victory and happiness was complete reverence and devotion to Jehovah, the unique God of the Israelites. In addition to the covenant Moses revealed God's will and sanction of the Ten Commandments and other laws that should guide the lives of his people. The Israelites finally came to the end of their journey around 1200 B.C. and arrived in the Promised Land where they were reunited with their kinsmen who had refused to join the emigration to Egypt 400 years before. These brethren had remained in Canaan, where many had become Canaanized or were assimilated with the Hittites who had come down from the north. The conquest of the land of Canaan was difficult and prolonged, though it was ultimately accomplished. Moses had died before the entrance into the Promised Land and Joshua, a military man, had become commander of the Israelites. A few generations after their victory over the Canaanites they had to struggle with the Philistines, who had invaded and were overrunning the country. These people, from whom the word Palestine is derived, were very formidable fighters and for a while compelled the Israelites as well as the Canaanites to submit to their rule.

The Israelite government was a primitive democracy consisting of two legislative houses, a number of elders acting as tribal administrators, a national supreme court and a selected judge as the chief executive of the nation. The twelve tribes enjoyed considerable autonomy and the power of the executive was limited by law, but in times of crisis they would surrender some of their rights and grant the chief judge complete authority.

As the military pressure of the Philistines grew more menacing and problems seemed insoluble the judges in 1020 B.C. decided to transform the republican government into a monarchy, and they selected a young man named Saul as the first king of Palestine. An army man, but unsuccessful, he was soon replaced by David as king and commander. More competent and far more fascinating than Saul, David defeated the Philistines and completed the conquest of Palestine. He established Jerusalem as the nation's capital, united the people more thoroughly than ever, tried to centralize the government and brought power and prestige to the little kingdom. Although he attained ascendancy over the tribes the king was still subject to the law, for the people opposed absolute monarchy.

At the death of David his son Solomon ascended the throne and the Israelite kingdom reached the peak of its power and glory. Solomon had a passion for luxury and splendor. A lavish builder of temples and palaces, he had to import, at great expense, an enormous quantity of various kinds of fine wood, precious stones, gold, silver, brass, iron and other materials. Most magnificent was the temple he erected on a hill at Jerusalem for the worship of Jahweh. To construct this lordly sanctuary the king pledged much of his own wealth but he also called on the people for contributions, and future members of the congregation from all over the land responded generously. Solomon also had a hobby of collecting horses, wives and concubines and it was said that in time he had gathered thousands of horses and hundreds of spouses, primary and secondary. To seal and fortify friendly relations with Egypt he married the Pharaoh's daughter and for reasons of commerce he consorted with a Phoenician princess and with the queen of Sheba. In fact, his harem contained numerous foreign wives and as a generous and gallant potentate Solomon ordered the erection of sumptuous palaces for their comfort and handsome temples where they could worship their own native deities.

The enormous cost of government and the military, the construction and maintenance of the many buildings and fortifications, the beautifying of Jerusalem and the general extravagance of the king resulted in heavy taxes and forced him to introduce conscript labor whereby every four months thousands of persons were drafted to perform the tedious unskilled work on the elaborate projects. These policies produced rumblings of discontent which culminated in the division of Palestine into two antagonistic tribal groups—the north and the south. Sectional differences, economic, social and religious engendered quarrels and violent conflicts, and finally the north seceded from the union resulting in the establishment of the kingdom of Israel in the north and Judah in the south. The northerners, comprising ten tribes, were successful farmers, traders and manufacturers—urbanized, worldly, and not averse to assimilation with their idolatrous neighbors, while the southern tribes were composed predominantly of poor and simple shepherds and farmers, provincial in their outlook and hostile to strange gods and customs.

The two Palestinian kingdoms continued in existence for about two centuries and then the Assyrians in 722 B.C. conquered Israel after a war that lasted ten years. Its inhabitants were deported and scattered over various parts of the empire where they were absorbed by other peoples, and so the ten tribes disappeared from history. The kingdom of Judah, however, managed to maintain a precarious independence until 586 B.C. when the Chaldean Babylonians, who had supplanted the Assyrians as the dominant power in the area, vanquished the southern Palestinians. Several thousand of the leading citizens were carried off into captivity in Babylon. About 50 years later the Persians, after overpowering the Babylonians, permitted those exiles who longed for Zion to return to Jerusalem where they enjoyed freedom of worship, though the state of Judah became a part of the Persian empire. In the fourth century came the conquering Greeks under Alexander the Great who subjugated the Persians and took over the land. Then in 143 B.C. the heroic Maccabees regained independence for the kingdom of Judah and for a while they ruled over all of Palestine. However, this restoration was only temporary as in 63 B.C. Judah was converted into a protectorate of the Romans, the successors of the Greeks as masters of the near East. The Romans also changed the name of the little kingdom to Judea—from which the word Jew is derived.

Unrest in Judea continued and finally rebellion broke out, first in the year six of the Christian Era, then again in the year 66. In the revolution of 66 all the Jewish religious factions, including the Christians, a newly formed sect, joined in the battle against the Romans and the city of Jerusalem held out until the year 70 after a siege lasting three years. Hundreds of thousands of men, women and children were slaughtered, burned, or crucified. The city, including the famous temple, lay in ruins and many of those who managed to survive were moved to other parts of the empire.

A tiny nation with a paucity of arms and equipment, the Jews fought bravely and furiously against the world's mightiest military power and won a number of battles. But it was a hopeless struggle since Rome's supplies and personnel were unlimited and they would prevail in the end by overwhelming the defenders. It was a victory gained at such a great loss of life and prestige that the Roman government found it necessary to restore its public image by an ostentatious victory parade and the construction of a triumphal arch as if a major power had been vanquished.

Two more Jewish revolts occurred in the second century, in 113 and in 132;the latter was incited by Hadrian when he started to replace the historic city of Jerusalem with a Roman colony and made plans to erect a temple to Jupiter on the site of the Jewish temple. He also promulgated an edict against the Jewish practice of circumcision. But both rebellions failed with an aftermath of destruction and butchery, exile and slavery. Judea now became a Roman province, Jerusalem was rebuilt and in 212 C.E. all the Jews in the Roman empire were given citizenship. Not until the twentieth century did the Jews again acquire an independent state, when a small number of them returned to the Promised Land—Israel.

Deprived of their homeland and scattered throughout the nations of the world, the Jews nevertheless retained their distinctive culture through a strict requirement of endogamy and a rigid discipline of religious training and inculcation. What motivated this tenacious cohesion was their passionate devotion to a singular God and a unique religion. All other people worshipped several anthropomorphic representational gods but the Jews believed in one spiritual Supreme Being—a god that could not be materially reproduced in the form of a man, statue, effigy or painted picture. This divinity, called Yahweh or Jehovah, was omnipotent and omniscient and required his worshipers to be upright in character and live a reverent and benevolent life.

The religion of the Hebrews had not always been monotheistic or so ethically oriented—but it had evolved over the years developing with changing circumstances and experience. Like other peoples the Jews had gone through the various stages of evolution—animism, idolatry, polytheism, anthropomorphism, monolatry or the worship of only one god, the greatest among all existing deities. Eventually came true ethical monotheism or the belief that in all the world there is only one universal god and his name is Yahweh or Jehovah. In the beginning Jahweh was a tribal deity converted by Abraham and Moses into a special and exclusive god for all the Hebrews. He had made a covenant with his followers. If they obeyed the Mosaic Code of Laws including the Ten Commandments, if they lived up to its moral standards and ideas of justice they would be rewarded with the land of great abundance where they would enjoy prosperity and happiness. In due time, the promise was fulfilled and the Hebrews did thrive in Palestine, though the wealth was not always well distributed, as some were rich and many were poor.

A number of Hebrews became affluent farmers and businessmen, the influential upper class, inclined to sumptuous and sophisticated tastes and habits. They often preferred the elaborate ritual and the thrilling, sensual ceremonies of the pagan worship to the plain and sombre liturgy of Jahweh's temple. Furthermore they asserted that the Hebrew religion was devised for simple shepherds not for wealthy farmers and worldly capitalists. It was obsolete and was in need of amendment and reform. As more and more Jews switched and joined the Canaanite cults and as attendance at the Hebrew temples declined, the priests became alarmed and introduced ritualistic forms and practices which modernized the religion and made it more compatible with contemporaneous occupations and aesthetic interests. Jahweh was now also given supernatural jurisdiction over vegetation, an addition to his power over pastoral affairs; and to honor the agricultural role of God they instituted agrarian festivals, appropriate sacrifices and even some of the licentious pagan rites and superstitions.

These sacerdotal concessions and compromises with strange gods pleased the landowners and the plutocrats but produced resentment among the orthodox Jews and among the poor, exploited masses. Some of these people wanted to return to the simple life of the desert where Jahweh protected the poor and the needy, deploring the situation in Palestine where the priests had evidently changed Yahweh into a Canaanite god who favored the rich and the privileged. However to revert to the nomadic pastoral life was neither feasible nor very popular.

It was during these years of corruption, class conflict and religious degeneration that there appeared a number of inspired leaders—ardent advocates of righteousness and eloquent champions of the downtrodden. These were the great Hebrew prophets, such as Elijah, in the ninth century B.C., Amos, Hosea, Micah, and Isaiah in the eighth century, Jeremiah in the seventh, Ezekiel and the unknown prophet, called the Second Isaiah, in the sixth century. Were it not for these prophets the Hebrews would probably have abandoned Jahweh and gone the way of their heathen neighbors and been completely Canaanized, for the reforms made by the priests were a convenient bridge to paganism. Not only did the prophets save the Jews from assimilation but they established true ethical monotheism, since Yahweh was no longer to be regarded as just one among many gods but as the only one that existed—the father of all mankind, a transcendent spiritual being, the lord of the universe, the God of righteousness, justice and goodness. The prophets denounced the greedy, the haughty, the arrogant oppressors of the poor. Right conduct was more important to Yahweh than ritual and sacrifice and He wanted men to be kind, humble, merciful, and to strive for social justice, for peace and human brotherhood.

With the return in the sixth century B.C. of great military powers on the world scene the Jews had little chance of restoring secular independence, yet they refused to be completely absorbed in the population of the conquerors. Unlike most vanquished nations the Hebrews were determined to retain their identity through a unique faith and religious organization. All Jews were expected to believe in Jehovah, the God of righteousness and justice and in the Mosaic code of laws as revealed in the first five books of the Old Testament. The Code contained ethical instructions and detailed regulations for every phase of Hebrew life and it comprehended religion, ethics, philosophy, history, and literature written by numerous authors.

The synagogue was introduced in the sixth century B.C. as a place of meeting to worship, to receive religious instruction and to learn, interpret and administer Biblical law. Other religious customs which distinguished the Jews from their neighbors were the observance of the Sabbath, the seventh day of the week, as a day of rest and prayer, the celebration of several seasonal and national holidays, the use of special forms of liturgy, the practice of circumcision and the avoidance of non-kosher foods. For a long time Jews, like the Greeks and Babylonians, had not been very much concerned about the end of the world, last judgment and immortality of the soul, but centuries of adversity, repeated distressful experiences, and contact with Persian and Egyptian theology probably caused many to begin to pray for some future divine dispensation of rewards and punishment. Henceforth Judaism would contain for some hopeful followers a belief in the existence of an evil spirit or Satan, who would eventually be overcome, of the Last Judgment or a final trial before the Lord of all mankind, and a heaven and a hell where justice would be vindicated. All adherents of Jehovah, however, believed that He had a plan for mankind which will someday bring redemption to all people—an ideal world society—a world without evil, without poverty, without war. Heralding the arrival of utopia, a paradise on earth, will be a Messiah who will establish the godly state of Israel dedicated to brotherhood and humanitarianism.

Out of Judaism there developed the religions of Christianity and Mohammedanism and from the Bible men derived many concepts of democracy—economic, social and political. All government officials from the king on down were subject to the law and must be impartial and just in their policies and judgments. The people were given the right to elect judges and other officers, and the people with the aid of the elders had the power of the administration of justice. The priests and prophets condemned oppression and exploitation and urged charity and liberality for the poor and the stranger. The Sabbath law provided all workers with a six-day week. All Jewish slaves were liberated after six years of bondage, all debts among Jews were released every seventh year, and every fifty years all slaves and debtors would be freed. No interest or usury was allowed and the principle of the sanctity of property was strictly enforced. Family and motherhood were exalted, marriage was compulsory for every one over twenty, and celibacy was regarded as a sin and a crime. Men were free to divorce their wives but public opinion generally disapproved of women divorcing their husbands. Polygamy was permitted among men of means and if wives proved to be unproductive of offspring concubines might be procured for the purpose.

The Old Testament contains some of the finest poetry and most admirable stories in world literature and its contents have inspired innumerable works of art and writing throughout the western world. The Hebrews were the first people to write interpretive history; that is, they would not only record happenings but tried to give meaning to the events of the past, which for the Jews had a religious and moral significance. The Old Testament was the Hebrew Bible, a sacred book of myth, legend, history and wisdom—the philosophy of the Jews in the ancient world. The ways of the Lord were sometimes mysterious and inexplicable, but the faithful Jew must always rely on the ultimate justice of God and the attainment of His plan for the world, regardless of their suffering and adversity.

Vocal and instrumental music, both religious and secular, abounded among the ancient Hebrews, but painting and the plastic arts were virtually shunned. Among the pagans painting and sculpturing were inspired by their religion but among the ancient Jews these arts were discouraged for fear that the prevalence of images might make the people revert to idolatry. Material works of art were mostly destroyed when a nation was destroyed but religious ideas and song were portable culture and could be perpetuated even by wanderers and refugees. Architecture and technology were still in the imitative or derivative stage and the Hebrews did not remain in Palestine as an independent nation long enough to develop an original style or skill. The study of science too was considered unnecessary, for the causes of all natural phenomena could be found in the Bible—everything happened by the will of God. So absorbed were the Jews in the Bible that they came to be called the People of the Book and henceforth manifested an uncommon propensity to love and esteem learning and intellectual pursuits.

Since religion was the central thought of the Judeans their children were carefully trained in the traditions of their fathers. At first they had open-air Bible classes and then they developed elementary schools attached to the synagogues. Attendance was compulsory for all boys while girls were given religious and household instruction at home. Subject matter in the public schools included reading, writing, counting, the Old Testament, history of Jewish traditions, Biblical law and poetry, and parts of the Talmud. The method of instruction usually employed was memorization.

However, it was not until the days of the Hellenistic Greeks, the Romans, and the cultural ascendancy of the Arabs in the Middle Ages that the Jews, achieved distinction in medicine, mathematics, philosophy and other secular fields; and not until the scientific revolution and the Jewish emancipation from the orthodox European ghetto did they begin to make their remarkable achievements in music, all the arts, literature, philosophy, and science as well as in practical matters.

Iran today is a small insignificant nation but in the sixth and fifth centuries B.C., under the name of Persia, it was the most powerful country in western Asia. Their first great king, Cyrus, conquered the Medes, the Lydians and the kingdom of Babylonia with all its subject states. His son, Cambyses defeated and added Egypt to their numerous lands. In the fifth century B.C. this empire was the largest in the world, extending from the Indus River in India to the Mediterranean Sea and from the Danube River to the Sahara Desert. Their soldiers penetrated southern Russia as far as the Volga River and invaded Greece where they were finally defeated.

The Persian kings were relatively generous and tolerant, permitting the subjugated peoples to retain their own languages as well as their own religious and social customs and in some cases even their own local government. The empire was divided into provinces or satrapies and each one was supervised by a Persian civil governor, a general and a secretary who would watch and check one another as well as all the people. Once a year the king would send out special inspectors, usually members of the royal family, to scrutinize the state of affairs in the entire realm and report to "the king of kings." There were also provincial garrisons of troops to maintain law and order, to spy on suspects, to ferret out and arrest seditious and rebellious subjects. Besides loyalty the national government required the conquered peoples to pay tribute and provide soldiers for the imperial army. In addition to money, the provinces had to send annually to the king all sorts of supplies, including such items as, corn, sheep, eunuchs and young horses. To facilitate the movement of troops as well as commerce and travel the government constructed an excellent and elaborate system of roads; for example, the Royal Post Road, running for over 1500 miles—almost the entire distance from the Persian Gulf to the Mediteranean Sea. This journey could be covered in less than a week by using a relay of fast horses traveling day and night.

Subject nations were not all submissive nor were the kings of Persia always lenient. If any member of the imperial organization became rebellious or tried to withdraw from the union the Persian ruler would quell the insurgents as brutally as any barbaric Assyrian potentate. Malfeasants, conspirators and recalcitrants were flayed, quartered, crucified or buried alive. The king ruled as an absolute monarch, his will was the law and all persons must prostrate themselves when approaching him. His authority was, of course, delegated to subordinates—to generals, priests and laymen; and sometimes he would have his mother or wife order the execution of a few troublesome dissidents. Rarely did anyone dare to criticize the king's acts or policies. One day a man saw his innocent son shot by the king and instead of remonstrating, the father complimented the monarch for his perfect marksmanship and at another time a number of persons, having been beaten by order of the king, thanked His Majesty for being aware of their existence. One shah took title to the throne after he had killed his father and seventeen brothers; however he died of remorse eighteen months later.

The priests were often the lawmakers and judges and since laws were divinely inspired a crime was also a sin. For minor offenses people were fined or flogged and for more serious crimes they might be branded, maimed, mutilated, blinded, imprisoned or put to death. Capital crimes were murder, treason, rape, sodomy, abortion, intruding upon the king's privacy, and approaching one of his concubines. Execution was by poisoning, impaling, crucifixion, hanging, stoning, burying one up to the head, crushing the skull between huge stones, or smothering the victim in hot ashes.

In their early history the Persians were reputed to be a very kindly, cordial folk, polite and hospitable. Their standards of propriety condemned spitting or blowing one's nose in public, eating or drinking in the street, and eating and drinking in excess. They enjoined cleanliness, fidelity to a promise, devotion to one's family and kindness to dogs, bulls and cows, especially pregnant ones. Boys and girls were ready for marriage when they reached puberty and their parents were the matchmakers. Both the government and the parents encouraged marriage and large families with many male offspring preferred, as boys were more valuable on the labor market and were always needed to replenish the king's army. Another source of supply for manpower were the numerous secondary wives and concubines found in all affluent and well equipped households. So eager was the government to further its policy of human reproduction that it strongly disapproved of contraception and regarded abortion as a serious crime. Although fornication and adultery were also unlawful the courts generally ruled that if a child was the result of either of the above misdemeanors both parties were forgiven. King Darius once rejected a request by a father of three sons to have one of them exempted from military service; instead he had all three put to death. Another man who had already sent four sons to the battleground begged King Xerxes to let his fifth son stay home and manage the family property. Xerxes not only refused but he had the son cut in two and then displayed the two halves before the army.

Before the fifth century B.C. Persian women were permitted to move about freely, to own property and sometimes to engage in business, but later upper class women were forbidden to mingle with men in public and if married they must not even see their fathers and brothers. Yet there were some very influential women at court and in the palace. In their days of opulence men and women in Persia dressed alike—both were covered from head to foot and both wore white underwear, a girdle and a gown with long sleeves. There were two visible marks of sexual distinction—a slit at the breast of the woman's garment and a long beard on the man's face. Wigs, curls, and long hair were worn by both sexes and perfume and cosmetics were frequently and strategically applied to enhance their scent and appearance.

Education in Persia was restricted—only the sons of the wealthy attended the schools which were conducted by the priests. The pupils learned to read, recite and memorize the Avesta, the sacred books of wisdom, and they acquired some knowledge of religion, medicine or law. A few were prepared for government work and all were given rigid physical exercises, trained in the arts of war and instilled with the virtues of austerity, loyalty and honor.

An Aryan-speaking people, the Persians readily adopted much of the culture of the nations they conquered. They learned to speak and write foreign languages especially Aramaic, a sort of international tongue; and they borrowed and imitated alien but talented sculptors and architects. A few Persians were familiar with literature and most people liked music and dancing. Science was not their forte; they imported the Egyptian calendar and a little mathematics and astronomy from the Babylonians. As in other nations the art of healing was hardly scientific but they tried to cure by medicine and magic. In the interest of the public, the government fixed the fees of physicians and surgeons though charges for treatment or operations varied with the patient's social rank. Interns gained their experience by practicing medicine on foreigners and evil persons. After three consecutive successful operations the young doctor would become a member of the guild and could then obtain a license to treat respectable God-fearing Persians.

Persia's foremost contribution to the world was in the realm of religion. The Persians had been worshipping many primitive deities—the most important being Mithra, the sun god, Araita, the earth and fertility goddess and a god of immortality symbolized by a bull. This bull-god would die and then come back to life; and so it was believed that the drinking of its blood would confer immortality. This primitive polytheism was the prevailing belief until Zarathustra or Zoroaster, a great preacher and prophet, introduced a kind of dualistic religious philosophy, known as Zoroastrianism. In the 6th century B.C. King Darius made this faith the official religion of the state. The Persians were taught to believe that the world is an arena in which two powers are at war—the forces of good and the forces of evil. The forces of good are led by Ahura-Mazda, who is the god of light and embodies the principles of truth, wisdom and righteousness while the forces of evil are led by Ahriman, the god of darkness, who represents wickedness, treachery and deceit. People are endowed with free will and may join one army or the other but Zoroaster urged them to fight for the god of light. This universal conflict would last twelve thousand years and its outcome would be a triumph for Ahura-Mazda. Zoroaster, who lived in the seventh or sixth century B.C. and who promulgated these doctrines, promised to come back again to reassure the good people of their future reward and announce the coming of the Messiah. Finally, at the end of the great victorious struggle Ahura-Mazda would proclaim the resurrection of the dead and the arrival of the day of judgment, when he would bring the virtuous to paradise and drop the wicked into the flames of hell. It was from the Persians that some of the Jewish sects, including the Christians, derived their concepts of satan or the devil, the last judgment, the Messiah, and heaven and hell. Zoroastrianism remained the Persian religion for over a thousand years but it underwent many modifications and adulterations. In the seventh century of the Christian Era Zoroastrianism was virtually stamped out when the Moslems conquered Persia. Those who refused to embrace the Mohammedan religion fled to India and their descendants called Parsees still adhere to the basic doctrines of Zoroaster.

When the Persians first embarked on their imperialistic course they were a homogeneous people with many brave and bold young men, vigorous, loyal and enthusiastic; and their military leaders employed methods of warfare that proved superior to those of their enemies. They often opened their battles by having archers disarray and soften the opposing army with a deadly storm of arrows and then they would follow this up with a devastating attack of the Persian cavalry to inflict a rout and complete collapse of the foe's troops. A favorite weapon frequently used by the Persians was the chariot armed on each hub with great steel scythes. And so they subjugated many lands, grew rich and powerful and culturally spirited and alive.

Persia flourished for about two centuries and then declined. The empire was composed of a motley of cultures with a number of subjected but refractory nations, reluctant to pay tribute and always seeking to restore their independence. Ambitious provincial governors would take advantage of incompetent kings by engaging in corrupt practices or participating in assassination plots and revolutions. Numerous wars and revolts drained the treasury and depleted the army, especially of its bolder and more patriotic personnel. Great wealth produced luxury, indolence and decline in national energy and vitality and a general demoralization set in. Concubines and prostitutes always accompanied the Persian troops to war whereas Alexander the Great, who conquered the Persians, did not permit his soldiers to make merry until after the battle was won. The Greek soldiers thus were better motivated—booty and pleasure were the reward for successful performance. In the fourth century B.C. military ascendancy in the Near East passed to the Europeans.

CHAPTER V

The Civilization of India

The earliest advanced form of civilization in India appeared about 5000 years ago—in the Indus River Valley in the northwestern part of the country. It was a culture similar to the one that flourished in Sumeria and it may have been brought to India from Mesopotamia; or perhaps Sumeria may have derived its knowledge from the Indus Valley. Archaeologists do not agree. But we do know from excavations that towns were meticulously laid out with paved streets of uniform width and the communities were provided with elaborate systems of aqueducts, drainage and sewerage conduits, public baths, temples, shops and a number of other buildings several stories high, nearly all constructed of burnt brick. There were many small houses and some sumptuous dwellings wih private baths and wells and a variety of household utensils and toilet articles. Many skilled artisans worked in copper and bronze, made pottery, knew how to spin and weave, and they transported goods in wheeled vehicles. The farmers raised wheat, barley and cotton and domesticated animals. The business men had a system of weights and measures and traded with the Sumerians, Egyptians, and Babylonians. They had a form of pictographic writing which has not yet been deciphered and they were familiar with games of dice and chess. They also made progress in the fine arts as is indicated by exquisite sculptures in marble, alabaster and terracotta by seals and toys, gold and silver jewelry, charms and other ornaments. Racially the people were mixed, white, brown and yellow, but the dominant group was the Mediterranean type of Caucasian. After an existence of about three centuries this Indus River civilization was either destroyed or abandoned. Probably floods and plagues befell the population or perhaps the climate changed. Whatever the cause India now passed through a kind of dark age which lasted about a thousand years.

About the close of the twentieth century B.C. Aryan speaking tribes akin to the Persians began to migrate from the Middle East and enter India, usually settling around the Indus and Ganges Rivers. They were not welcomed by the inhabitants already living there and had to fight them. After an extensive struggle the Aryans subjugated the Dravidians, as the natives were called, and they became masters of the land. These conquerors from the northwest were pastoral and agricultural and seemed to have a peculiar penchant for cows and often went to war to acquire more of these valuable animals. Cattle was the chief source of wealth, dairy farming was their favorite occupation, milk, butter and grain were their staple foods. Cow meat was not eschewed but was generally eaten only on festive holidays. The Indo-Aryans adopted some of the Dravidian customs and many of the invaders intermarried with the native women. After a while, however, the Aryan rulers began to foresee the disappearance of their race in India through assimilation and absorption, as the Dravidians greatly outnumbered the Aryans. They, therefore, commenced to denigrate the short, dark-skinned, broad-nosed natives as inferior human beings and began to restrict intermarriage between black and white people, hoping thereby to preserve the taller, fair-skinned, long-nosed Aryan race in India. This was probably the beginning of the notorious and unique caste system that was to exist in India until the twentieth century.

Caste, however, was not always based on race or color; it was also created by the barriers and differences of conqueror and conquered, of freemen and slaves, by sectarianism, and finally by the social grading of occupations. During the years 1000 to 500 B.C. when warfare was popular, warriors were admired and regarded as the highest in rank but when the land became peaceful and men returned to their farms, the priests or Brahmans became the most important social group; and after a struggle with the military autocracy the Brahmans assumed the highest position, socially and intellectually. The priests were the intermediaries between men and the gods and therefore indispensable to the farmers who were always dependent on the deities of the sun, rain and fertility. As educators of the young, the priests could inculcate in the minds of each generation a profound desire to revere and perpetuate the institutions of India and the leadership of the Brahmans. Next in rank were the nobles and warriors; then came the agriculturists and traders; and the fourth caste included the laborers, who were mostly non-Aryans who had been conquered and reduced to serfdom. In addition to the four fixed classes there were the miserable outcastes or pariahs who were offspring of unlawful marriages and the descendants of slaves or war prisoners. These were given the dirtiest and most degrading jobs, such as, the removal of dung and garbage. Originally these wretched "untouchables" were a small group but by the twentieth century there were almost fifty million of these lowest of India's proletarians whose touch or very shadow was enough to pollute an upper-class person. An outcaste must not come nearer than 24 feet from an ordinary workingman and not nearer than 74 feet from a Brahman. To remove the stigma of such contamination a person had to take a kind of ceremonial bath prescribed by law. The four castes were later divided and subdivided and grew more complex and rigid. The system was given religious sanction, that is, the people were taught to believe that caste membership is hereditary, is of divine origin and must not be altered. One must not marry outside of his caste, must not engage in another caste's type of occupation, must observe ceremonies associated with birth, marriage and death that are peculiar to his own group and must not eat or drink with persons belonging to another caste. Every detail of life, including diet, dress and manners, was fixed by strict rules, devised by a dominant elite—the Brahmans. This conservative social philosophy was retained and respected in India till the middle of the twentieth century, when the people were aroused from their traditional slumber.

The Indo-Aryans expanded eastward and southward but neither they nor subsequent conquerors brought complete political unity for any great length of time. India was generally divided into a number of petty states each headed by a king who allowed the communities to enjoy considerable autonomy. The country consisted of many diverse races, languages and creeds and since roads were poor, transportation and communication were difficult. However, occasionally an oligarchy or an individual emperor was able to centralize authority and unite much of the land.

In the sixth century B.C. the Persians conquered most of the northern and western parts and in the fourth century Alexander the Great subjugated a part of India. When the Greeks left a few years later the natives regained their independence and under the leadership of the Mauryan kings established a civilization comparable to that of the Greeks. The most famous king of the Mauryan dynasty was Asoka who ruled from 273 to 232 B.C. An ardent Buddhist, he aimed to govern his empire in accordance with the teachings of India's great prophet. He exhorted people to be kind, considerate, charitable and non-violent; set limitations on hunting and fishing and on the slaughtering of animals; and sent out missionaries to all parts of the country and to distant lands to preach and spread the gospel of Buddha, hoping to make his doctrine a world-wide faith. Asoka's policies brought prosperity and cultural advancement in art, literature, and learning. But not all the emperors were as capable, tolerant, and benevolent as he was and so after Asoka's death the empire began to decay; the Buddhist political union disintegrated into small warring states, and foreign invasions followed again. At the end of the fourth century in the Christian Era, the Gupta rulers, known as the warrior kings, reestablished Indian independence over a considerable part of the country and it managed to last over 200 years. This was a glorious period in Indian history when brilliant achievements were made in literature, science, religion, and the arts. It was during these years that Indian civilization spread throughout southeast Asia—to Indo-China, Malaya and Indonesia. This cultural imperialism greatly enriched and elevated the art, the literature and the religion in the smaller and less advanced regions of Asia.

In the fifth and sixth centuries of the Christian Era India was attacked by the Huns and later in the eighth century by the aggressive Moslems—first the Arabs and then by the more ferocious Turks, who slaughtered Buddhists and Hindus by the hundreds of thousands. The Mohammedan Turks were indoctrinated and trained to convert or kill the infidels while the Indians were taught to be tolerant and non-violent. Unfortunately non-violent nations are especially susceptible to conquest. The caliphs and the sultans made numerous expeditions subjugating one petty kingdom after another until the 14th century when they attained dominion over most of India. Buddhism became decrepit during the conflict and virtually disappeared from the land, but Hinduism managed to survive and continued to be the religion of the vast majority of the people.

Fierce and and ruthless, the sultans at Delhi rejoiced at the massacre of Hindus and other non-Mohammedans. Sultan Balban derived pleasure from the torture of infidels, rebels and bandits by having the victims trampled under the feet of elephants, by having them skinned alive or hanged from the gates of Delhi. Even more savage was Mohammed Tughluk who continued the truculent persecution, the plunder and butchery of Hindus in a wholesale manner. He murdered his father to become the sultan and later fed the flesh of a rebellious nephew to the rebel's wife and children. Yet in spite of his barbaric behavior and brutal policies Tughluk was an able scholar and writer, and displayed a dilettantish interest in art, science and philosophy. Subsequent sultans continued their ruthless religious persecution, offering rewards for Hindu heads and staging celebrations after every massacre of non-Moslems. Greatly outnumbered by the natives the alien conquerors sought to impoverish and decimate the Hindu population and make them submissive, and thus facilitate and perpetuate the power of the Moslems. But the sultans' policies were not all destructive for they did gradually reduce crime, abolish torture, they patronized art and literature, established towns, hospitals, colleges, mosques and dams.

In 1398, the notorious Tamerlane, a Turk, professing to be a descendant of the Mongol conqueror, Jenghis Khan, swept through India like a tornado, killing, destroying and plundering. He stayed in India for only a few months but his invasion was the most destructive the people had ever experienced. The Mongols slaughtered about 100,000 persons in cold blood, stripped Delhi of all its wealth and then departed, carrying away a multitude of slaves and women and leaving behind hunger, disease and anarchy. It took over fifty years for the Delhi sultanate to recover from the scourge. Toward the end of the 15th century, Babur, a descendant of Tamerlane and Jenghis Khan founded the Mongol or Mogul Dynasty. After a number of adventures and wars he restored the sultanate at Delhi and made himself the supreme ruler in the northern part of the country. He gradually extended his control over more territory until by 1605 his empire became the largest that India had ever known. The empire reached the height of its power in the 16th century during the reign of Akbar, the brilliant grandson of Babur. He was enlightened, humane and just, although it is said that at one time he had massacred 30,000 of his enemy and then built into a tower the heads of the victims. An efficient administrator, he curbed extravagance and corruption in government and maintained a surplus in the treasury through ample taxes, economy and a strict check on the honesty and competence of his officials. As a despot he could make laws, enforce them, and act as a supreme court, but he was benevolent and his code of laws were for the 16th century relatively lenient. Akbar forbade child marriage, permitted widows to remarry and prohibited compulsory suttee; and discontinued the practice of enslaving war prisoners and the slaughter of animals for sacrifice. He also put an end to trial by ordeal, reformed the currency, adopted a uniform system of weights and measures, and systematized taxation.

Eager to unify his empire and make all the diverse cults loyal and happy the great ruler issued edicts of tolerance and finally religious freedom. He abolished a tax traditionally levied on non-Moslem subjects, forbade discrimination against any race or creed in hiring and making appointments to jobs; and to attest to his broadmindedness he took into his harem several Hindu and Buddhist princesses to join his many Mohammedan wives. Deeply interested in religion he studied all the faiths of India, became conversant with their beliefs and frequently held lengthy discussions and debates with their respective priests and theologians. Over the course of years he gradually discarded some of the dogmas of Islam, declaring that all religion must be reconciled with reason, science and philosophy, and he prayed that all Indians would be united under one god.

He asserted that every faith has some merit in it and so he extracted a little from each and created a new eclectic religion with himself as the infallible head. From the Zoroastrians he derived sun and fire worship, from the Jains a predilection for vegetarianism, and to show his respect for the native sects and their idiosyncrasies he proclaimed a hundred meatless days a year, declared the slaughter of cows a capital crime and prohibited the eating of onions and garlic. When the Portuguese arrived in India Akbar invited Jesuits to his court, allowed them to build a chapel, to proselyte; he expressed an interest in the Christian gospel and even attended mass. But his religious policy succeeded in effecting only political unity, for after his death the followers of each creed returned to their own peculiar dogmas and prejudices.

As a young man Akbar had always preferred sports to school and so he never learned how to read or write. Instead of studying his lessons he would engage in rough and dangerous pastimes—riding fast horses, playing polo, learning sword craft, hunting lions and tigers, or training elephants. As an emperor his hobbies were collecting horses, elephants, deer and concubines. In spite of his illiteracy Akbar learned to love letters and art, he collected a large library containing 24,000 volumes and hired artists to illustrate and illuminate books and manuscripts. Then he had men read to him for hours at a time, as he imbibed facts and ideas that stimulated and cultivated his mind. He patronized poets, painters, architects and musicians. Surrounded by all this culture Akbar after a while became an extraordinarily edified, well-informed and wise emperor with a penchant for religion and philosophy.

After Akbar had reigned for forty years his son, the heir apparent, overly eager to become the ruler of India, hired 30,000 soldiers to help him expedite a change in administration, but Akbar quelled the revolt and persuaded his son to be more patient and wait a little longer. The emperor, saddened by filial disloyalty, died shortly after the abortive coup. Prince Jahangir, the rebellious son, had been forgiven by his father and succeeded to the throne. Not as able or dynamic as Akbar, Jahangir was devoted to alcohol, opium and sex and enjoyed watching men suffer tortures, such as, being impaled, skinned alive, or being torn to pieces by elephants. Yet in spite of his morbid cruelty Jahangir did follow the law in his severe administration of justice. He also learned how to read and write, left memoirs of his reign and was conversant with art and literature and displayed some intellectual curiosity. Unlike his father, Jahangir was not particularly interested in religion and so the people of India continued to worship in the traditional way attached to their particular bias and superstition; intolerance reappeared and spread over the land. His son, the crown prince, also tried to seize the throne before the king expired but he too was thwarted and had to wait a little longer before he was crowned Shah Jahan. Shortly after the coronation he had his many brothers ruthlessly slain to strengthen his security and tenure of office. Jahan's greatest interest was building and he was instrumental in the construction of hundreds of architectural masterpieces including mosques and palaces. His greatest and most magnificent structure was the Taj Mahal, a tomb for his favorite wife and for himself. The emperor employed thousands of laborers and artists who worked twenty-two years (1630-1652) to erect one of the most elegant monuments in the world.

Jahan was a capable and diligent ruler and a faithful Moslem, though his son accused him of being indolent and incompetent. He was undoubtedly lavish in his spending and taxes were heavy, which aroused discontent and Jahan was unable to finish his reign. One of his sons, Aurangzeb revolted and succeeded in deposing his father. The great builder was incarcerated in a prison located in a fort just across the river from the beautiful Taj Mahal, the home of his deceased wife and his own future resting place.

A very capable ruler and not as cruel as his predecessors, Aurangzeb was possessed of a fanatical zeal for Islam and pursued a policy of severe persecution of all non-Moslems, aiming to make all his subjects devotees of the Mohammedan faith. Hindus, Sikhs and Christians were forbidden to worship in public, thousands of their temples were destroyed and they were forced to pay higher taxes than Moslems. A man of morals, he prohibited strong drink, discouraged gambling, the voluntary burning of widows, castration of boys for sale as eunuchs; and he commanded all courtesans and dancing girls to marry or leave the country.

During the reign of Aurangzeb the Mogul empire reached the height of its power, but a few years after his death the great structure disintegrated. As a result of Aurangzeb's fanatical religious policy and the misery of the masses, many of the Indians became hostile to the government and the empire began to experience a trend toward religious and political separation. In the latter half of the eighteenth century internal dissension led to lawlessness, civil war and anarchy. The Moslem Mogul rulers were banished from the land and India fragmented into a medley of independent states. Meanwhile the Portuguese, French and English had commenced to take over parts of the country and India fell into the hands of Christian Occidental imperialists, who replaced the erstwhile Mohammedan intruders. The British East India Company ruled the land for many years and then by 1858 the Asian subcontinent was taken over completely by the English government and thus it became a possession of the British Crown. The natives were allowed to hold a few subordinate positions in the government but the educated Indians were very unhappy with their status and aspired to attain their national independence.

The chief occupation in India was agriculture. The people raised rice, wheat and other grains; vegetables, fruit, spices and cotton. Hindus held the cow sacred and would not take its life but many Indians did eat other meats including sheep, fowl, cats, rats, and lizards, and in time of famine, human beings. The soil also produced many minerals—coal, iron, copper, gold and diamonds. There were many skilled artisans and considerable manufacturing. Commerce flourished as Indians traded with Egyptians, Babylonians, Persians, Greeks, Romans, Chinese, Arabs and Italians. Cows were often used as money but by the fourth century B.C. metal coinage guaranteed by the government became popular. Business was hampered for a long time by the lack of contracts and an adequate credit system, by the failure to require security, by their religious objection to the charging of interest on loans. Taxes were usually very heavy, tolls and poor roads impeded transportation, famines were frequent and deadly especially after droughts.

The Hindu code of laws was formulated by the priests for the benefit of the Brahmans and was intended to strengthen and perpetuate the caste system. Priests were definitely the privileged class. They paid no taxes though they possessed an enormous amount of land and various kinds of property, received as gifts or fees for performing superstitious rites and ceremonies, for favors and services, or for intercession with the gods. For a price the priest could perform miracles, interpret dreams and omens, comfort the sick, give advice, and even render a barren woman fertile if she stayed overnight at the temple. In some parts of India a bride was expected to spend her first night of marriage with a Brahman, for which she paid an initiation fee. Brahmans were a social, religious and intellectual elite; they were the most privileged of aristocracy. Since they were the educated, they became the teachers, the lawyers, office workers, literary experts and philosophers, as well as the authorities on the holy books—the Vedas and the Upanishads.

Trial by ordeal generally prevailed in the courts. The accused might be required to plunge his arm into a vessel of boiling oil mixed with cow dung, and if his arm were not scalded he was innocent. Another ordeal required the defendant to be blindfolded and to retrieve a coin or a ring from a basket which also contained a poisonous snake. If the accused was not bitten he was innocent. Punishment was based on the principle of the law of retaliation. The guilty person might be beheaded, have his hands or feet mutilated, be thrown to the elephants or hanged on a hook by the chin until he died. Other cruel punishments included removing one's eyes, ears or nose, pouring liquefied lead into the throat, cutting or sawing men into parts or driving nails into the hands, feet or bosom. However crime in India was relatively rare as the people were inclined to be gentle and law-abiding.

The Brahmans however received special treatment as they were considered sacred and inviolate. If a man attempted to strike a Brahman the offender would suffer in hell for a hundred years; if he actually struck a Brahman, he would suffer in hell for a thousand years. If a laborer seduced the wife of a Brahman, the laborer's property was appropriated and his genitals were cut off. If a laborer killed a laborer the penalty might be a gift of ten cows to the Brahmans; if he murdered a member of the middle class he had to pay the Brahmans one hundred cows; if he killed a nobleman or a warrior he must give the Brahmans a thousand cows; but if a laborer killed a Brahman the laborer must die. On the other hand if a Brahman committed a crime he would have to pay more money than a person of lower caste. If a laborer stole something he was fined eight times the value of the theft; if the thief were a person of the middle class he would pay sixteen-fold; if a nobleman or warrior, thirty-two fold; and if a Brahman committed a theft he would be fined sixty-four fold.

A Brahman must bathe every day and must purify himself by ceremonial ablution after touching anything unclean or the person of a foreigner, or after being shaved by a barber. He had to follow strict hygienic ritual when performing physiological necessities of nature and he must always purify and sanctify his bedroom with a bit of the manure of the sacred cow. Brahmans refrained from drinking any beverage but water, abstained from eating meat, eggs, onions, garlic and mushrooms. Before each meal a Brahman would wash his hands, feet and teeth, then pick up his food with his fingers, and after eating he would wash his hands again, brush his teeth with a little twig and rinse his mouth seven times. They were expected to lead a righteous life and avoid greed, anger and sensual pleasures.

Marriage and family were prominent and esteemed institutions in Indian society. Bachelors and spinsters were very unpopular, for marriage and the legitimate production of children were considered religious duties and therefore obligatory. Early marriages were most prevalent and the wisest union was the kind arranged by the parents. In child marriages the couple would not live in cohabitation until the arrival of puberty. Marriage by purchase was regarded as more moral and prudent than one determined by affection because the former was rational and economically sound while the latter was the result of fanciful or transient physical passion. It was considered a compliment to be stolen and so a girl would pray for a young man to come and secretly carry her away as a bride to be. On rare occasions a man might offer his unmarried daughter for sale at a market place, draw a crowd with the sound of drums and trumpets and then display to potential customers the girl's uncovered rear and front parts. If the prospective patron was pleased with the price and the merchandise and the daughter was not too strenuously opposed to the buyer the deal was consummated and they became husband and wife.

Monogamy was preferred by the government but polygamy was permitted, on condition that the husband would show favoritism to his first wife. The latter must belong to his own caste while all subsequent mates were to be members of other castes and to be considered of inferior importance. A man could divorce his wife for adultery; but if she became diseased, alcoholic, excessively disobedient, quarrelsome or a spendthrift he was allowed to select another spouse to just supersede the first. Under no circumstance could a woman divorce her husband. The husband was the lord and master and was expected to be her protector but she was to be faithful and devoted and often an obsequious servant. Hindus believed that a disobedient wife would change into a wild dog after her death. A popular story of creation tells how God made the world and man and then found that there was no more solid substance left, so He had to make woman out of odds and ends. Though women in India were completely subordinate to men, mothers were always highly respected and revered, they had considerable influence over their children and often a mother would rule for her child.

The lowly status of women was partly due to Mohammedan influence for it was the Moslems who introduced the customs of *purdah* and *suttee*. Purdah was a system of seclusion of women while suttee was the practice of burning a widow on her husband's funeral pyre. Some widows preferred to be buried alive, which was permitted as an alternative for suicide by fire. Self-immolation was used as a manifest of sincere devotion to the master, to assure him of care in his next life, and to prove that marriage is eternal. Some believed that the custom was introduced to discourage wives from poisoning their husbands. However, suttee was not always widespread and obligatory and many widows chose not to follow their husbands to the next world immediately but to stay alive here on earth, as long as possible. In that case the law compelled the widows to shave their heads, to remain unmarried and to devote themselves to their children and to charity. Respectable women wore veils in public and could be seen at home only by their husband and sons. Prostitution in India was not common but was often restricted to the temples where sacred courtesans entertained the gods, that is, the Brahmans. They would also dance and sing and some of them made their services available to the general male public. The laymen, unlike the priests, had to pay and the girls would contribute a portion of their receipts to the Brahmans. In some parts of India city governments sometimes regulated the brothel house business and derived considerable income from this hustling libidinous traffic.

The Hindu religion was derived from the sacred writings of the Vedas and the Upanishads, but it was also influenced by the beliefs and practices of the non-Aryans in India. The Hindus worshipped many nature gods and on appropriate occasions they invoked an infinite number of divinities, but there were three supreme gods—Brahma, the creator, Vishnu the preserver, and Shiva the destroyer. Brahma is an impersonal divine spirit, an eternal and universal soul, from which the souls of all forms of life emanate. Every creature is charged with the spark of life, a spiritual element, introduced into every organism by Brahma; it remains in its assigned housing until death, when the soul departs while the body, which is material stuff (protoplasm), decays and ceases to exist. Material things are transitory and are really illusions; only that which is spiritual is real and immortal. A religious man must accept his lot, should not desire physical comforts and pleasures; he must fast and pray and thus free his spirit.

The most fanatic way of securing Nirvana or serene happiness was to practice yoga—a discipline that could bring about the union of one's soul with the universal spirit and thereby give the person wisdom and tranquillity. To effect this supernatural euphoria the yogis practiced self-mortification. A yogi might sit on the ground with his legs crossed, motionless, staring at his nose or his navel or he might look into the face of the sun for a few days until he went blind. Some of them would lie naked for a few years on beds of iron spikes, chain themselves to trees, live in cages, bury themselves in the earth up to their necks, hold up an arm or a leg until it withered and died, walk barefoot upon hot coals, or take a spiritualizing journey by rolling their bodies thousands of miles to a holy shrine. The perfect yogist posture was to squat with the right foot placed upon the left thigh or the left foot upon the right thigh, cross the hands and grasp the two big toes, rest the chin upon the chest and direct the eyes to the tip of the nose. These zealous practices were presumed to facilitate the attainment of wisdom, truth and redemption.

The soul of a dead man returns to Brahma to be recycled. It is then given a reassignment in a new material body on earth. This is called reincarnation or the transmigration of the soul. The kind of home that the soul is to occupy during its next sojourn on earth is determined by its conduct in the previous habitation. Thus a laborer whose record was morally excellent might become a merchant, a banker or a warrior. Sinful or wicked persons would be reborn as rats, pigs, hyenas or untouchables. In other words every soul is given an opportunity or a test to be virtuous or sinful and receive a reward or punishment accordingly. A person may move up or down the ladder of incarnations. Suffering on earth or low social status is the result of an evil ancestral background. Therefore one must, through constant renunciation of all desire, atone for his antecedents and thus build up a good basis for future existences, and he eventually may reach the highest stage in the physical world—that of the Brahmans. There the cycle of rebirth ends, the soul is liberated from the illusory material world; and when the Brahman dies his spirit rejoins the universal force from which the migration had started. Here the soul attains perfection and resides forever in transcendental bliss. It behooves all good

Hindus to be righteous and hopeful for then the next incarnation will be a happier one. Physical pleasure is an illusion and self-denial can be more rewarding than self-indulgence. In a land of perpetual poverty and deprivation rulers, priests and nabobs could utilize such a religion as a plausible philosophical rationale and as a spiritual placebo. It was a panacea for all social ills and a solution for all economic problems.

Few Hindus worship the lofty, remote and unapproachable Brahma, the creator of the world; most people prefer the more personal Vishnu or Shiva. Vishnu was a god of love who frequently came down to earth, assumed the form and nature of a human being, helped the sick, the poor, the unfortunate and raised men from their graves. Vishnu died and then rose to heaven, but he promised to return some day to judge the living and the dead. Shiva is the symbol of death and destruction but in association with his wife, Kali, they personify birth and reproduction. Devotees of this divine union adore idols representing the male and female organs. Phallic images adorn Shiva temples, they are carried in parades, and small figures or amulets are sometimes worn on the arms or around the neck. In one prevalent ritual the phallic figure was anointed with consecrated water or oil and then it was decorated with leaves. The goddess Kali had a consuming passion for men whom she devoured voraciously until the temple authorities ordered the introduction of goats as substitutes in the sacrificial rites.

The Hindus also made deities of animals, such as elephants, tigers, snakes, monkeys, crocodiles, peacocks and parrots, but the most sacred animal is the cow. Bovine figures are found all over the land, in homes, temples and city squares. The cow's dung was used as fuel or as a holy ointment and its urine was considered a miraculous detergent that could wash away all smutch and dirt and as a sacred wine taken internally it could remove inner pollution. The people would sometimes catch this precious liquid as it was discharged by the cow and collect it in pots and pans drinking it at times or applying it on their skin—hands or face as a kind of salve, or on their heads as a hair tonic. The cows were allowed to roam freely through the streets voiding where they will. Cows are never slaughtered and when they die they are buried with pomp and religious ceremony. No one is allowed to wear anything made of cow skin leather.

India is not unique nor peculiar in its religious customs. All nations have believed at some time in their history in similar superstitions—in the reverence of phallic symbols, in the deification of animals and in human sacrifice. India too had its magicians, soothsayers, necromancers and prognosticators. The new moon influenced economic prosperity, the shape of the holes in cloth eaten by mice determine the course of events, sunshine can make a menstruating woman pregnant, and when yawning a person should snap his fingers to the right and to the left to frighten away evil spirits that might enter the mouth. However, superstition and credulity do tend to diminish a little where modern education obtains and the freedom of speech is permitted to exist.

In the sixth century B.C. there arose among the Hindus a number of reform movements. They protested against the powers and privileges of the Brahmans and sought to modify the doctrines of the old faith. Of these heresies two developed into separate religions—Jainism and Buddhism, both of which have survived to the present day. There are very few adherents of Jainism but Buddhism, although not very prevalent in India, spread to all parts of Asia, including China, Japan, Indo-China and other lands of that continent.

Jainists believe that the universe was produced by the powers of nature—there is no creator, there is no world ruler. The aim in life should be the ultimate release of the soul from the physical body. To effect this liberation one must withdraw into a state of meditation and complete denial of the desires of the flesh. To be a good Jainist one must live right, that is, never injure any living thing, never tell a lie, never steal, never be unchaste, and never desire worldly possessions. Although to kill is forbidden, a person is permitted to commit suicide, preferably by slow starvation because in this way one can demonstrate the triumph of spirit over the desire for earthly existence, which is only an ephemeral sense pleasure. All living creatures, even insects must never be hurt. Thus zealous Jainists refrain from plowing the soil lest insects or worms be injured; they strain drinking water to save the visible little organisms; they protect aerial creatures from the heat of a lamp's flame and they cover their mouths when yawning to prevent flying insects from being swallowed. For fear of stepping on a bug a Jain carries a small brush to sweep the ground he is to tread or a chair before sitting down. There were at one time two sects of Jainists—the moderates who wore white robes and the extremists who wore nothing at all. Now they all wear the same kind of clothes as the Hindus, except for the saints who generally go about sky-clad or naked.

More important than Jainism was the religion that came to be known as Buddhism. It was founded by a man named Gautama who was given the honorary designation Buddha, the "Enlightened", when he discovered what he believed was the true road to redemption. As a young man he became deeply concerned over the problems of life and was dejected by the endless suffering of his fellow men. He studied the tenets of Hinduism and for six years he led a life of rigorous abstinence and self-discipline. During this ascetic period Buddha subsisted on seeds, grass, and dung; he pulled out his hair and beard, never washed or bathed, lay on thorns, and slept among rotting human corpses. But neither in Brahman teachings nor in self-torture could he find the cause of man's misery. What he wanted to know was how can a person escape from his agonizing and mysterious fate of the continuous vicissitudes of birth and rebirth.

One day while sitting in meditation under a shady tree he suddenly became enlightened—he found the truth about the secret of salvation and thus earned the title Buddha. For the next forty odd years he traveled through the villages of northern India and with his disciples, spread the message of hope to mankind. Selfish desire is the root of all evil, declared Buddha. To avert sorrow and pain a person must eliminate all worldly desires, all craving, and so attain the state of Nirvana—a place of complete peace and tranquility where one is released from the individual self or ego and becomes free from the anxiety of rebirth. But right conduct must accompany renunciation of desire, for this expedites deliverance. Right conduct contains five moral rules: Do not kill, Do not steal, Do not lie, Do not drink liquor, Do not be unchaste. Aphorisms of Buddha include: anger can be overcome by kindness, evil by good. Victory breeds hatred, for the conquered is unhappy. Hate can not destroy hate. Only love can destroy hate. Return good for evil and love for hate. He advocated moderation or the middle path of action, that is, the avoidance of fanaticism or extremes.

Buddha was not interested in theology, he seldom discussed the subject of God and immortality and was averse to dogma, ritual and prayer; the only thing about religion that mattered to him was right conduct. He was democratic, regarding all men equal; he invited all classes of people, members of any caste, to join him—the poor, the lowly, the rich and the high—salvation was open to all mankind. He wanted people to be less individualistic and more altruistic.

Buddha's ethical teachings spread over a great part of India and after his death in the fifth century B.C. his disciples made them the basis for a new religion. Buddha was now converted into a god, they revived many traditional rites and doctrines and devised many new ones. They created numerous legends and miracles about his life and career, venerated and worshipped his relics and statues, established cults, sacred places, monasteries, churches with all the paraphernalia and accoutrements necessary to equip such institutions. Buddhism flourished in India for about a thousand years, then it fell into decline and by the fourteenth century it was found only in Nepal and Ceylon. But in the early part of the Christian era it was brought to Burma, Thailand, southeast Asia, China, Korea and Japan in which countries it still abides.

Although religion was India's most important cultural achievement she also made significant contributions in secular areas. The priests were the leisured and the educated people and the monasteries were frequently centers of scholarship and learning. There Hindu and Buddhist schools and even universities developed and became so famous that they attracted students from many foreign lands. Schooling was for a long time restricted to the members of the upper classes with the exception of temple prostitutes who also were expected to procure an education as an essential requirement for their profession. Eventually all children except untouchables were given the opportunity to attend school. Basic courses included religion, character and proper conduct, as well as reading, writing and arithmetic.

India made remarkable achievements in mathematics and science. The Hindus were probably the first to use the so-called Arabic numerals, the zero sign and the decimal system. They were familiar with algebra, a little geometry and some trigonometry. They calculated the correct value of pi at 3.1416 and were acquainted with the radical sign, with square roots and cube roots, and the conception of a negative quantity. Their astronomers understood eclipses, solstices, equinoxes, knew of the sphericity of the earth and the daily revolution on its axis. They observed the moon and the stars and devised a lunar calendar. Indian physicists spoke of a force of gravity, delved into the phenomena of light and heat, wrote treatises on the mathematics and science of music, and invented a compass. Much progress was made in chemistry and its application to industry, and in the manufacture of various useful products. They understood the chemical processes of calcination, distillation, sublimation in the making of salts, alloys, dyes, glass, cement and fine steel.

Scientists in India studied anatomy and physiology by dissecting dead human bodies, describing the vascular system, the digestive and the nervous systems, ligaments and various organs. They thought the heart was the seat and organ of consciousness and that nerves ran to and from the heart. They learned a little about embryology, parental seed, birth control and some doctors even believed that the sex of an embryo could be influenced by food or drugs. Illness was attributed to disorder in one of the four basic body substances—air, water, phlegm and blood. Remedies prescribed consisted of charms, incantations, magical formulas, as well as herbs and drugs, though they also relied on fasting, diet, enemas, inhalations, blood-letting, hypnosis and the imbibing of a great deal of water. They knew about taking of the pulse, urinalysis, antidotes for poison, and they even employed a form of vaccination for smallpox. Their doctors warned against marrying anyone afflicted with tuberculosis, epilepsy, leprosy, chronic indigestion, hemorrhoids or loquacity. They performed many major and delicate operations, including cataracts, hernia, Caesareans and tissue transplantation. Surgeons used medicinal liquors as an anesthetic and sterilized wounds by fumigation. India's two most famous ancient physicians were Sushruta in the fifth century B.C. and Charaka in the second century of the Christian era. Sushruta wrote a book on medical education in which he discoursed on surgery, obstetrics, infant feeding, hygiene and the treatment of various ailments. Charaka compiled an encyclopedia of medicine and gave Indian doctors a kind of Hippocratic oath exhorting them to practice their profession not for monetary gain or prestige but for the good of humanity and he recommended that they treat the poor and the clergy, friends and relatives without charge.

There were numerous languages in India but the majority of the people spoke what were basically Indo-Aryan tongues. The Vedas and the Upanishads or the books of knowledge and wisdom were written in classical Sanskrit, an extinct literary language. They contain hymns and psalms as well as treatises on religion and philosophy. Writers were inclined to be didactic and sententious and so there were many maxims and homilies expressed often in the form of fables and fairy tales. Animals were greatly adored in India and so it is understandable why they were so often employed as human-like characters in their stories. This respect and reverence were not reciprocated by the animals as thousands of Indians were killed by tigers and snakes every year even as recently as the twentieth century. Many European fables, fairy tales and other popular collections of stories may have originated in India or they were influenced by Hindu narratives. Before the sixteenth century most Indian literature was oral—it was recited rather than read, and the Brahmans were the ones who did most of the reading. The Vedas were considered such sacred scriptures that if a serf or a workingman listened to the reading of the holy books they would pour molten lead into his ears, if he dared to recite some of the holy writ his tongue would be split and if he went so far as to commit the book to memory he would be bisected with an axe or a saw. The Brahmans regarded the contents of their holy writ as esoteric knowledge. Indian authors also produced lyric and epic poetry and dramas dealing in national legendary history, war episodes, and romantic love. Their aim was not only to entertain but to instruct in religion and ethics and so the epics and dramas abound in aphorisms, adages and other extraneous allusions.

As elsewhere religion inspired the development of the fine arts in India. Styles varied with the different faiths and character of the rulers and conquerors. The influences in mode included Hinduism, Buddhism, Mohammedanism or Persian and Greek artistry. Sanctuaries were often cut into solid rock in caves and cliffs and numerous free-standing temples were very impressive with their magnificent gateways, pillared porches, statues, friezes and reliefs. Buddhists early in their history built many dome-shaped memorial mounds called stupas. Made of earth, brick and stone, these shrines contained sacred relics of Buddhist saints and were found in many parts of the country. Islam was afraid of idolatry and so when the Moslems were in power they destroyed many statues and images, but most of the Indians felt that religious imagery was an indispensable component of their faith. Sculpturing and painting flourished if Mohammedan rulers were tolerant or when they were ousted from office. The Moslems built many superb mosques, tombs, palaces, and fortresses, simple and dignified in style, while Hindu architecture was often ornate, with highly lavish decoration, fanciful figures and grotesque design, depicting gods with several heads, arms, legs and breasts. The only surviving paintings are murals on the walls of cave temples which depict scenes from domestic and Indian court life and from the life and legends of Buddha. They also portrayed Hindu gods as well as animals and flowers, but unfortunately the colors have disappeared.

Hindus were fond of music—song and dance. Much of it was part of their religious worship that took place in the temple, but they had their secular music too. This was a kind of chamber music performed frequently before small gatherings in cultured upper-class homes. Instruments they were familiar with included drums, flutes, horns, cymbals, stringed lutes and harps.

. India was often conquered and controlled by foreign invaders but it was never destroyed; its people and its culture survived. The last alien rulers were the British, who surrendered their authority over the Indians in 1947, after enjoying economic, military and political dominion for almost 200 years. Because of religious animosities the country became divided into two independent states—the Republic of India which is predominantly Hindu and the Republic of Pakistan which is mainly Mohammedan. Both nations are hoping and striving to become modernized.

CHAPTER VI

The Chinese—Their Notable Achievements

The Chinese used to say that in the beginning there was chaos in a universe of water and then as a result of the rolling, the swelling, and bubbling of the waves there emerged from the liquid mass two forces, yang and yin, the active masculine and the passive feminine elements. The intimate association of these fundamental principles, yang and yin, brought into existence the first man, a little over two million years ago. They called him P'an Ku and he grew up to be a gigantic creature—hundreds of thousands of feet tall. Shortly after his arrival great blocks of granite appeared and floated in space and P'an Ku using a hammer and chisel began to build a world of which he was to be an intrinsic part. His head became the wind and the clouds, his voice was the thunder, his veins were the rivers, his flesh the earth, his hair the grass and trees, his teeth and bones the metals, his perspiration turned into rain, and all the insects that crawled on his body were transformed into the human race. P'an Ku completed his enormous task in 18,000 years and then he died; but they believed that he really lived again in the things he had created—the earth, the heavens and mankind. According to Chinese legend the celestial emperors who followed the great builder of the earth, P'an Ku, each reigned for 18,000 years also and conferred great benefits upon the people who gradually evolved from crawling insects to upright human beings.

Mythology aside, recorded Chinese history begins around 1500 B.C., that is, after the Paleolithic (Old Stone) and the Neolithic (New Stone) ages had been surpassed and supplanted by the Age of Metals. They began using bronze implements and some Chinese had learned to write. Considerable advance in civilization took place during the first historic regime, the Shang dynasty, although they still practiced human sacrifice. The Shang people lived in North China and were ruled by an emperor, the "son of heaven", who was the high priest; he decreed the laws and controlled the military. As son of heaven he was responsible to the gods and it behooved him to be benevolent, to promote the welfare of the people or else the gods and the people might unite, rebel, and remove him from office. On one occasion a blasphemous and brazen monarch defeated the Supreme Being in a game of chess, and for gloating over his victory, it is said, he was killed by lightning. The Shangs introduced the chariot in warfare, developed the writing brush, created beautiful bronze vessels, and invented chop sticks.

In 1028 B.C. the Shangs were overthrown by the Chous who were less civilized but better warriors. Semibarbaric but ethnically similar, the Chous intermarried and imbibed the superior culture of their predecessors. They expanded their territory and set up a strong central government. But then the emperor began to distribute different regions of the country among relatives and friendly local chieftains, who acquired so much autonomy that the nation's political system gradually evolved into a feudal type of empire. China thus became divided into many states and the central government with its royal power was weakened. The emperor was still regarded as the lord paramount by divine sanction, the Son of Heaven, the mediator between heaven and earth, who had influence with the vital and indispensable forces of nature. But his powers were ceremonial and religious while politically he became impotent. Actual authority was in the hands of the heads of states. The conflict among the feudal lords was chronic and resulted in a contest for supreme power.

In the third century B.C. there emerged from this struggle of the warring states a conqueror—the king of the state of Ch'in, Shih Huang Ti. After a few victories he made himself Emperor of Ch'in and as he subdued and annexed more territories Ch'in became China and the Emperor of China became a title that would last for over 2000 years. No other nation with such a large area and with so many people has ever been held together for so long a time. Under different dynasties the Chinese empire endured until 1912.

Shih Huang Ti had unlimited power. He stamped out all feudal institutions, changed the states into provinces and made all officials responsible to the Emperor. Although serfdom was abolished and the Emperor purported to promote the welfare of the community, he forbade freedom of thought and expression and instituted forced labor, conscription for military service, and compulsory migration and emigration of groups of people. He was hostile to intellectuals, especially if they disagreed with him, and so he ordered the works of Confucius, of Mo Ti and of many other authors to be burned. The imperial library, however, was allowed to preserve copies of some of the forbidden books including writings on agriculture, science, medicine and fortune-telling. Every subject was forced to bring his literature to the nearest government office where piles of these bamboo books were sent to the flames in huge bonfires. The Emperor also threatened to execute anyone caught with a book of the Confucian school or with any literature whose author believed that the power of a ruler should be limited by counsel or by moral restraint.

Nevertheless Shih Huang Ti united his country, gave the people uniform laws, standardized weights, measures, coinage and the length of carriage axles. He instituted a postal system, built many military roads and great tree-lined highways; embellished the capital with sumptuous palaces; simplified official ceremonies and unified China's style of writing. The most spectacular and most memorable project of the first Chinese Emperor was the building of the Great Wall of China. This huge fortress was intended to protect the country from invasions by the marauding Huns. It did not keep them out completely but the Huns were forced to take the line of less resistance, to move West and to conquer Rome instead. The construction of the Chinese Wall was one of the great feats of antiquity, comparable to the pyramids of Egypt. It is about 1500 miles long, forty to fifty feet high, fifteen feet thick, built of stone, brick and earth, with turrets and towers, arched gateways, and huge doors. The great structure also contained over a million bodies of workers. It was erected by forced labor, reinforced by criminals and merchants, and by scholars and writers who were not enthusiastic supporters of the emperor's regime. From time to time the thousands of weary workers had to pick up their bows and arrows to fight back the barbarian hordes sweeping toward them, but after ten years of involuntary toil the structure was completed.

The emperor's enormous success made him so conceited that he began to regard himself as indispensable, and to perpetuate his dynasty he thought it would be helpful if he were transformed into a god. But his ruthless, tyrannical policies, his heavy taxes and forced labor, had aroused enmity and hatred and there were several attempts to assassinate him. He kept a sword with him for protection and he slept in a different room every night so fearful was he of being murdered. His palace contained 10,000 rooms, his wives numbered 13,140 and he begot 2800 children. He was also in constant communication with magicians who professed to have the power of expelling demons and evil spirits that caused disease and death. However, the emperor's miracle workers were unable to keep him alive forever and he was not sufficiently popular to be deified. One day while on a distant trip searching for the elixir of life he passed away. On the long journey home the emperor's body became so malodorous that they had to counteract its smell with wagons of putrid fish. It was then interred in an immense tomb in a man-made cave with a bronze foundation, on the side of a mountain. To serve and keep the monarch company they buried alive with him all his family and relatives as well as a few hundred maidens, and since numerous workmen knew the path to the coffin and the whereabouts and the great value of a concealed treasure in the sacred sarcophagus they too were all left alive behind the walls to perish in the huge mausoleum.

The Ch'in dynasty did not last long—from 221 to 207 B.C. After the great emperor's death the government fell into the hands of a depraved but crafty eunuch who had the oldest but inept son of Shih's murdered; then he placed on the throne another incompetent son, who was also dispatched soon after, and finally the scheming eunuch crowned a grandson. But this grandson, suspicious and insecure, murdered the sexless kingmaker, abdicated, and then invited a rebellious general to take charge. The latter, an ambitious professional soldier, was Liu Pang who founded the Han dynasty which would endure for four hundred years.

The Hans were more popular than the Ch'in, at least in the beginning. The founder of the Han dynasty was liked by the common people because he was the son of a poor peasant, and the intellectuals were pleased because the new rulers did not persecute and execute scholars for trying to save books from the bonfires. In fact the tomb of Confucius now became officially enshrined and the emperor laid the ground work for the worshipping of the great philosopher. The government became relatively lenient and permissive, allowing freedom of speech and writing, and for over seventy years the emperors pursued a policy of laissez-faire which brought prosperity as well as peace to the Chinese empire.

But in 140 B.C. Wu Ti came to the dragon throne and the policy of non-interference was terminated. Strong central government returned and the quest for territorial aggrandizement and imperial control became its paramount goal. The Chinese conquered and annexed Korea, Manchuria, parts of Indo-China, Sinkiang, Turkestan and the rich Yangtze Valley, enormously augmenting the supply of valuable resources and greatly improving the means of communication in the empire. Acquisition of foreign land aroused interest in exploration and foreign trade and a bustling business between China and the West began to develop. It was during the Han dynasty that large caravans of camels loaded with precious rolls of silk moved across the desert sands through Persian and Arab territory and after an arduous journey of two or three years reached the city of Rome. As early as 36 B.C. the two great empires—the Chinese and the Roman, began to carry on a lucrative trade in which China exported such products as silk, furs, tea, paper, porcelain, gunpowder and playing cards. In exchange the Far East and Middle East usually received precious metals from the Romans since the latter had few desirable manufactured goods to offer, thus causing the West to suffer from an adverse balance of trade and a serious drain of Rome's supply of gold and silver. Barbarian tribes after a while made the overland route too hazardous and the merchants had to travel instead by way of the Indian Ocean and the Persian Gulf.

The economic policy of Wu Ti was revolutionary in that non-interference in business was replaced by a program of government regulation and control. To prevent maltreatment of the lower classes he nationalized natural resources, the production of salt, iron and fermented drinks. The state took over the ownership of the means of transportation, delivery and exchange, it regulated prices, limited profits and levied a five percent income tax. To provide jobs for the unemployed the government engaged in public works—irrigation projects, the building of bridges, canals, etc.

In the year nine of the Christian Era a usurper named Wang Mang, assumed the office of emperor. He abolished slavery on the farms, nationalized all the land and divided the soil equally among the peasants, and to prevent the concentration of wealth, forbade the sale or purchase of the land. He also took possession of the mines, established state control of the wine business and fixed prices. The government offered loans at low interest rates for prospective business men and lent money to the poor without interest for funerals and sacrifices. This mixed or partially socialistic economy brought prosperity and contentment to many but aroused opposition among the people of means—merchants, property owners, the high tax payers and the champions of rugged individualism. Revolt by these malcontents, insurrection and secession among the non-Chinese subject states, and attacks by barbarians on the border combined to overwhelm the illegal reform emperor. Wang Mang was removed from the throne, executed by the rebels, and his reforms were repealed.

In the year 36 of the Christian Era the House of Han returned to power and remained as the reigning dynasty until 220 C.E. These later Han rulers restored the provinces that had seceded from the empire and they extended their political power and China's cultural influence to many other parts of Asia. The government emphasized unity, stability, and the political and social teachings of Confucius and ordered everyone to religiously honor, respect and revere the famous philosopher. Sacrifices in honor of Confucius were made compulsory in the schools of the larger cities, his writings became classic and basic in the curriculum of every school and all applicants for jobs in the state service must be conversant with the precepts and tenets of Confucius. The young men who took and passed these examinations were sons of government officials or of landlords because training for civil service positions was expensive and the examiners were inclined to be partial to the gentry class.

The prevalence of moralistic philosophy notwithstanding, the later Han line declined, decayed, and after a succession of weak emperors came to an end. This was followed by chaos and political disunity, aggravated by invasions of Tartars and Turks. The south separated from the north and China was broken into sixteen kingdoms. Various war lords with their marauding armies, bandits and barbarians ravaged the land at will. And yet Chinese culture was not destroyed. Scholars continued to collect manuscripts and write books and commentaries and hold discussions on social and political philosophy. The writing of poetry, songs, novels and drama did not cease during the dismal age of strife and civil war. Basic Chinese institutions and traditions, city life and commerce continued to exist and Chinese civilization survived. Millions of unhappy people, finding hope and comfort in the mysticism of the then popular Indian cult, espoused the tenets of Buddhism. Buddha promised good people a better life in the future, in a reincarnation, which appealed to the poor and the downtrodden. Some of the Chinese converts were so fanatical that they would burn a finger, an arm, or the whole body as a sacrifice to Buddha and monks would sometimes soak their clothes in oil, sit on a platform, light a fire and slowly burn to death before thousands of wailing men, women and children.

The Dark Ages came to an end when in 589 the Sui emperor reunited all of China. There were two Suis and they ruled for 29 years. The first one curbed the petty war lords who were constantly fighting and ravaging the land, and he increased the proficiency of the administrative system by improving the civil service examinations. But his reign was cut short when his second son, Yang Ti, murdered him. Yang Ti had a penchant for travel and so he ordered the building of canals. Four canals were constructed including the famous Grand Canal that linked the Hwang Ho (Yellow River) with the Yang Tze, which not only enabled the emperor to take frequent trips but they greatly facilitated the transportation of food and other commodities as well as soldiers and government agents. The country was thus politically welded together more thoroughly, particularly the north with the south. However, these gigantic projects were very costly and required the employment of forced labor and cruel overseers. Millions of workers were pressed into service for a variety of public works and compelled to toil till they collapsed—often from hunger and sickness. This caused much discontent among laborers as well as tax-payers. Moreover the emperor was glaringly extravagant as evidenced by one of his journeys through the canals and rivers when the line of his boats extended for about a hundred miles. This time he brought with him his entire retinue of guards, servants and a myriad of concubines. The people who lived in the districts through which the grand voyage passed were forced to provide food and clothing for the emperor, his family and all his retainers. During one of these peregrinations a rebellion broke out and soon after, the second and last of the Sui was assassinated. This happened in 618.

The new dynasty was called the T'ang and it controlled China from 618 to 907. They were on the whole vigorous and brilliant rulers and the Chinese like to link them with the equally esteemed Han dynasty by calling themselves "The sons of Han and the men of T'ang." Outstanding cultural achievements during the T'ang dynasty included the development of printing and the production of some of China's finest art and poetry. The greatest of these emperors was the second member of the house, T'ai Tsung, who ascended to the dragon throne in 627 after putting to death two rival brothers. He drove away the barbarians and expanded the empire and instituted many domestic reforms. T'ai Tsung and his successor, Empress Wu Fu, extended China's boundaries to include more of Manchuria, Mongolia, Turkestan and all of Tibet.

Like some of his predecessors T'ai Tsung was concerned about the competence of the nation's bureaucrats. He saw to it that the civil service examinations were uniform and were offered at regular intervals in all towns and districts and to all young men of ability from every class of society. A thousand years after Confucius lived they still followed his advice for training and educating government officeholders before they were appointed. Not only must they learn to be proficient but they must also be cultured, that is, familiar with classical literature and philosophy. Though jobs were in theory available to all classes of society the highest grade of offices were generally given to scions of the most notable families while the more humble posts went to the sons of the lowly. Imbued with the teachings of Confucius T'ai Tsung was wise and humane by seventh century standards. He believed that by eradicating corruption and reducing the expenses of government he could lower taxes and so, as an economy measure and to demonstrate his sincerity, he released three thousand very dear ladies that had been brought to the palace to entertain him. The great emperor also believed in more humane treatment of criminals, that poverty is an important factor in the cause of crime, and that a ruler should fast three days before sanctioning a death sentence.

Meanwhile economic prosperity continued to develop on the farms and in the cities. The Tang rulers encouraged agriculture and were eager to keep the farmer happy since he was the chief source of food and revenue. Government favors for farmers included irrigation and transportation projects, an equitable tax system, and the occasional breaking up of large estates to prevent monopoly and force the distribution of land. The government gradually reduced the amount of forced labor from the peasants, and in the seventh century, by creating a standing army, freed them from compulsory military service, and in anticipation of future famines stored grain to be distributed among the poor, both rural and urban. During these years, however, most of the Chinese were well fed, well clothed and well housed. The middle class of people were increasing in number, growing wealthy as trade and industry burgeoned and expanded. Foreign commerce, overland and oceanic, attained remarkable proportions, greater than ever before. The riches of China, the abundance of desirable luxuries, the wealth of culture and ideas attracted and impressed visiting foreigners. Many merchants from various lands came to buy and sell and to learn about the civilization of the Chinese. Among these strangers, travelers and settlers were Arabs, Jews, Persians, Greeks, Hindus, and Japanese. Unlike its European contemporaries medieval China generally permitted foreign customs and religious ideologies to spread over the land. Zoroastrians, Mohammedans, Christians, and Buddhists broadcasted and endeavored to proselyte among their Chinese neighbors, but only the Buddhists met with any substantial success— Buddhism became the most popular faith in China.

In the 8th century the golden age of China reached the apex of its civilization, its glory and its brilliance. Only the Arab empire was comparable to China in wealth and power.

Emperor Ming Huang occupied the throne at the height of China's affluence and prestige and during the time of its widest territorial extent, but he also presided over the beginning of its decline. He was a warrior and a poet who encouraged music, art, literature, research and learning. Ming Huang, like his grandfather, thought that criminals could be rehabilitated and so he reformed the courts and prisons and abolished capital punishment. At the beginning of his reign in an age of great extravagance and luxury, he believed in sober living, in simplicity and temperance and even discouraged the wearing of jewelry, silk and ornamental fabrics. Then at the age of 60 he fell passionately in love with Yang Kuei-fei, the most beautiful woman in all of China. Yang Kuei-fei had been the mistress of his eighteenth son, but now the Emperor Ming Huang made her his own favorite concubine. So charming and beguiling was this young lady that through her influence the eminent ruler abandoned his interest in reform, public affairs and intellectual pursuits. The government was turned over to his sweetheart's brother, an incompetent and unscrupulous young man who now held the office of prime minister. Numerous other relatives of Yang Kuei-fei were granted sinecures, while the aged Son of Heaven gave himself up to sensual delight with his earthly goddess. But then there was the Tartar, An Lu-shan also a favorite and also in love with the enchanting Yang Kuei-fei. He was in command of several armies and was very ambitious, and so he took advantage of the situation at court. He instigated a rebellion and proclaimed himself emperor. Meanwhile the soldiers of Emperor Ming mutinied, arrested the brother of the informal empress and all her office-holding relatives at court, beheaded them and then they seized Yang Kuei-fei and slew her in front of the Emperor. The old ruler now abdicated and a civil war followed in which millions were killed. An Lu-shan, the Tartar who aspired to be the monarch never made it as he was assassinated by his son, but the latter was killed by a general, who in turn was then slain by his son. In 762 with the restoration of peace the old broken-hearted Emperor returned but he died a few months later. The T'angs continued to reign until 907 C.E. but they had lost their authority and the glory. The last century of the dynasty was characterized by dissension and civil war. Until 960 the country was divided into various independent states and five little dynasties tried to rule over China but failed as soldiers and bandits ravished the land. Some southern states separated from the union while in the north the barbarians again attacked and invaded the border territories. Amidst all the danger and chaos village elders and town fathers continued to maintain control over the local residents. And despite decay in the national government education remained alive and was promoted and disseminated when revised texts of the classics were promulgated by the newly invented method of block printing.

    The five little dynasties were not able to bring order out of chaos and so as usual a strong man appeared and seized the Dragon Throne. One day some soldiers gained possession of the yellow robe of royalty and when their general became drunk they threw the robe over him and proclaimed him Emperor of China. A new ruling house, the Sungs, thus came into power and remained sovereign from 960 to 1279.

The Sung emperors were not very powerful. They subdued the southern states that had seceded but were unable to contain the barbarian Tartars in the north; in fact, the latter forced the Chinese government to pay them tribute in the form of huge amounts of silver, silk and tea. These payments coupled with increasing monetary inflation resulted in a heavy drain on precious national resources and a financial plight bordering on bankruptcy. The consequent burden of paying higher taxes was particularly hard on the small farmers who had to bear more than their share while the large landowners cleverly evaded taxation.

Late in the 11th century the emperor appointed as prime minister an extraordinary reformer, named Wang An-shih. He had held other offices before, had improved the school system, had recommended the greater study of practical subjects, the revision of the civil service examinations, and had advocated the simplification of the Chinese language. Wang believed that the government should take over the management of agriculture, industry and commerce, and ought to provide the necessities of life for all its citizens and promote the welfare of all the people. In modern parlance he was a state socialist and as such he wanted to protect the working class from exploitation by the rich. Under Wang's guidance small farmers were aided by a reduction in taxes and by government loans at low interest rates and peasants would henceforth be paid for their labor on public works jobs. The government regulated wages, fixed prices, found work for the unemployed in agriculture or on public projects, bought up farm surpluses and redistributed land to the farmers. They also provided insurance for the unemployed, relief for the poor and pensions for the aged. Wang An-shih, philosopher, scholar and statesman was so devoted to and so preoccupied with his benevolent program for the people of China that he left no time for washing himself or have his clothes cleaned. His reforms were expensive and the people didn't want to pay the price, particularly the wealthy who felt they were being ruined by government taxes. Corruption spread through the enormous staff of officeholders, while conservatives denounced the radical innovations as unfeasible, contrary to human nature and oppressively harsh and unfair to the rich. Meanwhile wars, floods, droughts, a comet in the sky, all contributed to the failure of the experiment in economic planning and welfare statism.

Meanwhile the Tartar tribes continued their push against the forces of the Sung emperors until the barbaric nomads from the north reached the Yangtze River, and by the second half of the 12th century the Chinese held only the southern part of their country. Then the famous king of Mongolia, Genghiz Khan, launched upon his celebrated career of conquest, which included China and all its possessions; and by the 13th century became one of the world's greatest conquerors. After his death his invincible armies led by his sons and grandsons persisted in their successful sweep through most of Asia and eastern Europe. Genghiz Khan was so savage and brutal that he would sometimes order prisoners to be nailed to wooden statues, or be cut to pieces or boiled or skinned alive. He seemed to have a passion for cruelty and destruction and loved to massacre populations and reduce resisting cities to dust and ashes.

All Mongol males 15 to 70 served in the army of which the cavalry was the most important branch. Every soldier was equipped with four horses and if he became hungry or thirsty he might puncture the skin of one of them and suck a little of its blood. The Chinese held out against these ferocious fighters until 1279 when the last Sung emperor was overthrown. He was killed in an attempt to escape and reach Taiwan where he expected to set up a government in exile. Many patriotic Chinese resisted to the end and killed themselves rather than surrender. A general who was protecting the surviving boy emperor placed the child on his back and leaped with him into the sea. Historians say that at the same spot a hundred thousand excessively loyal Chinese drowned themselves rather than become subjects of a foreign nation. This was the first time China had been completely subjugated by alien conquerors. However the grandson of Genghiz Khan and his heir was no barbarian. He was Kublai Khan, a prudent and tolerant man, who became a Buddhist, imbibed Chinese culture and ruled over the huge empire which extended from Korea to Hungary. India was not included in this empire and the Japanese repulsed two Mongolian attempts to conquer them; otherwise virtually all of Asia and eastern Europe, including Russia, recognized the suzerainty of the Tartar ruler.

Peking was the new capital of China and from there, with the able assistance of the traditional mandarin bureaucracy, Kublai Khan governed wisely and effectively. This notable emperor improved transportation on the roads and canals and established a very efficient postal system which employed 200,000 horses with stations every 25 or 30 miles. The government stored food surpluses to distribute in times of scarcity and provided aid for peasants who suffered from storms, floods, drought or insects, and granted relief to the sick, to orphans, and to aged scholars. The great khan was very generous in his support of educational institutions, he had the calendar revised and he encouraged art, literature and building, particularly of palaces. In literature, it is interesting to note that the Mongols had a particular predilection for drama and the novel and were instrumental in popularizing these literary forms. Aware of the prevalence of order and prosperity throughout the realm and taking advantage of the liberal attitude of the Mongol rulers, travelers from Europe and Asia arrived in great numbers. Russians, Arabs, Jews and Italians came to trade and to see Peking, one of the world's most beautiful cities as well as other places, and to gaze upon a highly civilized land of great opulence and strange customs. Most famous among these visitors was the Venetian, Marco Polo, who spent almost 20 years in China, held office under Kublai and gave a detailed account of the then most fascinating and advanced country in the world. The Chinese also learned a little from the visitors who introduced a new food, sorghum, a few vegetables, the use of the abacus, and new ideas in art and religion.

The Mongol dynasty went through the same cycle as all their predecessors—strong rulers were followed by weak ones. Prosperity was followed by depression—the nation after a while became infested with bandits, pirates and partisans, guerrilla bands and finally organized rebellion. At the head of the insurgents was a former Buddhist monk—Chu Yuan-chang, who succeeded in driving out the last Mongol emperor and in 1368 established the Ming dynasty. The Mongol population disappeared among the more numerous Chinese who almost always assimilated their conquerors. The Ming remained in power until 1644 during which era China was fairly prosperous, was notable for extensive building and impressive for its voluminous literary and artistic output. Although for a while China engaged in exploratory, maritime expeditions in the Indian ocean and forced small weak nations in southeast Asia to pay her tribute, she no longer ranked militarily among the great powers. China was satisfied in just containing the Mongol menace on the northern border while the Japanese took advantage of her naval weakness and raided the Chinese coast repeatedly. On the west the overland commerce with Europe was closed by the Ottoman Turks and China abandoned her old policy of hospitality to strangers and began to manifest a growing hostility to foreign influence. But the Europeans—merchants and missionaries, persisted and came by sea to sell and buy and to spread the Christian faith. Moslems too, came to profit and proselyte and seemed to specialize in the travel business—inns, horses and camels.

Then the Mings, like all the other dynasties began to lose power when government corruption, heavy taxation and famine among the masses led to internal dissension and rebellion. Taking advantage of the chaos, the Manchus, who were unfriendly neighbors across the northern border, poured through the Great Wall and in collusion with Chinese rebels captured Peking. Decisively defeated, the reigning Ming emperor drank a toast to his family and then after stating that he was ashamed to meet his ancestors he hanged himself with a girdle. And so the Manchu monarch took over and China was dominated by foreigners again. However in due time the Manchurians too would be assimilated and disappear in the vast Chinese population. The dynasty that the Manchus set up was known as the Ch'ing line. They stayed in power from 1644 till 1912 when China became a republic. Of the many emperors that were on the throne two were very able and outstanding—K'ang Hsi (1661-1722) and Ch'ien Lung (1736-1796), grandfather and grandson. China reached its widest extent and became more populous than it had ever been before.

The Chinese continued to produce an enormous amount of art, literature and enlightened philosophy, but their civilization remained conservative, dormant and static, for they had made no advance in science, in medicine or in technology. In fact Chinese culture was basically and essentially the same at the beginning of the nineteenth century as it had been in the third century. The Europeans, on the other hand, had been transformed and were still undergoing revolutionary changes in almost every field of thought and endeavor, thanks to the Renaissance, the Scientific Revolution, and the Industrial Revolution. Europe had not only caught up with China, it had surpassed the Orient and had become the most civilized area in the world. Around the opening of the 18th century Emperor K'ang Hsi was sufficiently prescient to warn his people to beware of the white peril coming out of the west that might someday destroy the Chinese civilization—its traditions and institutions. However, most of the Chinese regarded Europeans as barbarians who had nothing very useful or profound to offer them.

About eighty per cent of the Chinese people were engaged in farming or were in occupations connected with agriculture. They were familiar with the rotation of crops and employed composts and leguminous plants as well as the usual animal dung for fertilization of the soil. The Chinese also returned to the fields human excreta instead of wastefully conveying it into the rivers and the ocean as modernized nations do today. They developed many irrigation projects, maintained public granaries to provide food in times of famine and sometimes granted financial aid to farmers in distress. China's farmers cultivated a vast variety of grains, fruits, and vegetables and they raised numerous pigs, goats, sheep and fowl. Many Chinese earned their living from fishing or from the production of spices and tea, which was the national drink. But the standard of living among the peasants was miserably low, as the farm population constantly multiplied while the land was inadequately divided. About two thirds of the farmers crop was needed to feed the family and the value of the balance was hardly sufficient to pay for the remaining expenses. Famine occurred annually and millions died of hunger each year. Peasants lived mostly on rice in the south and millet, a cereal grass, in the north, ate some fish and occasionally bits of pork. Beans were also an important source of protein. Milk, butter and cheese were not used, the Chinese believing that one should not wait for vegetable products to go through the animal before obtaining their benefits. The rich enjoyed a variety of foods, including vegetables, soy beans, fruits, macaroni, vermicelli, seaweeds, silkworms, grasshoppers, and other insects, and watersnakes, fish, poultry, pork, mutton, goats, horses, rats, cats and dogs. Tea was their favorite beverage.

Although agriculture was the chief occupation, many were engaged in industry and commerce. The most important commodities manufactured in China were paper, porcelain, lacquer ware, spices, silks, tea, cotton goods, gunpowder, playing cards,—all produced by the simple handicraft methods in small shops or in households. Artisans were organized into guilds which regulated wages, prices, and hours, limited competition and discouraged the introduction of labor-saving machinery. They enacted strict rules for their members and settled all disputes of employers and employees through mediation boards. There were also a few household slaves and in time of famine girls and orphans might be sold as bond servants. Merchants ranked below the scholar and farmer in the social scale and were not very popular because they were regarded as parasites—middlemen who grew rich selling products made by other men's hard labor. But traders were indispensable members of society who paid a great deal of money to the state treasury and contributed considerable to the wealth of the nation. The Chinese used copper and silver coins and paper money, drafts, bills of exchange, banks and pawnshops. Transportation was by cart, horse, donkey, camel, wheelbarrow, sedan chair, or by a pole balanced on a person's shoulders.

The Chinese people were governed by the Emperor who in theory was the ruler of all mankind because non-Chinese people were considered inferior and subordinates but also subjects of the Son of Heaven, who represented the Supreme Being on earth. He decreed and enforced the laws, was chief justice, and head of the nation's religion. Actually his power was frequently limited by a grand council, an inner cabinet and numerous administrators. Furthermore laws were often unenforced because of the vast size of the country and the slow, inadequate means of transportation and communication, the incompetence and dishonesty of officials, and the inefficiency of the military and police agencies. Besides there were intrigues of eunuchs and women of the court, civil strife and rebellion, and finally invasions by foreign armies which sometimes conquered a part and sometimes all of China. For administrative purposes the country was divided into eighteen provinces, each headed by a governor and his assistants. The provinces were subdivided into townships with administrators in charge of courts, police, taxes, and a few other functions. Officeholders or mandarins were chosen through the civil service system and jobs were open to all young men regardless of social class. Eligibility to office was determined by competitive examinations which emphasized character, judgment, and knowledge of the writings of Confucius. At the national palace the Emperor often employed eunuchs as officers of state and as attendants in the royal harem. It was customary for some parents to physically qualify and ensure a son employment in the government or palace by having him mutilated before the age of eight.

Most men and women in China felt that their primary loyalty was to the family rather than to the national government. The Chinese family was usually large, for the sons would bring their wives to live at or near the paternal home and so it would after a time embrace several generations and so expand until entire villages consisted of a single clan. It was then a well organized unit governed by the elders and providing for the welfare of all its members. They took care of their poor, sick, aged, and unemployed and provided education for the young. It was a patriarchal family where women were subordinate to men and boys were preferred to girls. Sons were better workers and fighters, girls became producers of labor and laborers for other families when they got married. When food was scarce female infants might be left in the fields to die or be eaten by animals. To please the men, who like their women to walk elegantly, parents would have their daughters' feet bound at the age of seven and thus keep them tiny and dainty. In public only females of the demimonde were permitted to mingle socially with the men. The Chinese believed in the struggle of the yang and the yin principle and the yang or the male element must prevail; for it represents light, warmth, activity and righteousness, while the female or yin element denotes weakness, passivity, darkness and evil. The symbol of male strength is the rooster crowing in the rising sun. Nevertheless love and devotion abounded in the Chinese family, women were sometimes very influential in public affairs, often dominated their husbands and their homes, and were always revered by their sons.

Monogamy was the rule in China but a husband was allowed to possess concubines, especially if a wife failed to give birth to a male heir, and sometimes she might even help procure a mistress to obtain a son for her spouse. A wife might also urge her husband to bring home and marry his supplementary concubines. Emperors were uncommonly polygamous. Kublai Khan would have, in addition to his four empresses, a hundred young women brought to him every two years and with the aid of expert judges he would select 30 or 40 to serve him for a period of time in sundry capacities. They were all inspected for beauty, temperament, body aroma, sweetness of breath and quiet sleeping habits. Parents considered it an honor to provide a daughter for the royal harem.

Marriage was compulsory and at one time there were officials that enforced the custom whereby every man must be married by the age of thirty and every woman by twenty. Marriages were arranged by the parents or by matchmakers. The bride was brought to her husband's home and she would live there for a three month period of probation and in the meanwhile wedding presents were exchanged between the families. Sometimes a bride would take along as a gift for her husband a younger sister or a cousin to serve as a supplementary spouse or as a substitute in case the bridegroom changed his mind. Prearranged unions of children sometimes took place shortly after puberty and occasionally even before birth. The children would live with their respective parents and might not even see each other until the unveiling of the bride at the marriage ceremony. Divorce was rare but it was allowed for men only and for almost any cause including inability to bear children or for talking too much. When the husband died she was expected to remain unmarried and on rare occasions might commit suttee as they did in India. The last of the Ming emperors, anticipating suicide, requested his wife to kill herself also and she followed his wish.

Excepting the subjection of women the Chinese were inclined to be socially equalitarian, for they avoided the caste system and rigid class distinction. But many of their customs were quaint and quite bizarre to Westerners, to wit: A person was a year old when he was born. Meals began with dessert and ended with the soup. They paid their doctors only when they were well. Women wore trousers and men wore skirts. They shook their own hands instead of the guest's hand. Generally a man covered his head indoors and went bareheaded outdoors, but when gentlemen wore hats and glasses and met on the street they would remove their spectacles and not their hats. Humor was not supposed to elicit laughter. White and not black was the color of mourning and the highest form of revenge against a personal enemy was to commit suicide on the enemy's doorstep.

In the fine arts the Chinese were most gifted in painting. They created charming ink sketches and water colors on woven silk and painted superb frescoes, generally using a single color with different shades. The artists expressed with extreme delicacy and restraint a sense of mysticism often inspired by religion. Their style was generally impressionistic. Their favorite subjects were scenes of nature—mountains, water, flowers, birds and horses, but seldom were there pictures of people. Chinese sculptors worked with stone, bronze and clay, and were also inspired by Buddhism, but sometimes they carved grotesque dragons, dogs and other animals. There were also vivid and vigorous sculpturings of scenes from mythology and from everyday life as well as delicate figurines of human beings and animals. Chinese artists were also talented in the carving of wood and ivory in lacquer and bronze work. Buildings were made mostly of wood and brick and their most impressive structures were temples, palaces, archways, pagodas and arched bridges. The roofs of some of their buildings were often unique in their curved massive shape with figures of fantastic phoenixes and dragons and with ornate, colorful tiles. They were skilled in the development of porcelain ware, in carving glass and in the making of exquisite vases and articles of jade.

Music was associated with religion, dance and drama. The Chinese were familiar with harmony and tonality and they used such instruments as drums, bells, gongs, cymbals, castenets, tambourines, flutes, trumpets, oboes, whistles, ocarinas, viols and lutes.

China produced a vast amount of literature. The best poetry appeared in the T'ang period in the eighth century and the two greatest poets were Li Po and Tu Fu. Chinese poets generally wrote brief, simple, sometimes subtle verse, portraying melancholy moods, the mystic beauty of nature, the evils of man, the injustice of poverty and the cruelty of war. Drama started with solemn ceremonial dances accompanied by music of the flute and drums at the temples and at court, where entertainers amused the emperor and his friends with stories, jokes, dances and acrobatic feats. The Mongols introduced popular plays for the masses that dealt with dramatic episodes in Chinese history or in the current life of the common people. In the Chinese theater scenery and stage props were scarce but the actors wore elaborate costumes, heavy makeup or masks and employed a great deal of pantomime, gesticulation, even acrobatics and dancing to convey intent and meaning. Sometimes they drew pictures on cardboards which were shown to the audience to illustrate and clarify the players' charades. In other words, the people in the audience had to stretch their imagination as well as their necks immensely. The lines were written in verse and were sung by the actors and accompanied by an orchestra which sat on the stage. While the play was going on the spectators would eat, drink, smoke and talk to one another and even the performers would sit on the stage and sip their tea while waiting for their cues. It was considered socially debasing for one to become an actor and women were generally excluded from this profession although prostitution was legal and widespread in China.

Stories were told before they were written and in ancient China there were many professional storytellers. Often a glib and imaginative vagrant would spread a mat at a convenient street corner, sit down and amuse passersby who would stop and listen. At the conclusion of the story he would pass around a hat or cup and the people who listened to the tale might reward him with an appropriate gratuity. Other professional narrators performed in tea houses or at fairs and sometimes the tales were so long that they had to be recited in installments as serial stories. This novel way of earning a living required a constant supply of material and so it led to the appearance of short-story writers and subsequently to lengthy forms of fiction. These were romances that portrayed in detail interesting escapades, adventures, wars, intrigues, historic events, and an occasional diversive discourse on contemporary public affairs. The real Chinese novel developed during the Mongol dynasty. The authors displayed skill in character analysis and were often humorous and satirical and realistic. The Chinese also wrote essays, literary criticism, histories, biographies, encyclopedias and commentaries on religion and philosophy.

China did not have free public education but there were a few small schools voluntarily organized and maintained by villages or clans. Middle class parents sent their sons to these schools and affluent families engaged private tutors for their children. Wealthy girls might receive a literary education also but more often girls would specialize in training for wifehood and motherhood. All pupils had to read and memorize large quantities of literature, Chinese history and the classics, particularly the writings of Confucius. Teachers aimed to inculcate the old standards of literary style and to perpetuate ancient ceremonial institutions and the traditional ideals of Confucius and his disciples. Rules and regulations in the elementary schools were strict, discipline was severe, independence and originality of thought were discouraged. For those young men who wished to enter the civil service there were state schools for further learning, where students would receive very intense scholarly training. Here the courses were more advanced and the young men were expected to study and compose poetry and write intelligent essays on the problems of moral and political life. There were periodical examinations and those that passed received degrees and became eligible for public office in the bureaucracy—national or local. These well educated officials called mandarins were held in very high esteem, as all scholars in China were. Some educated young men entered less prestigious careers, such as, the army or teaching or they became Buddhist monks after some special study and training in that religion. However, more than half of the population of China remained unschooled and illiterate.

The Chinese admired the beauty and enjoyed the pleasures of nature but never bothered about its secrets or its laws and never tried to control its forces or powers. They were inclined to leave nature alone and so pure science and the scientific method were virtually unknown until the advent of European culture. Yet the Chinese were practical minded and they did introduce a number of useful mechanical inventions. They contributed the compass, paper, paper money, silk, block printing, porcelain, gunpowder, hand grenades, the water wheel, the wheelbarrow, wallpaper, upholstered chairs, coal and gas for heating, cold storage, finger-printing and a taximeter. They wrote a number of treatises on geography, mathematics, astronomy and agriculture but their attempts at pure science were adulterated by superstitious admixtures. China had numerous medical schools though most of their healing practices were based on experience with the efficacy of ancient herbs combined with the popular superstitions about demons and evil spirits. The state held annual examinations for prospective physicians and fixed their salaries in accordance with their grades on these tests. Chinese doctors wrote medical encyclopedias and many treatises on fevers, dietetics, surgery, the pulse, and on diseases of women and children. They used a wine for anaesthesia, inoculation in treating small-pox, and mercury for syphilis. Technologists dreamed about flying cars, iron ships, self-moving vessels, and they invented a primitive seismograph, but knew very little about hygiene, public sanitation and sewage systems.

In most countries people adhered to one religion and excluded all others but in China they often worshipped at many altars, for it was considered prudent and advantageous to be eclectic in one's religious beliefs and thus have optional and sundry roads to heaven. In fact the vast majority of the Chinese were Confucianists, Taoists and Buddhists at the same time and they also retained a number of superstitious traditions that came down from the distant past—from the days of nature gods and animistic spirits. At funerals all three religious organizations sent their representatives to participate in the ritual. Some people did adopt one of the three major faiths and gave it exclusive adherence but these devotees were in the minority. Buddhism was the only foreign religion that became popular among the Chinese though there were a few million Christians and Mohammedans and a few thousand Zoroastrians and Jews. The Chinese were not concerned with rewards and punishments in an afterlife but wanted a guarantee of profit and happiness here on earth. They were inclined to be skeptical about religious doctrines that were so specific and categorical about heaven and hell. China was usually tolerant toward foreign teachings though Buddhists were at times persecuted, Nestorian Christians and Zoroastrians were once driven out of the country and Moslems were even massacred, but such occasions were rare.

During their remote antiquity the Chinese believed there were spirits everywhere—in every nook and cranny on earth, in heaven, and throughout the universe, in every animal, in leaves, in trees. These spirits were ominous and terrifying, causing disease, accidents, floods, earthquakes and other misfortunes. Hence priests devised a set of rituals and ceremonies to guard against or to expel the malevolent beings. To keep spirits out of their homes orthodox animists would place a screen inside the front door which necessitated a left or right turn after entering and the zealots were told that the divine phantoms could move only in straight lines. The masses also believed in witchcraft, good and evil omens in messages conveyed through mediums, and in divining the future by magic formulas or by reading the stars. The priests introduced the wearing of charms and amulets to bring good fortune and prophesied by observing the movements of the stars, and declaring days lucky or unlucky. They also informed persons of their fate under all possible circumstances and contingencies by shaking up marked bamboo sticks in a container and then rolling one out; the one that came forth would reveal the judgment of the spirits on coming events. Another method of divining the future was to have a priest scratch a question on a bone (called oracle bone) or on a tortoise shell with a little round hole on it. Then with a poker he would hold the object over a fire and burn it until lines and cracks appeared that resembled written characters. These symbolic marks were interpreted by the priest and the divinity's reply was imparted to the suppliant. Rulers frequently consulted these oracles before adopting a policy or embarking on an expedition and thus man's destiny depended on which way the bone cracked.

Another noteworthy religious practice was ancestral worship, which made funerals and burial very important. Nourishment and valuable objects were placed in the grave of the deceased and when parents passed away the custom was for their children to mourn for three years. Mourners wore white garments and abstained from meat, wine, and attendance at public gatherings. It was customary to be buried where one was born. They burned incense and supplied the soul with all the needs for a voyage to Paradise—paper imitations of a horse, food, clothes and servants. It was believed that the spirit of an ancestor might come back to the house of his descendants and if he were not properly revered he might bring disaster. They therefore would prepare a wooden tablet on which the name of the dead person was inscribed and place it opposite the entrance of the main room because the spirit was supposed to descend into his tablet. On festival days the members of the family would burn incense and place sacrificial food before the tablets, thus propitiating the soul of their ancestor. Like all agricultural people—the Chinese in their early history worshiped the deities that controlled the relevant forces of nature—the sun, the earth, winds, rivers, rain, fertility, vegetation and the soil. Prosperity was the farmer's primary aim in life, but hard work alone would not guarantee abundance and success; one must also have the friendly approval of the gods. Accordingly the farmers, aided by the priests, offered sacrifices of bowls of cereal, burnt animal flesh, wine or beer and in very early times even resorted to human sacrifice. During the spring festival, when elaborate fertility rites were performed, young men and girls would dance and copulate in the fields to illustrate the significance of their petition.

Chinese priests were not considered sacred or superior; they were ceremonial aids or ministers and the emperor too was called a priest-king although he was also referred to as the Son of Heaven. When the winter solstice began, December 22, the emperor would purify himself by fasting. At daybreak, wearing a sky-blue gown suggestive of the blue heaven, he would come before a national sacred altar which contained a deep-blue jade tablet consecrated to the most majestic god or Heaven, the supreme deity, Shang Ti. He bowed and prayed while a young ox and twelve rolls of blue silk were burned as a sacrificial offering. Then incense was burned, followed by music and dancing. At the summer solstice festival dedicated to the earth goddess, the emperor was clad in a yellow gown like the color of the clay in the soil, and he again officiated at a similar ceremony of sacrifice and prayer. Lesser officials held sacred observances throughout the land in provinces, cities and other political units and offered their prayers and oblation to the divine elements of nature—fire, water, wind, thunder, mountains and streams.

Intellectual Chinese preferred Confucianism or the ethical teachings of Confucius. His doctrines were taught in the schools, read in the temples and carved on monuments. They were memorized by scholars and were selected as standards for examinations in schools and universities. The celebrated Chinese philosopher who lived in the 6th and 5th centuries B.C. was venerated as a great religious teacher but he never claimed to be divinely inspired. The people, however, built temples of worship to honor him and offered sacrifices to his spirit. Scholars and other educated persons, even agnostics and atheists, revered him as a sort of substitute for a god. Confucius himself had believed that there must be a guiding force—Shang Ti, a vague impersonal supreme being that maintains order and stability and rules the universe. He also often spoke of or referred to heaven or T'ien, another Chinese term for the almighty celestial deity. Confucius asserted that authority and leadership are indispensable in every administrative division, whether it is the family, the village, the province, the empire or the cosmos. In each case the lord sovereign helped his people in their difficulties and chastised them for iniquities. Confucius also favored the observance of ceremony as a form of discipline and as a manifestation of faith which made for peace and harmony. He also recommended that people should on regularly specified days demonstrate love and reverence for their ancestors, not by religious worship, but by a commemorative ceremony. The great philosopher was skeptical about life after death and avoided reference to the supernatural, but esteem for one's antecedents would contribute to the perpetuation of basic customs and institutions and thereby promote order and stability. Confucius was no theologian and his teachings were not a formal set of dogmas but just a system of morality or ethical principles. He was neither a prophet nor a messenger of the Lord; he never saw visions, never performed miracles, never held conversations with God; he was just a great moral leader. But his views on virtue and good government were so highly cherished by the people, the emperors, and the mandarin schools for bureaucrats that the philosopher was virtually deified and worshipped as a kind of god.

The Confucian code of cardinal virtues included filial piety, propriety of conduct, and historic tradition; and he exhorted people to be honest, truthful, sincere, moderate, reasonable, faithful and well informed. Good manners and a love of music would promote benevolence and righteousness. He emphasized the importance of ceremony and etiquette and even at an execution one should observe the rules of proper conventional decorum. In driving with a woman a man should drive with one hand, but, cautioned the philosopher, one must keep the other hand behind his back. He believed in the effectiveness of education and conditioning—that character and human nature can be improved and perfected and that rulers could and should be properly trained and enlightened. However experience must have disillusioned him, for at one time Confucius was employed to be the instructor and adviser to the governor of his home state of Lu, (now called Shantung). Under the noble philosopher's guidance the ruler became benevolent and conscientious and so all of Lu became faithful, law-abiding and prosperous—a model community. But a nearby jealous rival contrived to overthrow the government of Lu and its celebrated teacher. He sent twenty beautiful horses and eighty charming girls who were skilled in music and dancing, to divert the prince from his serious duties and responsibilities. These creature comforts proved to be so enchanting that the ruler of Lu made merry with the young ladies and neglected his public functions. But a happy society, according to the great sage, depended upon the sobriety and righteousness of the ruler; so Confucius was forced to resign his post and leave the state. Commenting later on the conduct of his pupil-politician he remarked that he had never seen a man who loved virtue as much as he loved beauty.

Selected passages from the thoughts and doctrines of Confucius were collected by his disciples and published as the *Analects* or conversations. He often expressed himself in aphorisms, such as: The good man is serene, the bad is always in fear. To be poor without being resentful is difficult; to be rich without being arrogant should be easy. Return kindness with kindness but recompense injury with justice. Learning without thought is useless, thought without learning is dangerous. Those who know the truth are not equal to those who love it. Learn the past and you will know the future. Never do to others, what you would not like them to do to you.

Confucianism was rational, ethical and wise, and appealed to those who believed that knowledge, truth and behavior should derive from logic and reason. But in their religion most people preferred the heart to the brain, they loved feeling more than mind and had a predilection for a faith that was rich in myth, mystery and the irrational. Therefore more popular with the masses and with many highly imaginative religious persons were Taoism and Buddhism. Taoism was based on the philosophy of Lao Tze who lived in the 6th century B.C. Lao Tze taught that truth and reality can be obtained through intuitive contemplation. Happiness comes with peace of mind, which can be gained only by withdrawing from worldly interests, by the renunciation of the pursuit of power, wealth and material things. Harmony, tranquillity, long life and immortality are the rewards of self-effacement, suppression of desires, the renunciation of science and intellect. He prescribed leading a simple rustic existence. A wise man must sit, meditate and contemplate nature; he must not try to reform the world but accept things as they are. A benevolent ruler should interfere as little as possible in the life of his subjects; he should pursue a policy of laissez-faire and allow his people to follow their intuition. To govern well the prince must keep the people simple and ignorant; he must beware of intellectuals for they favor more and more government regulation, and legislation which will ruin the nation. Intellectuals may have an abundance of knowledge and ideas but too often lack wisdom and a capacity for action. Philosophers must never be rulers for they are impractical and dangerous to the state; and it is easier to govern the naive and uneducated than the sophisticated and well-informed.

Lao Tze urged people to refrain from quarreling, fighting and going to war. Among his many precepts were: Recompense injury with kindness. It is right to take away from those that have too much and give to them that have not enough. To the good be good, to those who are not good also be good in order to make them good.

Long after Lao Tze's death his philosophy of passivity and quietism was combined with mysticism and superstition and transformed into a popular religion—Taoism. To please the masses the pagan theologians introduced the customary features of common creeds: belief in many gods, (Lao Tze himself was converted into a deity); guardian spirits, evil spirits, saints, monks, witch doctors, sorcerers, elaborate ritual and public worship in temples. There were medicine men who sought to drive out demons from sick people and animals employing magic divination, charms, chants and highly dramatic performances involving snakes, tigers and grasshoppers. And from Buddhism Taoists adopted the doctrine of transmigration of the soul and the belief in thirty-three heavens of joy and eighteen hells of torture. These afterlife abodes were nationalized, that is, they were given Chinese names and were to be administered by Chinese gods. Taoism permitted their clergy to marry and thus enabled them to retain the highly cherished tradition of ancestor worship. The Chinese believed that a ghost would return to earth in search of food, which was supposed to be supplied in a sacrificial offering by a descendant of the deceased. To die without offspring was the worst kind of fate and a hungry ghost was extremely dangerous. Celibacy was therefore generally shunned. Some members of the Taoist cult engaged in the practice of disciplined diet, breathing exercises and spiritual meditation. Millions of Chinese joined the organized religion of Taoism, which lasted until the twentieth century.

Buddhism was at first disliked by the Chinese because many of its doctrines were alien to their nation's tradition—the concepts of transmigration, asceticism, celibacy and contempt for the physical world. Some of the emperors persecuted the Buddhists, destroyed hundreds of their monasteries and tried to eradicate the foreign Indian faith, but as poverty and discontent among the Chinese population increased the principles of Buddhism became more attractive and expedient. These doctrines offered the weary toilers, the oppressed proletarians of China, hope, comfort and tranquillity; they taught their devotees how to mitigate a life of pain. Suffering is caused by desire, therefore one must overcome desire; material things are transitory and unimportant; the less one wants the easier it is to forgo it. Furthermore Buddhism was more democratic than the other two major religions, for it promised the downtrodden that by right living on earth they could improve their chances in a future existence through the process of reincarnation. So millions of Chinese flocked to the big beautiful temples inspired and entranced by the colorful, gorgeous ritual with candles, incense, impressive images and mysterious ceremony. Both Taoism and Buddhism played very important roles in the inspiration and development of Chinese art and philosophy.

Among the many other schools of thought, outstanding were the Mohists or the followers of Mo Ti who lived in the fifth century B.C. His philosophy was a combination of religious idealism and material utilitarianism. He believed that the universe is governed by Shang Ti, a personal god who loves mankind and expects people to be altruistic to all their fellowmen. A person who devotes his interests to the welfare of others will involuntarily promote his own well-being. He believed in free will and self-perfection but the ruler, as a servant of Heaven, should assist in improving the economic condition of the people. Selfishness is the source of all evil and so we have greed, avarice, exploitation and war. Mo Ti recommended state regulation of the production and distribution of the necessities of life while luxuries, elaborate ceremonies, non-useful commodities and customs and activities that serve no practical purpose should be eliminated. The simple life, universal love and enlightened government will assure mankind peace and security.

Another eminent philosopher was Mencius who, like Confucius and Mo Ti, was a native of the state of Lu. A disciple of Confucius, Mencius lived about a hundred years after his master. He wandered around the land teaching and preaching against poverty, luxury and war and urging governors to always work for the welfare of the masses. Crime and disorder are the result of poverty and ignorance; and it's the duty of government to provide education and equality of opportunity for all, regulate economic activities, assist the farmer in particular, and avoid forced labor, tariff and heavy taxes. Men are by nature good and if the rulers are just their subjects will be virtuous. If the princes are tyrannical and unjust the people have the right to rebel and depose them. Rule by one man is more feasible than rule by the people because wisdom and learning are prerequisite qualities for good governors and it is easier to educate one than many men. The ruler must be a philosopher or he should be guided by a philosopher.

There were many other schools of thought in China. In disagreement with Confucianists were the Legalists who believed that people are not naturally good nor will they follow the example set by a virtuous and benevolent prince; for human beings do not become righteous and altruistic by association. People are inclined to pursue their own interests unmindful of public welfare, and the only way to alter their disposition and conduct is to enact laws which are firmly and justly enforced. They disapproved of laissez-faire but they agreed with the Taoists that the common people are too simple and ignorant to rule themselves and must be governed by an aristocracy. Some Legalists favored the socialization of capital, a government monopoly of commerce and the enactment of laws to prevent the manipulation of prices and the concentration of wealth. The realists declared that man is by nature savage, evil and avaricious—that the good develops in man as the result of social custom, laws, training and education. The epicureans believed that the chief purpose in life is pleasure, that one should gratify his every impulse. People are just the puppets of insensible and unsympathetic forces of nature; there is no god and there is no life after death. Yang Chu asserted that morality and universal love are deceptions and delusions; that the wisest course of conduct is sensible sensualism. Idealists would escape from a complex, turbulent existence, from civilization with its machinery, artificialities and pretentiousness, and return to primitive nature, to live in simple peace and harmony and freedom as the birds and the beasts in the woods. Life as a man on earth is transient and death is only a change of form. But Confucius remained the favorite philosopher and so conservatism and stability generally prevailed in the history of China.

Chinese culture was not the oldest in the world but it was the most durable. It had a continuous existence for about thirty centuries and at times it surpassed all others in art, literature, manners, and philosophy. But tenacious devotion to their ancestors and excessive pride made the people hostile to foreign influence and averse to new ideas and innovations. Thus when the Europeans discovered science and technology—the key to success in the modern age and the means to a higher standard of living, the Chinese regarded it with scorn. Meanwhile Europe advanced and became progressive and aggressive, while China remained weak, old, stagnant and miserably poor. The mortality rate was very high and the average life expectancy was the late twenties or the early thirties. Not until the end of the 19th century did the ancient and dormant power finally awaken from its slumber and begin to break away from its attachment to the past. Heretofore the Chinese had been defeated in wars from time to time and had been ruled by culturally inferior foreigners or barbarians, but these invaders had been either absorbed or driven out. The imperialists who attacked China in the nineteenth century, however, were not barbarians, nor were they altruists either, but they did introduce ideas and expedients that could promote the well-being of the Chinese. Transformation finally came in the twentieth century—first the democratic revolution of Sun Yat-sen and then the violent collectivistic revolution of Mao Tse-tung; and China was on the way to modernization and hopefully to a better way of life.

CHAPTER VII

(Part 1)

The Greeks
The Story of Sparta, Athens and Alexander the Great

The civilizations so far described were Asian or North African, but henceforth this book will deal with the European peoples and their culture. Of these, the earliest and one of the most important, was the Hellenic or Greek civilization, which appeared on the scene about 3000 years ago. Originally inhabitants of the Danube River valley, the Hellenes, named after a mythical King Hellene, migrated south in search of new homes and more food for themselves and their animals. When these primitive immigrants arrived they found a people already living there, on the mainland, on the island of Crete in the Mediterranean and on numerous small islands in the Aegean Sea. The Hellenes are better known by their Latin name—the Greeks. Their language was Indo-European and they were predominantly members of the Alpine branch of the white race. They were mostly of medium height, with broad heads, brown hair and brown eyes.

The language of the earliest known inhabitants of Greece has not yet been deciphered but racially these people have been classified as Mediterranean whites, similar in appearance to Egyptians and Babylonians, that is with short and slender bodies, long heads, dark eyes and dark hair. These Aegeans, the first nation in Europe to be civilized, flourished between the thirtieth and the twelfth centuries B.C., contemporaneously with the Mesopotamians and the Egyptians. Their world had been centered on the island of Crete which so dominated the eastern Mediterranean that historians referred to the entire area as the Cretan civilization, and sometimes they called it the Minoan after the legendary King Minos.

At river valleys where the soil was fertile they raised cattle, grain, olives and grapes; in the cities they made and sold olive oil, wine, honey, textiles, gems, bronze products, fine pottery and many other commodities. The main source of wealth was the maritime trade and the Cretans were the leading carriers between the Near East and Europe for many centuries before the Phoenicians. Commerce with Egypt was particularly extensive, but the Aegean navigators also sailed to Italy, Spain and perhaps England. Business was privately owned and even the king was an enterprising capitalist who engaged in manufacturing and selling various products at an adequate profit. But the government regulated and controlled all industry and also supervised labor.

The ruler was a monarch whose power was limited by an aristocracy; in fact, all the people seemed to enjoy relative freedom and equality, even the women. With an economy that was mostly commercial and industrial there was little need for slaves, and being a maritime nation they relied on a large fleet to protect their country; in naval warfare very few prisoners are taken. In theory the king possessed power over all functions of government—legislative, executive, judicial and military, but, since there was no compulsory military service the army was very small and so an absolute monarchy could not have been very viable.

Royalty and the wealthy Minoans built splendid stone palaces, town houses and country mansions equipped with running water, baths and flush toilets. There were also thousands of humble but comfortable dwellings several stories high constructed of brick. Palaces were decorated with elegant furnishings—exquisite statuettes, stone carvings, beautiful vases, frescoes and reliefs. Minoan painting was mostly naturalistic and their sculpture was usually done in miniature—delicate, graceful and refined. They excelled in painting of murals and in their sculpturing of animals. Excellent work was also done in spinning, weaving, engraving, metal ware, pottery and carpentry. Artists as well as the people in general were individualistic, gay, free and happy, and peacefully inclined. The Aegeans enjoyed music, dancing, hunting, fishing, chess and prize fighting. There were light weight, middle weight and heavy weight boxers and sometimes they fought with gloves and sometimes with bare fists. The most thrilling and most popular sport to watch at the arena of an ampitheater was baiting and grappling with a bull. The animal would be tormented and forced to charge with its head down, then an acrobatic toreador would grab the animal by its horns, leap into the air, somersault over its back and then land feet first on the ground in the arms of a female athlete. Women enjoyed complete equality with men; there were not only assistant toreadors, but also female prize fighters, and they were permitted to engage in virtually every occupation.

The average Cretan male wore only a loin cloth or short skirt, unless it got very cold, of if he had to attend an important ceremony when more bodily covering was required. Notables and rich men covered their bodies completely, wore turbans and even leather shoes. Women dressed in long bell-shaped skirts, tightly compressed around the waist, they wore an attractive hat and much jewelry. The female face was unveiled and the breasts were bare—a remarkable exhibition of the freedom of Aegean women. The female deities created by sculptors and other artists were dressed in the same style.

In Crete God was a woman—the Earth Mother, the source of all life—ruler of the universe. She represented creative fertility, the mysterious power of reproduction and so the people venerated the bull and the snake, animals which they believed were connected with generative fertility. Sometimes the mother goddess is depicted holding a divine child born in a mountain cave. This holy son later dies and then rises from the dead. The people sacrificed animals, grain and fruit to Earth Goddess and since the Cretan religion was matriarchal the rites were administered by priestesses. There were prayers, hymns, processions and several holy symbols including the double ax, the swastika and the cross. Aegean gods were unconcerned about man's concepts of right or wrong and Earth Goddess was the source of evil forces as well as good. Cretans believed in life after death, for in their graves one finds food, lamps, razors, mirrors, toilet articles, toys and hobbies, such as boats, chess sets, and musical instruments which would give the ghost comfort and entertainment if and when life after death became boring.

Around the opening of the twentieth century B.C. the Hellenes, vigorous and warlike, invaded the southern part of the Balkan peninsula. They moved slowly, but after a few hundred years they succeeded in occupying all of the mainland of Greece, the islands to the south and east, and some even moved into the western coast of Asia

Minor in what is now modern Turkey. The Aegeans were all subjugated, their cities were ravaged and plundered but their arts of civilization were preserved and then gradually absorbed by the invaders. The surviving Aegeans and the barbarian conquerors intermarried and produced the Greek or Hellenic people who would after a time of transition achieve their outstanding fame and glory. It was a new, superior civilization, using the Greek language, though the Minoan influence must have been considerable.

From 1150 to 800 B.C. there was a period referred to as the age of darkness because of the chaotic conditions that prevailed; law and order broke down, the people lapsed into illiteracy and art became crude and primitive. There was economic collapse. The people tried at first to make a living by herding sheep and cattle, then by raising grain, olives, figs, grapes, and a few other farm products, but the fecundity of their women always exceeded the fertility of the soil, which was uncommonly barren. Landless and unemployed peasants began to move to the cities. Food became scarce. Some people turned to robbery and piracy but more went into business, into industry and trade. Others were persuaded to emigrate and the government established colonies in Italy, France, Spain, Libya, Asia Minor, on the coast of the Black Sea and in Byzantium or modern Istanbul. These settlements would serve as sources of food and raw material, as outlets for surplus goods and population, and opportunities for enterprising farmers, laborers, business men, for malcontents and adventurers. After a few years these efforts proved fruitful and engendered a veritable economic revolution. The switch from farming to commerce and success in the colonies led to prosperity and affluence for the Greeks. Large estates employing slave labor began to appear. They produced commodities for export, particularly olives and grapes, which netted huge profits.

Contact with the nations of the Near East brought new ideas and new techniques, such as; the introduction of weights and measures, the use of gold and silver and then coins as mediums of exchange, greater knowledge about the textile industry, metallurgy and ceramics, and about the arts of sculpture and architecture. Very important too was learning how to write by using an alphabet, which was borrowed from the Phoenicians. The word alphabet comes from the first two Greek letters—alpha and beta which in turn were derived from the Phoenician aleph and beth; and gamma evolved from gimel. The Phoenicians wrote from right to left and so did the Greeks for a while, but they subsequently found the left to right practice more convenient. The Romans modified these letters a little more and the English alphabet is virtually the same as the Roman or Latin. Writing was first used for business records but as literacy spread the Greeks also began to record their myths, legends and important events. Trade and social intercourse sharpened the mind, stimulated intellectual activity, and thus civilization was revived in the Aegean world, only now it was Greek instead of Cretan.

Before 800 B.C. the prevailing system of government was the clan organization, a kind of cousins club governed by heads of the families. Then as a measure of defense the groups of kinsmen united under the leadership of a king, one of their men who was highly respected by the chieftains for his ability as a warrior. Members of the clan had held their wealth and lands in common but under the new system of government the clan leaders emerged as owners of most of the land and as a privileged aristocracy and as advisers of the king. This political unit or city-state, called the polis, developed during the period from the 8th to the 6th century B.C. The English words politics, police and policy are derived from polis. The Greek city varied in size, ranging in area from about 25,000 to 400,000 persons, and there were over a hundred of them in the country. The polis consisted of the acropolis, an elevated site that contained fortresses, temples and a few other public buildings and the agora, which was at the foot of the hill and served as a trade and shopping center and a place for political assemblies. Around the market place were homes and beyond that were farms, and pasture lands. Sometimes they built a wall around the city and in time of war all the people would take refuge inside the stronghold.

For hundreds of years the only government the Greeks had was local city government. There was no national, political organization—the topography of the land made it difficult to unite the country, as it was divided by mountains and valleys and plains, bays, gulfs and seas. A national state comes into existence when people who have a common territory, a common language, common customs and beliefs find it advantageous to unite under one government or when one tribe is strong enough to conquer all the kindred and neighboring tribes. Neither of these conditions prevailed and so the ancient Greeks never achieved national statehood; instead the nation was politically fragmented into small independent local or city kingdoms, oligarchies or democracies. Although they had common customs, one language and one religion, the Greeks had no national government. Each city made its own laws, had its own courts, coined its own money, levied taxes, maintained its own army, waged wars against other cities, and foreign countries and made treaties with them. This was an aspect of freedom as the individual could participate more easily and more intelligently in local politics than in national affairs. In the fourth century B.C., however, an ambitious neighbor, Macedonia, took advantage of the disunity and lack of national patriotism among the Greeks, overwhelmed them and annexed all the states to the Macedonian empire.

All freemen born in a Greek city were citizens of that polis, provided their antecedents were, and all citizens were presumed to be descendants of a common ancestor. They were protected by a patron god and by the king who had come down from heaven to guard the people and lead the army into battle. The king was also the high priest, the supreme judge, but his authority was limited by a council of nobles, the great landowners; and to declare war or make peace he had to get the consent of the popular assembly, a meeting of the freemen in the market place. In fact royal political power did not last very long, for about 700 B.C. it came to an end in most Greek cities and was replaced by aristocracies or governments by landholding nobles. In some cities, the king's powers were restricted to religion and the council assumed complete control of secular affairs; in others monarchy was discarded completely. Forms of government changed with economic change. When the Greeks were mostly farmers an oligarchy or clique of landed aristocrats dominated the government; when the Greeks became predominantly commercial, an oligarchy of wealthy capitalists or plutocrats exercised complete authority. And when the middle class and the poor felt intolerably oppressed and exploited they put into power a tyrant or dictator who brought relief to the masses. In a few cities, such as Athens, tyranny was finally supplanted by popular rule or democracy.

The two largest and most important of the Hellenic city states were Sparta and Athens. Shortly before 1000 B.C. the Spartans settled in southern Greece and concentrated on farming since their land was relatively fertile. But in due time as the population began to increase faster than their food supply they decided to augment their city-state not by colonization of distant lands but by seizing their neighbor's land. Commerce did not appeal to them; they preferred aggrandizement through contiguous territorial expansion. The Spartans conquered and annexed a number of adjacent communities and persuaded others to become protectorates in a confederacy or a sort of league of cities dominated by Sparta. The members of this little league had to supply troops for the army which was controlled by Spartan officers. The people in the towns that were completely subjugated and absorbed were divided into two groups: those that were submissive and those who were stubbornly resistant. The former called the perioeci, became the middle class. They conducted trade and industry, engaged in some farming, paid taxes, but had no political rights and were not allowed to marry with the ruling class. The intractable, rebellious group, known as helots, were serfs or slaves, who worked as laborers and as servants, and occasionally were called on to fight for the state. As a reward for war service they might be granted their freedom; however if they displayed unusual courage and military proficiency they would be secretly dispatched. The Spartans themselves were not only the landowning aristocrats but also the rulers of the state although they never exceeded five per cent of the total population. They were the privileged, the only citizens, they held all the political offices and they comprised the professional army. The military was needed not only to wage foreign wars but also to prevent the unhappy and hostile helots from rebelling against their masters. In constant fear of revolution, the government had to maintain rigid discipline, military efficiency and a cunning secret police. There were revolts, arrests, murders and executions of malcontents and potential insurgent leaders; strong and intelligent helots were always suspected and were usually killed. But the 20,000 Spartans continued to thrive from the exploitation of almost 300,000 state slaves and from the taxes paid by the alien middle class.

At the head of the government of Sparta were two kings who inherited their crowns and who frequently clashed with each other over policies and personal relations. Their powers were mostly military and religious and their political authority was very slight. Much more important was the council, composed of the two kings and twenty-eight nobles, sixty years of age and over, elected to serve for life. The council formulated the laws and submitted them to the assembly or the lower house. It also advised and supervised the administrators and served as the supreme court for serious cases. The general assembly met on each day at the time of the full moon. All male citizens, aged thirty or over, were permitted to attend these meetings but their power of law making was only nominal. They were allowed to listen to the declaration of the proposed law and then without discussion or debate approve or reject the measure, but as obedient soldiers they generally ratified the recommended statute of the elder legislators. However they did enjoy the elective power, since they chose the members of the council, except for two kings, and they selected all public officials. Candidates who wished to fill a vacancy in the council were required to pass silently and in turn before the assembly and the one who was greeted with the loudest and longest oral applause was declared the winner. All measures were approved or disapproved by acclamation. The executives or ephors, five in number, were elected annually by the assembly. The ephors presided over the two houses, exercised a veto power over all legislation, controlled the educational system and the distribution of property, censored the lives of all citizens, determined the fate of new-born infants, decided disputes at law, commanded the armies, and conducted foreign affairs.

The primary concern of the ruling group was to maintain a military machine strong enough to keep in perpetual suppression a discontented servile population which outnumbered the Spartans twenty to one. To safeguard their continued existence they instituted a unique social organization whereby every individual was made subordinate to the state and every male Spartan was born and raised to be a soldier. Every father had to submit his child soon after birth, to an inspection by government officials and if they found it sickly or defective it would be thrown from a cliff or left to die of exposure on the side of a mountain or in a cave. At the age of seven the healthy boys were taken from their mother and placed in an army school where they received their basic training and patriotic indoctrination for about twelve years. They played games in the nude, marched, took vigorous physical exercises, practiced boxing, wrestling, swimming, running, jumping, hunting and learned to use weapons of war. They were taught to be brave, obedient and sly, to endure pain, hardship and punishment silently. Youths would compete with one another in bloody religious scourging or whipping bouts as a test of strength and fortitude at the altar of Artemis. Sometimes a contestant would endure the flogging till he fainted or died. Boys were also taught to steal without being caught and not to confess the theft. A Spartan boy once stole a live fox and hid it under his clothing. When questioned by his supervisor he let the fox gnaw at his belly until it killed him rather than admit his guilt. Life in camp and barracks was made as uncomfortable as possible to make the trainees tough and hardy. They must sleep in the open, winter and summer, swim in cold water, wear scanty clothing and no shoes and must not bathe very often, for cool air and an ample amount of dirt make one's body strong and resistant. The young men were taught also to read and write but arithmetic was left for the business men; soldiers didn't need it. They recited patriotic ballads and sang martial music, but books were scarce in Sparta and the authorities frowned on intellectual and cultural pursuits. When he reached the age of twenty the young man became a warrior, began more specialized training and joined one of the military eating clubs. To be admitted among this elite he had to contribute a membership fee and his own share of food, such as cereal, oil and wine, cultivated for him by helots. At the age of thirty the Spartan young man became a full citizen, he was given some land and helots, and he received the right to vote in the assembly and hold political office. He also was allowed now to live at home with his wife but he still must eat his main meal in a public dining hall where the food was coarse and simple and he was still required to participate in drills and gymnastics. Obesity was considered unpatriotic and the government might publicly reprove men for being persistently overweight and sometimes sent excessively fat Spartans into exile.

As mothers of future soldiers, the girls of Sparta had to be strong and healthy and so they received an equally rigorous physical training, which was prescribed by the state. They engaged in such sports as running, wrestling, throwing darts and quoits and they performed public dances, held processions and sang serious songs all in the nude before male audiences. Such occasional public display of their bodies, it was thought, would inspire the girls to be in good physical shape in order to receive a high rating from the authorities. Conditioned to be callous, mothers of sons off to war would tell the boys they must win or die—"Return home with your shield or on it."

The ideal age of marriage in Sparta was thirty for men and twenty for women, but younger marriages were not prohibited. A man was allowed to marry when he was twenty but he was not permitted to live with his wife until he was thirty. The young husband had to stay in the barracks while his bride remained with her parents and he could visit his wife secretly by eluding the guards, escaping from camp and being absent without leave. Marriage for males over thirty was compulsory; to be unmarried was a disgrace and so celibates were penalized. They were not allowed to vote, nor to watch the public parades when young men and women danced in the nude; in fact, the bachelors had to march in public, naked themselves, singing a song about how just and deserving was their punishment. Confirmed bachelors were sometimes assaulted in the streets by groups of women and were severely battered. Usually marriages were arranged by the parents but a quaint alternative was to select several men and an equal number of girls, push them into a dark room and let them pick their life mates in the darkness; on the theory, no doubt, that love was blind anyway. There was a great deal of sexual freedom before and after marriage and so divorce and prostitution were rare in Sparta. Many husbands were persuaded to share their wives with friends and brothers and a married man whose health was declining was expected to lend his wife to a more robust and virile male to assure the state of vigorous offspring. The women of Sparta enjoyed more freedom than those of any other Greek city. They inherited and bequeathed property, they were very influential, and owned about half of the wealth of Sparta and lived in comfort and luxury at home while the man ate simple food in army mess halls and had to endure the hardship and agony of frequent wars. At the age of sixty the Spartan male was finally allowed to retire from military service and if he were capable and popular he might become a member of the city council.

Spartans were forbidden to engage in trade and industry and of course to labor with their hands, for they were military aristocrats. They were not allowed to leave the city except to fight or perhaps spy for their homeland, and outsiders were discouraged from visiting

Sparta. If non-Spartans did come their stay must be brief and they were closely watched. In this way new and foreign ideas were kept out and the status quo would not be disturbed. The Spartans were fervently proud of their political system, firmly opposed to change and fearful and contemptuous of strangers, since two-thirds of the city's population were unhappy slaves and potential revolutionaries. Sparta had no art, no literature, no science or philosophy and no freedom, but it had the best trained, the bravest, the finest army in the Greek world. Intellectually the city was stagnant. The Spartans were often admired by the other Greeks but they were never imitated.

Northeast of the Peloponnesian peninsula where Sparta was located lay Attica, also a peninsula, where a group of villages united to form the famous city of Athens. Here there was no oppression of the vanquished by the victors, no bitter conflict or hatred among the various tribes and towns that belonged to the polis. The process of transition from tribal to monarchical rule was gradual and comparatively peaceful. The soil of Attica was rocky, poor and scarce but there were mineral deposits, the coast was near the city and excellent harbors were abundant. The people were predominantly conservative farmers but a few progressive planters emerged, usually specializing in the growing of olives and grapes, which were in great demand throughout the civilized world and therefore considered the money crops. To raise these products and to convert them into oil and wine required much time, labor and capital and only those entrepreneurs with ample means and capacity could become rich and influential. Farmers who lacked the wherewithal were thus left behind in the race for wealth and many of them often became indebted, impoverished, and enslaved. The aristocracy of great landowners, highly pleased with their success and eager to insure their wealth and economic power, decided to gain complete control of the government. They gradually divested the king of his authority and seized all important offices of state. Henceforth an oligarchy of privileged nobles dominated the government.

Meanwhile specialized agriculture became big business and the planter-processors, seeking foreign customers, arranged to have foreign grain dumped on the Greek market. Financially powerless to grow great quantities of grapes and olives and unable to compete with the prices of imported grain, farmers began to sell their land or lose it to creditors. Many of them became sharecroppers on the farms or laborers in the city. More and more Athenians turned to business—to selling, to manufacturing, to foreign commerce and before long they, like the nobles before them, demanded a share in the government to protect their interests. Now, fortunately for the middle class, the technique of warfare was changing. Before the seventh century B.C. the Greeks fought mostly on horseback or on chariots, and only the aristocracy or rich knights, who usually owned horses, were eligible for the cavalry or the charioteers. But this method of battle by individual champions was replaced by the heavily armed infantry or hoplites—a military machine, which required a number of men in the fighting force. Needing many more soldiers than the aristocrats could furnish they had to call upon the lower classes of citizens. But the latter would not serve in the army unless they were granted some political concessions—the right to vote and to hold a few offices. And since military preparedness was indispensable the oligarchy of nobles was forced to yield and enfranchise the middle class, that is to say, those men who owned a pair of oxen and had enough money to buy the hoplite's equipment. Laborers were also allowed in the army but only as light-armed foot soldiers and to perform menial tasks.

The majority of Athenians, however, were still excluded from political rights, wealth and power were still concentrated in the hands of a few. Unemployment and poverty increased as free laborers were replaced by less expensive slaves. These conditions led to widespread social unrest, cries of distress and threats of revolution. Whereupon the rulers summoned a wealthy nobleman named Draco to check the growing turbulence. As a conservative statesman, Draco sought to restore order in Athens and his first important step was the establishment of a fixed, clearly written code of laws, replacing oral customs which had been interpreted by usually biased judges. The traditional blood feuds were abolished, a distinction was made between accidental and intentional homicide and all freemen could now expect a proper trial before being punished. However the Draconian criminal laws were so severe that the common people thought Draco had them written in blood since he imposed the death penalty for acts of petty theft, e.g., stealing an apple or a cabbage. Property owners were still favored over the masses and the Athenian rich still exploited the poor as the administration of Draco did nothing to correct social and economic conditions.

The situation grew worse, mobs demanded the redistribution of wealth and there was rampant talk of a violent revolt, when finally in 594 B.C. a progressive aristocrat named Solon, was appointed chief archon or prime minister with extraordinary powers. First he tried to solve the economic problem by enacting a number of liberal measures: the abolition of the practice of enslavement for defaulting on loans, the voiding of all debts secured by the debtor's person, freeing men enslaved for debt, restricting mortgages on land, and limiting the amount of land an individual might own. Solon also encouraged commerce and manufacturing by subsidizing certain industries, by inducing artisans and merchants to reside in Athens, promising citizenship to skilled aliens, and requiring that all boys be taught a trade. Since agriculture was not very profitable for most people Athens was forced to become industrialized. Athenians had to rely on foreign countries for farm products and to pay for these imports they would export their own manufactured commodities.

Solon also reorganized the government and amended the constitution, making it more democratic. The exclusively aristocratic and wealthy council, which had dominated the government was now opened up to the middle class—to all citizens over thirty who could afford to buy infantry equipment and enlist in the army as hoplites. The council's function was to prepare all measures, domestic and foreign, to discuss them and if deemed meritorious submit them to the assembly. All free Athenians who had reached the age of twenty, regardless of wealth, were admitted to the popular assembly to pass on all matters presented to them and to elect or remove the archons or chief executives and the administrative officers. The most important innovation was the establishment of popular courts whose judges were chosen by lot from all ranks of the citizenry. This random type of election involved drawing white beans instead of black beans mixed in a jar, and was the method employed in choosing most of the government officials. There were no formal civil service examinations but every officeholder had to pass a physical and mental fitness test and there were provisions for the quick removal of an incompetent or dishonest person.

Solon also enacted a number of moralistic reform measures which condemned ostentatious ceremonies, costly religious sacrifices, immoderate mourning at funerals and the overstocking of graves with supplies for the dead. Another law of Solon's provided that sons of soldiers killed in war should be reared and educated at the expense of the government. He limited the size of dowries and the size of women's wardrobes, and made it a crime to be habitually idle, to speak ill of the dead, or to speak ill of the living in public buildings or at the athletic games. In order to reduce sex crime and to give young men carnal release Solon legalized prostitution and provided for state licensing, the taxing and the supervision of all public brothels. The revenue derived from this gainful business was devoted to the erection of a temple dedicated to the goddess of love and beauty—Aphrodite.

The reforms of Solon started Athens on the road to popular government and the great lawmaker was regarded as the father of democracy, but the conservatives thought he was too radical and the radicals thought he was too conservative. Civil strife continued and dictatorship became necessary. But unwilling to set himself up as a tyrant, Solon voluntarily retired, left Athens and went to Egypt to observe and study the history and civilization of the Near East. In the meanwhile a nobleman named Pisistratus, a champion of the masses, employing demagoguery and political trickery, seized control of the government. He exiled the hostile aristocrats and divided their land among small farmers, while in the city he undertook public works projects to give jobs to the poor laborers and provide business for the middle class, particularly the building interests. He patronized the artists, brought poets and philosophers to his court, and enhanced the city's appearance by an elaborate building program. He fostered industry, trade and colonization and gave the people social and economic harmony, and brought peace and prosperity to Athens. Pisistratus was a capable and benevolent tyrant but his two sons, who succeeded him, were incompetent and oppressive. The first was assassinated and the second son was removed from office by exiled conservative aristocrats aided by Sparta.

This was followed by two years of civil war and then, in 508 B.C., Cleisthenes, a progressive aristocrat supported by the masses, ousted the conservatives from office, expelled the Spartan soldiers and came into complete power. The Athenians were now granted a thoroughly democratic constitution. The city-state was divided into ten geographic electoral constituencies or districts—regardless of clan or tribal affiliation. Members of every class—farmers, artisans, business men, rich and poor, were evenly divided into the ten territorial units. The council or upper house, would contain 500 members, over thirty years of age and each district would send fifty delegates elected by universal suffrage. The term of office was one year and no one could be a councillor more than twice. This legislative body controlled all activities of the government—commerce, finance, public works, foreign affairs and the supervision of all administrative functions and personnel. To expedite progress they were divided into ten committees, the members of which took turns in presiding over the lower house and acting as chief executive for one day. On occasion the council had the power to impeach government officials.

Ultimate power rested in the popular assembly which would debate all measures submitted to them by the council and then ratify or reject the proposals. By the middle of the fifth century B.C., during the administration of the great Pericles, it also acquired the right to initiate legislation. Members of the assembly discussed and voted on domestic and foreign affairs, decided on war and peace and audited the accounts of retiring officials. They also employed the device known as ostracism whereby they would cast a vote secretly deciding by a majority what citizen was a danger to the state, that is, threatened the security and the stability of the country, and he would be forced to leave Athens and stay away for ten years. This was to prevent tyranny and to demonstrate the sovereignty of the people. The assembly also elected the ten members of the Board of Generals—one from each tribe—that served as a kind of cabinet or executive department replacing the archons. These men were commanders of the army who also possessed legislative and executive powers, but their policies were subject to review by the assembly and they could be impeached. The generals' term of office was one year but they were eligible for indefinite re-election. Pericles, the eminent statesman and orator, served as the chief member of the board for over thirty years. The judicial system was also democratized. Every year six thousand citizens over thirty years of age were elected to serve as a popular judiciary. This court in turn was divided into panels which varied in size from 201 to 1001 and acted both as judges and jurors, each one trying particular cases. They would decide all legal matters by a majority vote and there was no appeal from their decision.

The Athenians thus enjoyed a form of direct or pure democracy but it must be remembered that more than half of the population were not citizens and had no political rights. Excluded from the privileges of voting and holding office were women, metics or resident aliens, and of course thousands of slaves. The power of the masses was only theoretical, since laborers could not afford to leave their jobs—they were too busy earning a living to practice politics; and farmers were too far away from the civic center where the assembly met. Pericles did introduce pay for jury duty and for attendance at the assembly, but as a rule only men of leisure had the time and the inclination to participate in political deliberations; the number of members present at the popular assembly seldom exceeded 5000.

Sessions were held under the open sky and business began at dawn after prayers and the sacrifice of a pig to Zeus. In case of a storm, an earthquake or an eclipse, which were regarded as omens of divine anger, the meeting would be postponed. Normally there were about forty sessions every year. To address the assembly one was required to be a moral and patriotic Athenian citizen, a landowner, legally married, dutiful to his parents, and must not be delinquent in the payment of his taxes. Furthermore, to be a participant in the debates and discussions at the meetings one had to be fluent and articulate, for the members were ruthless in their heckling, and would frequently shout and whistle and ridicule speakers and roar with laughter at a mispronounced word. There was a time limit on speeches and voting was done by show of hands though the secret ballot was employed occasionally. A mass gathering, the assembly was naturally susceptible to the influence of eloquent and histrionic demagogues. Nevertheless the Athenians rejoiced in their freedom of thought and speech—a rare and precious privilege in ancient times.

Not all Greek cities were as democratic as Athens; at Locri, for example, they were always very wary about reform and change in customs and so they required that any person who wanted to propose a new law must speak with a rope around his neck, so that, if his measure was not approved by a majority of the legislators he might be ejected and hanged with ease and dispatch. Other Greek states had popular governments but the Athenian citizens enjoyed the greatest amount of freedom and were relatively liberal toward aliens and slaves.

The Greeks had been establishing colonies in Asia Minor since the eighth century B.C. but when Lydia became a dominant power in western Asia she took possession of these Ionian Greek colonies; and later when the Persians replaced Lydia as a leading world empire they also annexed these Greek cities. In 499 the Greek colonists revolted against their Persian masters and appealed to the European Greeks for help. Only Athens and Eritrea responded. The Spartans too were willing but could not send aid immediately because the time for embarking on a foreign war was inauspicious, that is; the moon was not yet full.

In 490 B.C., to everyone's great amazement, a small Athenian force defeated a huge army of Persians led by the sovereign of the world's greatest empire. When the Persians landed on the beach at Marathon the Athenians dispatched their long distance runner, Pheidippides, to Sparta asking for aid. In overdue time the reluctant Spartans arrived but the greatly outnumbered Athenians (20,000 against 100,000) had already won a brilliant victory in driving the Persians back into the sea whence they came. The same messenger was now sent to Athens, which is twenty-four miles away, to herald the great news. He announced the incredible and signal triumph of the Athenians and then the great courier collapsed and expired.

The Battle of Marathon made the people of Athens proud and it inspired all Greeks, encouraged them, made them more confident. The Persians were no longer invincible—their expansion to the west was checked and their economic competition could be curbed. But the war was not yet over. Emperors Darius and Xerxes returned with enormous armies and fought on. At Thermopylae a small Spartan force made a heroic stand defending the strategic narrow pass where the soldiers died almost to the last man.

The Persians then attacked and seized Athens, pillaged and burned it; but the people had fled the city and presently rallied under the leadership of Themistocles, a great navy enthusiast and statesman. They then fought on the water at Salamis where the Athenian fleet outmaneuvered and routed the Persians while the disappointed King Xerxes watched the battle from the shore. This great victory and two more Greek triumphs, one on land and one on sea, forced the Persians who survived to abandon Greece and return to their home in Asia. This freed the Greeks from the Persian peril though the fear of invasion did not end completely until the advent of Alexander the Great in the fourth century B.C. In the meanwhile as a security measure against the Persians and as an aid to their own imperialistic expansion—economic and political, the Athenians organized the Delian League in 478 B.C. It was a voluntary confederacy with a common treasury located on the island of Delos but it was led and dominated by Athens. More than 200 cities joined the organization and each one paid an annual tribute of about a half million dollars or they contributed ships and oarsmen for the league's fleet. Athenian leadership was greatly strengthened by this maritime union and before long the members began to suspect and fear Athenian imperialistic, selfish ambitions. When one of the unhappy cities in the league tried to secede the Athenians overwhelmed it by force and converted it into a tributary possession. Now Sparta, a rival of Athens for leadership over the Greeks and envious of the growing Athenian wealth and hegemony, also formed a defensive alliance of Greek city-states—the Peloponnesian League.

Changing economic conditions in Greece made self-sufficient cities no longer feasible. There was a trend toward economic specialization which led to commercial interdependence and the need for cooperation to replace rivalry and antagonism. A larger political organization of the city-states was imperative, but who would be the leader—Athens or Sparta? The Spartans favored a loose organization of independent states each governed preferably by an oligarchy but all of them regarding Sparta as their guide and leader. Athens, on the other hand, wanted to establish an imperialistic Hellenic state dominated by Athens but permitting each city to have a local democratic government. In addition to the economic and political rivalry between Athens and Sparta there were definite cultural contrasts. Athens was urban, intellectual and progressive while Sparta was provincial, unintellectual and conservative. Devoted to commerce, the Athenians built up a strong navy while agrarian Sparta had the best army in Greece.

Pericles, the famous Athenian statesman, believed that since rivalry between the two chief cities would inevitably lead to an open and widespread conflict it would be wise to launch a fast preventive war. So in 432 B.C. Athens began to provoke Corinth, a leading commercial competitor by interfering in a quarrel that city was having with one of her colonies. Since Corinth was an important member of the Peloponnesian League Sparta came to her aid and before long almost all the Greek states were involved on one side or the other. Thus the tragic internecine Peloponnesian War was started. It was a struggle for supremacy among the Greeks and it lasted from 431 to 404 B.C. The war was for some time indecisive as Athenian sea power was balanced by Sparta's superiority on land, but the Athenians made two serious mistakes. Attacked by the Spartans Athens took in thousands of refugees behind its walls and soon the city became overcrowded and unsanitary. As a result a plague broke out, decimating almost a third of the population, including their greatest statesman, Pericles. The second mistake was their rash, ill-planned attempt to conquer Syracuse in Sicily, a colony of Corinth, in order to get control of the trade of the western Mediterranean. Sicilian Greeks aided by Corinth and Sparta almost annihilated the Athenian soldiers and sailors led by incompetent and bungling officers. The expedition to Syracuse turned out to be a disastrous adventure. The remnants of the erstwhile great Athenian fleet was subsequently defeated by the Spartans who built up a navy of their own. The Persians who were glad to see the Greeks fighting with one another and were particularly happy over the humiliation of Athens, sent financial aid to Sparta. Sparta not only accepted Persian gold but also agreed to assist in returning Greek colonies in western Asia to the Persian king. With almost half of her citizens enslaved or dead, bereft of all her foreign lands, and her funds exhausted, Athens surrendered to her perennial rival and Sparta became the dominant power over all the Greeks. But the Spartans, although very proficient as fighters were not very adept as statesmen and their ascendancy was short-lived. The city of Thebes supplanted Sparta as the preeminent state but its rule too was brief. From 362 to 338 B.C. incessant strife and intercity warfare kept Greece in turmoil and hopelessly divided.

The Greeks needed a strong man, a commanding leader with a large army capable of subduing all the city states and imposing unity upon the country. Greece did not produce such a paramount figure, but Macedonia, a kindred northern neighbor with a semi-civilized but hardy and warlike people, happened to have a clever monarch named

Philip, who possessed the necessary qualifications. This king was a shrewd politician, a cunning diplomat and a highly skillful militarist. He also had great admiration for Greek culture. As a young man Philip had lived in Thebes as a hostage in the home of the greatest Greek general where he learned much about the Greeks including the Theban phalanx method of fighting, at that time the best in the world. Returning to Macedonia he improved on the Theban tactic. This sort of military organization consisted of a massed body of pike men eight to sixteen ranks deep with a cavalry force on each wing of the phalanx, the infantry and cavalry operating as a unit. Philip introduced longer spears (18 feet long) to the rear rank, and added archers, slingers and siege trains. The king had plenty of horses, well-disciplined soldiers and an ample supply of gold and thus built up the most formidable army in the world. Already a united nation, Macedonia under Philip's rule conquered adjacent territory and became larger and then the king introduced some Greek civilization among his more intelligent subjects.

His next great step was the invasion of Greece and the conquest of the constantly quarreling city states. The decisive battle was fought at Chaeronea in 338 B.C. and it was a triumph for Macedonia. After this victory, Philip imposed unity upon the Greeks, which they had been unable to achieve themselves. To perpetuate this unity he organized the Hellenic League of which he was the master. The city states were allowed considerable autonomy but they all must furnish soldiers and arms to a national army of which Philip was the commander. His next objective was the subjugation of the old Asiatic menace—the Persians, and he made plans for a conquering expedition in Anatolia, but unfortunately the great king did not live long enough to see their fruition. A much married monarch, he had a passion for women, drink and debaucheries and was often involved in clandestine affairs and feminine conspiracies. There were many family brawls, and one day while celebrating his daughter's marriage and in the presence of many notables, he was assassinated by an agent of one of his ex-wives.

Philip's son, Alexander, only twenty years of age, succeeded to the throne. Conspiracies and rebellions greeted the young ruler but Alexander crushed all opposition and the Greeks began to respect him. Thebes, one of the unsubmissive cities was burned to the ground, only the temples and the home of Pindar, the poet, were left standing. The men were slaughtered and the women and children were sold into slavery. Then Alexander led his armies into Asia Minor and as reports of his sensational victories arrived in Greece describing the Persian defeats and the freeing of the Greek cities, Alexander was hailed as a national hero—the ideal Greek youth—handsome, athletic, a skillful horseman, a fearless hunter and valiant soldier. An ingenious general, who never lost a battle, Alexander required his soldiers to shave their whiskers lest the enemy be tempted to use beards as convenient handles. He thereby introduced in Europe the custom of shaving one's beard. The philosopher, Aristotle, was his teacher who instilled in him a love of learning, an interest in science and philosophy, intellectual curiosity and a cultivated taste. The young king often supported artists, scientists, and explorers. At night beneath his pillow, alongside of his dagger, he always kept a copy of the *Iliad* annotated by Aristotle. But Alexander was not always cultivated and urbane. He could be civilized or barbaric, he could be kind and considerate or cruel and ferocious, and he loved both science and superstition.

His father had wanted to subjugate the Persian empire but Alexander's ambition was to conquer the world and then to Hellenize it. Using the old phalanx cavalry combination, he succeeded in defeating the Persian army in Asia Minor, then in subduing Phoenicia, Egypt, Palestine, Syria, Babylon and Persia itself. He led his invincible army into northwest India and moved across the Indus River but finally his troops refused to go any further. They could no longer endure the unhealthful climate and they were not eager to tackle the enemy's wild, savage cavalrymen equipped with hundreds of elephants. Suffering from thirst, heat and fever, they retreated and returned to the city of Babylon. Here Alexander remained for two years planning explorations and further conquests though he also turned his attention toward the organization and administration of his huge empire. Almost everywhere he was deified or he ruled by divine right and in Egypt the priests proclaimed him the son of their god Ra. All his subjects were expected to prostrate themselves in his presence. As a champion of integration and the fusion of the races, he married a beautiful Bactrian princess, Roxane, and later wedded two daughters of the Persian king. His officers and thousands of soldiers followed his example and married native women. Alexander and many of his officials adopted Persian customs and manners. He hoped that eventually the nations of the world would unite and form a universal brotherhood of man dedicated to justice and reason. In the meanwhile he thought it was necessary to Hellenize the Asians by settling Greek immigrants in strategic places—commercial centers, military bases and centers of culture and learning. About seventy-five new cities were founded, old ones were rebuilt and a number of them were named after Alexander. Two cities were named after his horse and after his dog. The mixture of Hellenic and Asian culture continued for many years but Alexander's reign only lasted 13 years, for he died in 323 B.C.

Some of Alexander's officers had begun to question his policies and his excessive predilection for alien customs. There were disparaging remarks, criticism of his godlike behavior, mutinous talk and even conspiracies to assassinate the illustrious commander. Suspicion led to torture, confessions and executions. A nephew of Aristotle's was suspected of being involved in a conspiracy, he was imprisoned and died a few months later. Relations between Alexander and the famous philosopher which had been very amicable for years, now became unfriendly. When the king's most intimate and beloved companion, Hephaestion, took ill and died, Alexander was so overcome with grief that he lay on the corpse weeping for hours and expressed his sorrow further by cutting off his hair and fasting for days. His friend's physician was put to death for being insufficiently diligent and devoted to his patient. On his next military campaign Alexander had an entire tribe slain as a sacrifice to the ghost of Hephaestion; he spent sixty million dollars to build a colossal funeral pile in memory of his friend, and even considered the worship of Hephaestion as a god. He was overwhelmed by the enormous amount of work he had to do and the strain began to take effect. He also was suffering from old battle wounds and he began to drink very heavily. At one of these drinking parties an intoxicated officer delivered an invidious tirade belittling the king's military achievements. This so enraged Alexander, who was also drunk, that he hurled a spear at the officer and killed him. This general had once saved the king's life in a battle with the Persians and when Alexander calmed down and become sober he was stricken with remorse, refused to see anyone, refused to eat; he became morbid and tried to commit suicide.

The king ultimately recovered from his sorrowful state of mind but he resumed his intemperate drinking habits and he attended one bibacious banquet after another. At one quaffing orgy one of his generals ingested twelve quarts of wine and then died three days later. At another spree Alexander imbibed six quarts of wine and the next night he drank immoderately again, fell sick of malarial fever and died a few days later in Babylon at the age of 33. When asked to whom he bequeathed the empire, Alexander replied "to the strongest." His mother and brother survived him and a month later a son was born to his first wife, Roxane, but all potential heirs were slain within a few years.

For more than forty years the Macedonian generals fought over the division of the Alexandrian empire, the greatest the world had ever seen. Early in the third century B.C. three large kingdoms emerged as the strongest. These were: Macedonia-Greece which was taken by Antigonus, the Asian territory seized by Seleucus, and Egypt ruled by Ptolemy. The Antigonids were unable to govern either Macedonia or Greece very well as they faced almost constant revolts and civil war at home and threats from neighboring countries. The liberty-loving Greeks would not tolerate absolute or divine right of monarchy and demanded and received considerable autonomy. In the third century B.C. the Romans began to intervene in the quarrels of Macedonia and Greece and in the wars between Ptolemy of Egypt and the Seleucid kings of Syria. By 188 B.C. all the eastern Mediterranean lands became Roman protectorates. But gradually over the years they were all converted into provinces or colonies in the empire—Egypt not until 30 B.C. Alexander's Macedonian-Greek empire became a part of the Roman empire.

CHAPTER VII

(PART 2)

The Greeks
—Their Customs and Cultural Contributions

During all these political and military vicissitudes the peasant, the laborer and the merchant continued to toil and to trade and provide the necessities of life. As late as the fourth century B.C. agriculture was still regarded as the most honorable economic activity, and it supported the majority of the people, even though it was not the most profitable occupation. Olives and grapes were grown on large estates but most of the farms were small and the land was poor. By the fourth century B.C. they learned how to prevent soil exhaustion by the three field system and they were able to raise a wide variety of vegetables, fruits and animals, but they had to import most of their wheat and other cereals.

To meet the demand for necessities and to pay for imports the Greeks developed their own industries. Shops, like farms, were generally very small though there were a few large factories that employed about 100 or more workers. But most of the craftsmen labored at home or owned a small workshop. For a long time production was limited by definite consumer orders but gradually they began to manufacture for the general market, domestic and foreign. The workers might be Greek citizens, slaves or metics, that is, resident aliens; and sometimes they all worked side by side even with the master craftsmen. In Greece doctors and artists were also considered craftsmen and were of the same social and economic rank as painters, masons and carpenters; in the democratic communities of Greece manual labor was not generally held in disdain. The only work that was unworthy of a good Greek was the kind that did not provide him with a bit of leisure, some mental and physical relaxation so indispensable to civilized living. For example, mining silver or copper was a necessary form of labor but it was toilsome, injurious to mind and body and so fit only for slaves or foreigners.

Trade too was a comparatively disrespectful economic activity. Bartering had not been so bad, for that was just an exchange of commodities equal in value, but with the introduction of money trade became profit-making at the expense of the customer. However, highly successful businessmen who became enriched by investing in either manufacturing or selling and by employing others to do the tedious routine work involved, were always regarded as superior merchants or industrialists and were accepted as equals in rank to wealthy landowners. Buying and selling were transacted at artisan shops, public markets and at fairs. Most of the people engaged in middle class pursuits were non-citizens, that is, Greeks from other cities, foreigners, such as, Phoenicians and Jews, and an occasional freedman. These non-equal denizens were not permitted to own land and therefore earned their living by becoming artisans, merchants, manufacturers or professional men. Foreign commerce was opened up in early Greek history by pirates who carried on a lucrative enterprise selling their precious plunder. The Greeks in those days had no love for the sea but economic necessity forced them to become sailors and shipbuilders, skills they learned from their neighbors, particularly the Phoenicians, and by the sixth century B.C. they were the dominant maritime people in the eastern Mediterranean region.

Hellenic business was usually small, individual enterprise with a little government regulation and some public ownership, as the mines, for example. The earliest bankers were the priests, who loaned money to individuals and governments at a moderate interest. Although the taking of interest was regarded as an evil there was no compunction about using the treasure amassed in the temples to earn a profit for the gods.

In the Hellenistic age, that is, the period from the death of Alexander to the Roman conquest of Egypt in 30 B.C., the economic life in Greece underwent a great change. The most flourishing centers of commerce were no longer to be Athens and Corinth but Alexandria,

Rhodes and Antioch. Many venturesome and enterprising Greeks migrated from their home towns to the new or rebuilt cities of the empire where the opportunities were abundant for becoming rich and influential. Alexander's successors invited Greek businessmen to come to the eastern lands to organize, to develop, and to manage commercial, industrial and financial enterprise. The governments made commerce more attractive by eradicating piracy and brigandage and by building roads, canals, harbors, lighthouses and warehouses. It was an age of large scale capitalism with big corporations, numerous banking companies, expanded credit, widespread speculation and investment, and government regulation of prices and marketing. As for agriculture, the lands seized by the Macedonian-Greek imperialists became either part of the royal domain or they were presented to favorites who frequently leased the farms to tenants. But small scale farming like small business could not successfully compete with large landowners or wealthy corporations. Agricultural tenants usually failed and were forced to become serfs and the small businessmen became bankrupt. The Hellenistic age was remarkably prosperous but the wealth was concentrated in a few hands as the upper classes became more affluent and the lower classes became more impoverished. It was necessary at times for city governments to provide public relief by furnishing the unemployed with cheap or free grain.

Slavery was regarded as a labor-saving device that relieved citizens from drudgery in domestic service or in industry. The slaves were condemned malefactors or prisoners of war; they and their offspring were acquired by purchase. They were not expensive during the Hellenic period but in Hellenistic times hiring free workers was often cheaper than buying and maintaining slaves; consequently manumission was very prevalent and slavery declined. The treatment of slaves in Greece, as elsewhere, depended on the master but on the whole, particularly in democratic cities it was relatively humane. A slave was sometimes whipped or tortured and was not allowed to defend himself when struck by a freeman. But the law did protect the slave, for it did not permit a master to have the right of life or death over him and he might escape from constant cruelty by fleeing to a temple, whereupon his owner was compelled to sell him. When he was ill, old or unemployed his master took care of him. Many slaves worked for wages, were allowed to keep part of their earnings and were even permitted to go into business and to buy their freedom. A freedman possessed the same rights and restrictions as a metic or resident alien. Although these underprivileged people had to pay taxes and were subject to military service they were denied the right to vote or hold public office; they were forbidden to own land or marry into citizen families. However with the exception of agriculture they enjoyed complete economic freedom, religious freedom and the freedom of speech. Many of them achieved distinction and fame in commerce, industry, the professions and in the intellectual world. Citizenship was an inherited privilege though on very rare occasions this high honor was conferred on a distinguished alien or a former slave. Such a meritorious reward however was bestowed on persons for unusual service to the state and it could be done only by decree of the assembly.

Greek cities were known for their many beautiful public buildings but their residential sections were notoriously dingy and depressing. The streets were narrow and crooked, they had no pavement and no sidewalks. They were dark, dirty and smelled bad, for all refuse, garbage and slop were thrown into the street and they had neither sewerage nor a sanitation department. Not only were the cities polluted with offensive odors but they were unsafe at night since there were no public lights and no professional policemen. The houses of the average Greek family were flimsy, humble and unattractive, built close to one another, mostly of sun-dried brick and occasionally of crude stucco. They were generally one story structures though there were some with second floors that had a few windows with shutters or lattices but no glass. They were all built around a court which was used to the full for work, play and conversation. Entrance to the house was usually from the court while the front of the building facing the street might have a door but was mostly a blank wall. Wealthy Greeks of course had more elaborate dwellings but the average family led a very simple life and their home was plain and unadorned. Floors were either hardened earth or were paved with cement and stone and covered with mats or rugs and the walls were plastered or whitewashed. Braziers or portable fire-places provided heat for the house but there were no chimneys and so the smoke would escape through random openings. Furniture included hard chairs, three-legged tables, chests of drawers, and beds without springs. Richer families however did possess cushions, pillows, mattresses, springs and even a few decorations, such as, vases, paintings, tapestries, mosaics and arabesques. To light up the house they used candles, torches, and clay or bronze lamps that burned olive oil. They did their cooking over an open fire until the Hellenistic period when stoves were first introduced.

Most Greeks ate twice a day and their food was simple, consisting of bread, fish, honey, eggs, and a few vegetables and fruits; they drank water, wine and goat milk and boasted about their delicious cheese cake. They ate with their fingers, scooping up the food with chunks of bread and then rubbed off the grease and dirt from the fingers with pieces of bread and finally washed their hands in a finger bowl. Discarded food was thrown to the dogs under the table. Clothing too was simple, consisting of a tunic without sleeves fastened at the shoulders with a kind of safety pin and with a rope around the waist. A second outer garment or mantle was draped around the body when the weather was cold or inclement. They wore no stockings or socks but some did wear sandals or shoes. Covering for the feet or the head was optional and there were many who were bare-headed and bare-footed. After the Battle of Marathon it became stylish for men to cut their hair short and to shave their beards, and a mustache without a beard was taboo. Motivation for this cosmetic reform was military as well as aesthetic. In hand to hand fighting long hair whether on the head or face could be an encumbrance and provide an enemy with helpful leverage.

Women wore their hair long, but braided with colorful bands and ribbons and allowed to fall around the neck, breasts and shoulders. They beautified their eyes, skin and complexion by applying creams, powders, oils, ointments, rouge, lipstick, lampblack and perfume; and they sometimes dyed their hair. Jewelry too, helped to make them attractive and so if they could afford it they wore rings, bracelets, necklaces, earings, brooches, and anklets. At one time the city of Miletus quickly stopped an epidemic of female suicides by issuing a decree which required that self-slain women be carried naked through the market place and be displayed to the public before burial. In Greece as in Asia the women were subservient first to their father and then to their husbands. For men the home was only a place to eat and sleep but a wife lived and worked there almost all the time. A lady of the upper class lived in seclusion in the female quarters of her home, kept busy with domestic duties, supervised the slaves, and reared the children. She must always stay away from the windows and must retire to her section of the house when ever the husband had male guests. She was allowed to leave the house to go shopping, to visit relatives, to attend a wedding or a funeral, and occasionally a tragic play, but when she did venture into the streets, she must have a chaperon older than herself. On the other hand, the women of the working class were free to engage in economic activities and were often bakers, shoemakers, innkeepers, barmaids, and salesgirls.

Young women generally married at the age of fifteen or sixteen and were selected by the young man's father or by a matchmaker. The husband-to-be was usually ten or fifteen years older. Marriage was seldom the result of a romantic love match; it was considered a business arrangement involving a satisfactory dowry and other sundry possessions, and sometimes the bride and the groom had never seen each other before the wedding day. Betrothal took place in the home of the girl's father; then several days later there was a feast where the men of both families would sit on one side of the room and the women on the other and they would all consume much cake and wine. Then the groom escorted his veiled and white robed bride into a carriage and took her to his father's dwelling. The couple was accompanied by a procession of flute-playing girls and friends carrying torches and singing hymeneal songs. When they arrived he carried the girl over the threshold, a traditional custom which symbolized bringing home the seized booty. After a religious ceremony, performed without a priest, the guests escorted the couple to their bedroom and stood by the door singing appropriate melodies until the bridegroom emerged and announced that the marriage had been consummated. Men usually got married because it was a religious requirement to have children who would tend and protect departed souls and after a war it was also a patriotic duty to help replenish the depleted male population. Boys were preferred not only because the army needed them but because it was less expensive to bring them up and marry them off. Outside of Sparta where they were disposed of immediately, feeble, deformed or just undesirable children might be left in a container at some conspicuous place where they might be rescued and adopted.

In this thoroughly masculine world concubines or secondary wives were legally recognized though their offspring were not considered legitimate. The husband was allowed to divorce his wife if she was barren or if she committed adultery, but male adultery was not considered a very serious crime and if he was a sterile husband it was customary for him to enlist the services of a relative and appoint him as a surrogate spouse. Children born of this arrangement were considered the legitimate descendants of the original husband. Sometimes a wife was granted a divorce when her husband was flagrantly cruel and iniquitous. When husband and wife separated their children remained with the father and the wife got back her dowry and her personal property.

Greek men spent their days working or enjoying themselves away from home. They might go to the gymnasium for physical exercise, attend the theater, athletic games, meet their friends at a club to eat, drink and discuss politics, philosophy or sports or they would relieve the monotony of monogamy by visiting a courtesan. Prostitution was licensed, taxed and supervised. From this commercialized and profitable recreation the government at Athens was able to erect a temple to the goddess Aphrodite, that only temple harlots were allowed to attend. There were three kinds of daughters of joy, who offered men sexual relaxation for an appropriate price. The lowest class lived in common brothels identified for the convenience of the public by the display of a phallic symbol and they charged twenty-five cents for admission. The madam of the establishment allowed patrons to inspect the diaphanously clad wenches and then would rent a girl by the hour, the day, the week or the year. More refined courtesans were the female flute players who provided prefatory entertainment in the form of dancing, singing and the interchange of thoughts and feelings. These preliminaries were followed by amorous flirtation and a night of coitus. Retired strumpets sometimes established charm schools where girls were trained to be alluring, to play the flute, to sing and dance lasciviously and to entice the male through social intercourse. The highest type of courtesan was the hetairai, or female paramours. Unlike the above harlots who were foreigners, these were daughters of Greek citizens who left their homes to lead independent, uninhibited lives, informal and unconventional. They learned how to read and many of them became self-educated in poetry and philosophy and were able to carry on intelligent and sometimes witty conversations with men of culture and learning. They were very discreet and discriminating and they consorted and were intimate only with men of superior quality. For example, Pericles didn't like his wife and so he found her another husband and lived with Aspasia, an attractive and talented hetaira.

The Greeks realized the importance of education as well as indoctrination and started the process very early in the life of the child. The Spartan method was almost exclusively military but Athens recognized the value of a general or liberal education and sought to develop the pupil not only mentally but also physically, morally and esthetically. Up to the age of seven boys were trained at home and from seven to fourteen they went to school and there learned to read, write and reckon. They read Aesop's fables, stories about the exploits of national heroes, memorized poetry and recited it to the accompaniment of music. They learned to sing and to play the lyre, a seven string instrument. The curriculum in the higher schools also included arithmetic, geometry, drawing, history, ethics, literature, rhetoric and public speaking. From eighteen to twenty they were enrolled in military service where they learned how to defend their nation or the science of war but also the duties of citizenship and how to govern themselves democratically. The education of girls outside of Sparta, was domestically oriented, that is, they must be trained to perform their household duties, though they were allowed to study music and dancing and also how to read, write and figure. Most girls were not permitted to go off to school but at home they often picked skills and knowledge from their mothers, nurses or slaves. Sappho, the great Greek poetess, had a kind of finishing school for girls, on the island of Lesbos, where they were prepared for entrance into society, and Aspasia, the common law wife of Pericles and an ardent champion of female emancipation, established a school of rhetoric and philosophy to give the Greek women an opportunity for higher education. Outside of the military, schools were privately owned and operated.

The gods of Greece were a heavenly family who dwelt high on the top of Mount Olympus in the northern part of the country and Zeus was their father. They were not supernatural, as gods generally are, but were just supermen and superwomen; larger, stronger and more capable, possessing human forms and human attributes. Like people, these divinities had to eat, sleep and reproduce and they had frequent family quarrels, but unlike ordinary people, they never died permanently because they subsisted on nectar and ambrosia. Unlike Jehovah who was eminently versatile, omniscient, and omnipotent, the Greek gods were specialists, i.e., each one was usually knowledgeable and efficacious in one field of a life situation. Athena was the goddess of wisdom, Aphrodite gave advice and help to the lovelorn, Demeter could effect fertility, Aesculapius was the god of healing; Ares of war; and Hephaestus would resolve industrial and labor problems. When the farmer needed help he might consult one of several gods—Zeus, the sky god, could bring rain; Apollo by controlling the sun, supplied and regulated light and temperature; Demeter and Dionysus would assure him good crops; farm animals were protected by Apollo, the woods and trees were guarded by Pan. Some gods were endowed with more than one aptitude and potency and could assist in two or three areas; for example, Hermes had jurisdiction over athletes and sports but he was also a guide to travelers, Poseidon masterminded the sea and was also the supreme authority on horses. In addition to the powers mentioned above, Apollo possessed divine expertise in music, poetry and in the art of prognostication.

Deities were as innumerable as the stars. Belief in these gods made the mysteries of nature and the unhappy human situations less terrifying and more endurable. The Greek religion had no ethical content; there were no commandments and no sermons emanating from Mount Olympus; their code of conduct was the product of social custom rather than spiritual or divine inspiration. To be religious one must please the gods and that meant their devotees must observe the traditional ceremonies and be ritualistically correct. To win the aid of these gods worshipers would go to the temple to sing and pray and sacrifice something of value—material possessions, such as, farm goods, animals, vases, statues, ornaments or clothing, anything that might appease or bring help from the divine powers. The priest who was the middleman between mortals and deities fixed the price for favors granted by the gods and collected all the articles contributed, conveyed some to the appropriate god and kept the remainder for himself. In very perilous times they might sacrifice human beings but in the course of time, by the seventh or sixth century B.C. the offering of humans as scapegoats was replaced by the sacrifice of an animal—a bull, sheep, goat or pig.

The Greeks also believed that the gods indicate their intentions by signs and omens as manifested by thunder, lightning, eclipse, storms and other natural phenomena, by the behavior of animals or through dreams. One could foretell the future or discover the will of a god by interpreting the flight of birds, examining the entrails of sacrificed animals or by consulting a specially gifted priest or priestess who could communicate directly with the god and obtain an appropriate response to the suppliant. Such agencies of divine communication or revelation were called oracles, the most famous of which was situated at Delphi and was the shrine dedicated to Apollo. Near this temple was a fissure in the earth where there lay the decomposed serpent that Apollo had once slain, and over the cleft stood a high three-legged stool on which there sat a priestess named Pythia who officiated at the services that took place once a month. She would chew laurel leaves and inhale the divine stench that issued from the remains of the serpent. The foul gas emanating from the carcass of a snake combined with the juice of the laurel leaf produced an inspired or narcotic effect—a delirious and convulsive trance. While in this ecstatic state Pythia was able to converse with the god Apollo and then give vent to incoherent utterances, kind of esoteric remarks, which attendant priests translated into comprehensible Greek, and the people believed. For hundreds of years Greeks and sometimes foreigners visited the Delphic oracle to find out what the future had in store for them, whether their plans would succeed or fail, to seek Apollo's advice on all sorts of matters. A king wanted to know if his country should go to war; a woman wanted to know why she couldn't have a baby; a business man was uncertain about investing his money in real estate; a young man wanted to know what career to pursue; another, how he could stop stammering and stuttering. The priests' replies to inquirers were composed cryptically in hexameter verse and expressed in ambiguous terms; and thus having a double meaning the answers were seldom wrong, and there was always an alibi. In fact the priests were commended and admired for being clever. They were highly intelligent and adroit and very well informed on personal problems, on political issues and public affairs; they were a kind of think tank of the ancient world. The Delphic oracle welcomed gifts from the grateful supplicants, was not averse to bribery and occasionally showed personal favoritism or political partiality, but on the whole it was reputed to be honest and wise.

Another all Hellenic religious center was Olympia the site of the temple of Zeus where the Greeks came to witness the famous Olympic games dedicated to their chief god, the ruler of the heavens. Beginning in 776 B.C. and every four years thereafter in the midsummer they would hold the contests to demonstrate the national esteem for young men of health, strength and athletic skill. These sporting events were considered an important sacred festival and were opened up with a solemn religious ceremony including sacrifices to Zeus in front of the temple. A sacred truce was proclaimed throughout Greece, all wars were to cease for the duration, which was for a period of one month, and all athletes, pilgrims and spectators traveling to and from Olympia were promised safe conduct. The great happening was somewhat commercialized as merchants were allowed to set up booths and sell almost any commodity they pleased, money changers facilitated trading, food and drinks were made available and there were all sorts of amusements including acrobats, magicians, jugglers, fire and sword swallowers. Artists exhibited their creations, authors recited excerpts from their works, orators displayed their eloquence, holding forth on various topics and heralds publicized treaties recently made among the Greek states. The stadium could hold about 45,000 spectators and they usually were all male, though only married women were specifically prohibited from attending the festival. Girls had their own intercity athletic tournaments and beauty contests in the nude.

Participants in the Olympic competitive events must be of pure Greek descent, free and thoroughly law-abiding young men. The athletes were naked as they engaged in foot-racing, jumping, leaping, discus-throwing, spear-throwing, swimming, bareback horse races, chariot races, boxing, wrestling, and male beauty contests. Greek boys at times also played ball games in which the ball was thrown, passed, bounced or batted with the hand or with rackets. There was no weight classification among boxers; they wore leather gloves and fought without rest or rounds until one was knocked out. There was one contest where two men could fight fiercely and freely by combining wrestling and boxing; they were permitted to jump on the adversary's body, kick each other in the stomach, break the foe's fingers or toes, strangle him, pierce the opponent's flesh and even to drag out his intestines. Unlike the Spartans, Athenian rules prohibited biting and eye-gouging. Greek fighters would rather die from strangulation than admit defeat. They told the story of how one popular athlete developed his strength by carrying a calf until it became a full-grown bull and then dropped the practice. One of the great runners, it was said, raced a horse for about twenty miles and beat it and another outran a rabbit, though he won only by a hair. Other competitive events included the display of poetry, musical compositions, trumpet playing, drama, the arts, oratory and drinking contests. The Greeks took their sports very seriously and the athletes were all amateurs. They crowned the winner of each event with a wreath of the sacred laurel and his home town would welcome their hero with parades and celebrations. On his arrival he was feted by the entire population and was usually rewarded by being supported for the rest of his life at public expense. An Olympic victor might have poems dedicated to him by famous authors, statues were erected in his honor, and some cities even made their local hero a general. In all the games and contests the runner-up would receive a wreath of pine leaves, and the one who finished third was crowned with leaves of parsley.

When the Greeks were prosperous and happy they didn't seem to be concerned very much about life after death though there were ceremonies not unlike those of other nations. Before burial, the body of the dead person was bathed and dressed meticulously, then sprinkled with perfume and flowers. It was customary to place a coin between the dead man's teeth so he could pay for the ferry ride across the river to Hades, the abode of departed spirits. On the grave they poured wine, laid flowers on it and sometimes food. After the interment there was a funerary repast for the mourners. To die meant the soul must move to another world, to a state of perfect happiness if the person were an exceptional hero; to a very deep infernal region if he were a heinous sinner. But the ordinary mortal was relegated to Hades, a subterranean land of dust and darkness—dull and indifferent, and thus a joyless outlook for persons who had been prosperous and happy in this world. And for the poor man Hades offered no comfort or consolation for all the pain, sorrow and disappointments in his life on earth. So to make life after death more agreeable and to compensate the unfortunate for their hitherto hapless existence the priests introduced the mystery religions with their attractive and optimistic promises of better times, personal immortality and a euphoric hereafter. The two most popular of these mystery cults were the ones involving Demeter, the earth mother and goddess of grain and Dionysus, the god of wine and vegetation. Primitive Greek peasants believed in the mythological story of Demeter—how her daughter was abducted by Death and taken to Hades, a gray and gloomy realm, where she was kept in captivity through the winter and then allowed to return to earth in the spring. The people celebrated at a festival where secret and sacred rites were performed that demonstrated the mourning of Demeter when her daughter was carried off in the fall when vegetation died, and then came the joy of recovering her in the spring when plant life was reborn. This ceremony came to signify a mystical relationship to the death of a person and the resurrection of his soul followed by eternal happiness. The Dionysus myth was somewhat similar. As a child this wine god had been torn to pieces by evil deities, killed and then brought back to life as happened to gods in Egypt, Babylonia and other lands. The son of god died to save mankind. There was frenzied and impassioned singing of hymns and then the Dionysian worshippers, the majority of whom were women, celebrated the festival by roaming around at night dancing wildly, singing, screaming and drinking—all accompanied by the beating of drums and the clashing of cymbals.

 Dionysus was the god of agriculture who stimulated the power of fertility, impregnated the soil and brought the joyous season of the spring with wine, gladness and intoxicated abandon. The boisterous festivity in his honor featured processions displaying the human symbols of reproduction while the officials relaxed conventional moral restraints and granted the devotees complete freedom of speech and sex for the occasion. The phallic emblem as a symbol of fertility was also flaunted at rites and processions in the worship of Demeter and Hermes. During the revelry a bull, a sheep or a pig was slain, sacrificed and by a magic formula the body and blood of the animal were transformed into the god Dionysus. The worshippers poured wine upon the body and then drank it and ate the flesh of the victim in divine communion. Having consumed consecrated flesh and blood of a reborn god who was imbued with the power of eternal life the communicants themselves mystically acquired blessed immortality and like Dionysus they too would live forever.

The Greeks were exceptionally talented in the arts. They had a passion for beauty and progress and they had an abundance of material to work with—timber, bronze, brick, stone and marble. Inspiration came from a rich religious mythology and from patriotic or civic pride and a profound desire to have beautiful temples and public buildings. Their homes could be plain and ordinary but the houses of their gods and places of assembly for citizens must be superfine. Contemporary writers refer to the excellence of their paintings—murals and mythological portraits used to enhance the architecture; but these were virtually all lost over the centuries. In the arts of sculpturing and architecture the achievements of the Greeks have never been surpassed and a few of their buildings and statues have survived, though badly damaged. Greek art was at its best in the fifth and fourth centuries B.C. and the city of Athens was at this time outstanding in all cultural and intellectual pursuits. On the Athenian citadel or acropolis there stood some of the most magnificent public buildings the world has ever seen. The central edifice and the finest example of Greek architecture was the Parthenon. It was a religious temple dedicated to the goddess Athena and was used by her as a temporary residence whenever she visited the city of Athens. Unlike churches Greek temples were shrines where people would come to offer sacrifices to the god or goddess in anticipation of a reciprocal favor. Other cities had their own patron deities and also built shrines or temples which the gods graced with their hallowed presence from time to time.

The Parthenon, built entirely of white marble, and in the Doric style, has been regarded by architects as an exquisite structure, a masterpiece, representing technical and aesthetic perfection. It possessed the dominant characteristics of classical Greek buildings— perfect proportion, harmony, order and moderation. Beautiful works, they believed, must be simple, graceful and dignified, and have nothing in excess, either in ornamentation or in size; and so the Parthenon was not too heavy and not too light, not too long nor too short and the building was decorated with restraint and in good taste. Greek temples were generally rectangular in plan, the roof sloped slightly from the center and was supported by a single or double row of columns on all sides. There were doors but no windows, the pediments and the upper part of the walls had some statues and sculpturing. Usually there were two porches, one at each end of the building, and two rooms inside—one for a statue of the patron deity and the other for the treasure and sacrifices given to the god. Two types of columns were used in the classical period—the Doric and the Ionic. The Doric was sturdy, solid and severe, with a simple capital and without a base, while the Ionian was more slender and elegant; the capital was decorated with a spiral or scroll-like formation and the pillar rested on a base. Three great names were associated with the construction of the Parthenon—Pericles supervised the project, Ictinus was the architect and Phidias was the chief sculptor.

Fifth century or classical sculptors generally sought to attain the ideal or the perfect rather than the real; therefore the subject matter usually embraced gods, heroes and athletes and the traits that were portrayed were strength, beauty, serenity and dignity. Besides statues that adorned the temples there were superb and exquisite mythological and historical scenes of religious festivals and processions carved on pediments and walls. These carvings were colored in gold, black, red and blue and the sculptors usually worked in stone and bronze. The most renowned Greek sculptor was Phidias who sculptured the majestic figure of Athena that stood in the Parthenon and of Zeus seated on the throne at Olympia. Both statues were colossal and both were constructed of gold and ivory laid over a framework of wood. With Praxiteles in the fourth century the style of sculpture became less severe, more human, emotional, contemplative, showing character and facial expression. And during the Hellenistic period sculpture became very realistic, more highly individualized, intensely emotional, depicting tragic incidents, realistic scenes from everyday life, and sometimes the extravagant and grotesque. This epoch produced many beautiful buildings too but they were much larger and more ornate and elaborate than the Hellenic. The Greeks were also skillful in the minor arts—in the making of vases, some painted, some embellished with reliefs, exquisite ornaments and jewelry, and charming terra cotta statuettes. These objects were often buried with the dead where they remained safe and unimpaired over 2000 years.

The Greeks loved music and they were proud of their achievements but nearly all of the records have disappeared and so we know little about their technical proficiency. But we do know that the study of music was required in the schools and even as a part of military training; the pupils were taught to sing and to play string, wind or percussion instruments. Music was not an independent art but was a counterpart of poetry, drama, and dancing; choral singing was very popular especially at religious festivals, musical strains accompanied the pronouncements of the oracles, and martial music was an important feature of army routine. Every cultured person learned to sing and to play a harp and enjoyed the competitive singing and playing contests at the Olympics and at other sporting festivals. Music, it was believed, could affect a person's morale, make him joyous or melancholy, brave or gentle; music would stimulate or tranquillize; it might even possess therapeutic power.

The literature of Greece began with epic poetry, stories about gods, kings and heroes. The most prominent works were the *Iliad* and the *Odyssey*, the products of Homer, a blind poet who lived in the ninth or eighth century B.C. It is not absolutely certain whether these books were written by Homer or whether they were a collection of ballads composed by many poets. These narratives in verse apparently had been recited and sung for about three hundred years before they were written down and they had been kept alive and embellished through the many generations by musicians who traveled about the land with their guitars entertaining kings and nobles. The *Iliad* describes the heroic, legendary figures and dramatic events in the closing years of the Greco-Trojan war. The Greeks, considering themselves an up-and-coming world power, eager to gain possession of the strategic city of Troy on the Dardanelles, fought and besieged and finally overcame the Trojans. Romantic poets rendered the conflict more palatable. According to these authors the war started when Paris, a prince of Troy, carried off the beautiful daughter of Zeus and so the Greek warriors immediately took steps to retrieve the lovely abducted lady. It took ten years and the lives of thousands of men to recover and repatriate the divine princess, Helen. The city of Troy, we are told, was finally captured by a ruse involving a wooden horse which concealed a fifth column of Greek fighters. The *Odyssey* relates the fantastic adventures of Odysseus, king of Ithaca, who wandered for ten years after the defeat and destruction of Troy before he returned to his native land and his beloved wife, Penelope—who had waited faithfully during his long absence of twenty years. These great epics contain not only the account of the melodramatic exploits of the famous Hellenic heroes but much information about everyday life in early Greece. The author also pauses and frequently digresses to make discerning observations and moral reflections on various topics.

After Homer the next great Hellenic literary figure was Hesiod who lived in the eighth century. He was known mostly for his poems of farm life but he also wrote about the origins and character of the gods and the universe. His verse was often moral, didactic and philosophical. Besides the work of Homer and Hesiod there was a considerable amount of lyric poetry. Expressing the feelings of the individual, these poems were recited or sung to the accompaniment of a lyre. Distinguished among the authors of lyrics was Sappho of Lesbos, the woman poet who was directress of a combined parochial and finishing school for girls, dedicated to the goddess of love, Aphrodite. She had great affection for her pupils and wrote passionate love poems, wedding hymns, and simple, graceful lyrics on the sublimity of nature. Equally outstanding and a master of craftsmanship was Pindar of Thebes who differed from Sappho in theme, style and technique. He was more interested in choral lyrics which expressed the feelings of the community; he composed numerous odes honoring the victors of the athletic contests and he was devoted to traditional religious and moral purity. There were also authors who wrote poems about politics, pleasures, and court life, and others who composed hymns and charming pastoral poetry.

The greatest literary achievement of the Greeks was the tragic drama. It arose in connection with the worship of Dionysus at the annual spring festival in honor of the vine and vegetation deity. The wild orgy of the ceremony was tempered and changed into a ritual where the worshipers acted out the myth of the god in a religious musical tragedy composed of songs, dances, and a choir led by a narrator or cantor. The first known playwright was Thespis who lived in the sixth century B.C. and from whose name the word thespian is derived. He devised a more theatrical performance which included spoken and musical recitations by the leader and dialogue between him and the chorus. The narrator would appear at the altar at various intervals wearing masks and costumes and impersonating different characters, but there was no action and no conflict.

A few years later there appeared on the scene the great dramatist, Aeschylus, who introduced a second actor and diminished the role of the chorus by reducing its number of members and by lessening the amount of singing in general. He retained background music and interspersed the play with lyrical passages and musical dialogue. He also introduced essentials of dramaturgy—clash of interests, verbal collision and the conflict of emotions and circumstances. The characters in the dramas of Aeschylus, which numbered about eighty, were mostly gods and other lofty and heroic figures; the theme was religious and the dialogue was majestic and ponderous. Aeschylus believed that life was determined by fate which is controlled by the laws of the gods and any violation of these laws inevitably leads to punishment and death. The author himself was destined to be a fatal victim of a singular and outlandish accident. The famous playwright was killed in Sicily when an eagle dropped a turtle on his bald head mistaking it for a stone. Sophocles went further than Aeschylus in the development of technique, increasing dramatic dialogue and introducing a third actor and the use of scenery, as well as the theatrical elements of suspense, climax, and conflict. He emphasized the importance of character, was more moderate and restrained and more skillful in character and emotional delineation; his style was more elegant and artistic and he was more profound in his exhorting and philosophizing. Affirming his stark pessimism he asserted that the fortunate person is the one who has never been born, the next happiest is the one who dies in infancy. Sophocles wrote over one hundred dramas, yet he had time and energy to become skilled as a musician, a ball player, and a wrestler; he also was a soldier, a priest and a political officeholder, and he was very fond of women and money. The third great writer of tragic dramas, Euripides, believed that the fortunes of men are not determined by the powerful and inevitable will of the gods nor is tragedy the result of the hero's weakness of character. It is the fault of the individual, of human passions, love and devotion; it is engendered by one's inability to adjust to moral, religious and political customs. Euripides was a rebel, a radical and a humanitarian who expressed sympathy for the heretic, the common man, the disadvantaged, the poor, the women and the slaves, all of whom he realistically portrayed. He ridiculed popular prejudices and popular heroes and bemoaned the woes and horrors of war and was an advocate of reform for the exploited. Euripides was a champion of change—political, social, economic and recommended the union of all Greeks.

The foremost author of comic drama was Aristophanes, a conservative aristocrat who ridiculed contemporaries he disliked: progressives, radicals, liberals, democrats, corrupt politicians, but also imperialists and war makers, particularly if they fought against other Greeks. In one of his plays he has the women of Athens stage a strike against the war with Sparta. The strikers promise to withhold physical love from their spouses until peace is made with the enemy and they invite the women of Sparta to also impose a sex ban and join the lockout. The men order their wives to come home and when they refuse, the husbands besiege a convention of the female strikers but they are driven off by torrents of hot water and a stream of abusive words. Negotiations are finally arranged and after a conference of delegates from the warring states a treaty is signed. The play ends on a happy note as the chorus sings a hymn to peace. Aristophanes could write excellent lyric poetry and his plays were witty and subtle but they often were also vulgar and pornographic abounding in ludicrous farce, wild burlesque and gross obscenity. He even caricatured the Greek religion and profaned the divinities in asserting that there are brothels in heaven maintained by the gods. There were other Greek dramatists but none was as talented and as profound as the four above who lived in the sixth and fifth centuries B.C.

Greek plays were performed outdoors where benches were usually placed into the side of a hill forming a semicircle of tiers. The theater of Dionysus in Athens accommodated about seventeen thousand persons. The seats were built of wood or stone and had no backs except for a few in the front rows that were made of marble and were reserved for high priests and prominent local politicians. Many people brought cushions with them as the performances lasted three days; there were sometimes five plays in a day and they began early in the morning and ended at dusk. At the bottom of the hill of seats was a circular dance floor called the orchestra, behind the orchestra was a platform that served as a stage, and just beyond this was a small building called the *skene* which was used by the actors to house their props and to repair to when offstage. The performers, called *hypok-*

rites, were all male, were organized in a guild or union (the Dionysian artists) and they were exempt from military service. With the exception of the chorus they were all professionals who composed plays and music, made their own costumes and set up the stages. Although acoustics and visibility in Greek theaters were purported to be quite adequate, the actors found it necessary to make their voices more audible and resonant by using crude loud speakers or mouthpieces of brass and to enlarge their stature by wearing high headdresses, padding and thick elevated shoes. The price of admission to the theater was about thirty-five cents but a few hundred citizens on welfare were admitted free of charge. Women were allowed to attend the serious plays but they had to sit apart from the men while courtesans were assigned a restricted section of the theater, and at the comedies, which were often lewd and salacious, the only females in the audience were women of easy virtues. People generally brought refreshments with them and ate great quantities of nuts and fruit and drank wine continuously throughout the performances. Actors employed claques and the audience was often noisy and could even become riotous. They applauded and cheered, they booed, hissed and jeered and pelted the stage with olives, figs and even stones. Prizes were awarded to the dramatists who produced the finest plays. In early Greece they gave the writer of the best tragedy a goat, one of Dionysus' favorite animals, and the author of the most entertaining comedy was presented with a basket of figs and a jug of wine. But by the fifth century the winning dramatists were rewarded with grants of money provided by the government.

Historians were among the first prose writers of Greece. Herodotus, known as the father of history, wrote about the invasion of Greece by the Persians and seasons his account with the numerous strange, interesting facts, exotic customs, and amusing anecdotes of the peoples in the Middle East. For example, Herodotus states that inscriptions on the pyramids are not so memorable for they convey the amount of garlic, radishes and green onions paid to the workers who built them; that Egyptian cats are so fascinated by fire that they compulsively jump into the flames; and that the semen of Ethiopians is black. To illustrate the irresponsibility and danger of dictators Herodotus related the story of a Persian absolute monarch who, caught in a storm at sea, advised the captain to lighten the ship. He then summoned his courtiers and commanded them to jump overboard. When the ship reached land he decorated the skipper for saving his life and then beheaded him for causing the death of his courtiers. Less charming but more accurate and intellectual was the famous work of Thucydides—the history of the struggle between Sparta and Athens. It is a statement of facts based on evidence scientifically collected and weighed and it contains objective comment and analysis of the leaders' motives and policies—political and psychological reasons for their thoughts and actions. Another very competent historian was Xenophon, who wrote an exciting story of the retreat of a Greek army through Asia Minor. During the Hellenistic era the best historian and prose writer was Polybius who was objective and scientific, but unlike Thucydides, he was interested in and recognized the importance of not only political factors but social and economic forces as well. Other outstanding writers of noteworthy prose were the eloquent orators, Demosthenes and Pericles, and Aesop the author of common sense animal tales. Literate farmers enjoyed reading the patriotic, heroic poetry of epics but urbanites often showed a predilection for the witty dialogue and clever fables of Aesop.

    The Greeks knew more about science than any other people that lived before them but their scientific knowledge was infinitesimal comparative to that of the modern world. Their greatest contribution in this area of enlightenment was an open-minded inquiry, a secular and scientific attitude toward nature and man. Many Oriental pundits from Egypt to China averred that the primary substance in the world was water but they all believed that this elemental material was manipulated and processed into a multifarious world by a variety of supernatural beings or by an omnipotent creator. In the sixth century B.C. Thales, a Greek of Phoenician parentage, and a successful speculator who dealt in salt and oil, who had traveled and studied in the eastern lands, reiterated the water hypothesis—that everything ultimately comes from water. But he disregarded divine participation and declared that there is a natural cause and a rational explanation for all physical phenomena. He is therefore called the father of science. His thesis, he said, was logical and rational, for water is a liquid, a solid and a gas and it is indispensable to life for both plants and animals. Others believed the original material from which all things come is fire, or air, or earth. Still others taught that there were four basic elements—earth, air, fire and water.

Doodling and drawing angles and circles led the curious intellectual Thales to introduce geometry into Greece. He originated a number of geometric theorems: a circle is bisected by its diameter; the angles at the base of an isosceles triangle are equal; if two straight lines cut one another the vertically opposite angles are equal. Pythagoras, a little younger than Thales, discovered the theorem that in a right angled triangle the square of the hypotenuse equals the sum of the square of the other two sides. No other significant achievements were made during the Hellenic era but much more was accomplished in Hellenistic times and in both periods the Greeks made much use of the knowledge they acquired from Egypt and the Middle East. Around 300 B.C. Euclid of Alexandria wrote the *Elements of Geometry* which was used as a textbook in Europe until the nineteenth century. Other Hellenistic mathematicians divided the circle into 360 degrees, dealt with geometry of conic sections, invented plane and spherical trigonometry and developed a system of algebra. Archimedes of Syracuse was regarded as the most eminent mathematician of antiquity. He delved and commented on spheres, cones, cylinders, and other figures and made a close calculation of the value of (pi), the ratio of the circumference of a circle to its diameter.

Thales, the founder of science, was not a great astronomer but he was so curious about the heavenly bodies that once while observing the stars he fell into a ditch filled with his favorite original element—water. Later after much studying he learned enough astronomy to accurately predict an eclipse of the sun and he also divided the year into 365 days. Pythagoras was the first to declare the earth is a sphere and he and his followers tried to prove that it moves in a circular orbit. Anaxagoras described the sun as a mass of burning iron, he explained the waxing and the waning of the moon and stated that its light is a reflection of the light of the sun. The earth, he said, turns on its axis and along with the sun and all the planets, moves around a hypothetical fire. Democritus believed that the milky way is composed of a vast number of small stars. During the Hellenistic period when men were more interested in materiality and science there were at least three eminent astronomers. In the third century B.C. Aristarchus expounded the doctrine that the earth and the other planets revolve around the sun—the heliocentric system of the universe. However this theory was considered too radical since virtually all people continued to adhere to the traditional anthropocentric view of the cosmos, that man was the gods' favorite creation. Ptolemy of Alexandria worked out a more plausible and agreeable geocentric system, that the earth is the center of the universe, a notion that was also more in harmony with the prevailing religions. This incorrect Ptolemaic theory was universally accepted until the sixteenth century. The third great astronomer of the Hellenistic era was Hipparchus who invented the astrolabe, catalogued over a thousand stars, and prepared a celestial map and globe.

Greek scientists dealt with the state and properties of matter and speculated and reflected on the laws of physics. Thales believed that water is the primary element—uncreated and imperishable; others thought it was air, or earth, or fire; still others declared there were four original sources—earth, air, fire and water. Anaxagoras asserted that at first there was only chaos in the world—an aggregate of infinitesimal particles. Then by a whirling motion, a process of integration, differentiation or evolution the cosmos arose. Leucippus and Democritus reasoned there is space and there is tangible substance, that all things in the world whether animate or inanimate are composed of atoms, which are invisible and indivisible physical, material particles of different size, weight and shape, which like a jig-saw puzzle combine to form the various tangible things that exist. Democritus also believed in the conservation of mass, that is, the quantity of matter remains always the same—none is ever created, none is ever destroyed, only the atom combinations change. More practical-minded was the great mathematician and physicist, the Hellenistic Greek, Archimedes, who lived in Syracuse. He discovered the law of floating bodies and devised a method for measuring specific gravity and he experimented successfully with a number of mechanical devices, such as the wedge, fulcrum, lever, screw, and pulley. Heron of Alexandria was a physicist and engineer who invented a siphon, an air pump, a fire engine, a slot machine and a rudimentary steam engine. However no industrial revolution resulted from these inventions, as labor and slaves were cheaper and the Greek businessmen could see no profit in machine production.

Anaximander, a pupil of Thales', was a very early Greek geographer. He made the first map of the earth, which he depicted as a cylinder, the top of which was inhabited by the people. It had been generally taught that the earth was a round flat disc, though Pythagoras, a contemporary of Anaximander, thought it was globe-shaped. Much geographical knowledge about Europe, Asia and Africa was acquired from the extensive travels and descriptive writings of the historian, Herodotus, and from the expeditions of Alexander the Great. Greek sailors had reached India in the East and England in the northwest. The Greeks were a commercial people and some of their scientists were telling them that the earth is round and by Hellenistic times they were making more accurate maps and were learning more about the technology of navigation. The first scientific geographer was Eratosthenes who estimated the diameter and circumference of the earth almost correctly at 7850 and 24,682 miles respectively and was the first to show latitude and longitude on his maps. There were other eminent Hellenistic geographers after the Romans took over the Mediterranean world.

Like most of the Greek scientists Anaximander was very versatile, but he was the first of them to manifest an interest in biology and to develop a general theory of evolution. He believed that originally the earth was in a fluid state and all animate objects lived in water. Even man was once a fish, for that was the only way to stay alive at that time—one had to adapt himself to his environment. But as environment changed the forms of life evolved from lower to higher beings by a compulsive desire to survive and by a process of adaptation. Other scientists modified and elaborated on the theory, stating that as the water receded from its original position it made land and mud and from the slime heated by the sun living things appeared. From this arose the belief in spontaneous generation or the production of living things from inanimate matter, an hypothesis that was not disproved until the seventeenth century. Empedocles also believed that lower forms of life develop into higher forms and he alleged that at one time both sexes were in the same body but in the process of evolution they became separated and now each possesses a magnetic desire to reunite with the other. Adam of the Hebrew Bible, it is said, was also originally both male and female.

The real founder of biology was Aristotle, a scientist as well as a philosopher. He carefully observed, dissected, and collected information about all kinds of animals from sponge to man; he classified them, described their structure, their organs and their habits. He introduced the study of comparative anatomy and by observing and describing the development of the embryo of the dogfish and of the chick in the egg he began the study of embryology. Aristotle subscribed to the theories of evolution and spontaneous generation; he studied the problems of heredity, sex, nutrition, growth, adaptation and the struggle for existence. People had generally believed that the male parent was the sole source of human seed, that the role of the mother in procreation was only domestic, that is, she provided a home and nourishment for the embryo, but Aristotle proved this to be an erroneous conception and showed that the female ovum or reproductive cell is equally important in the generative process. He also rejected the theory that the right testicle produces male and the left testicle female offspring, by showing that a man whose right testicle had been removed had continued to beget boys and girls. Aristotle's *History of Animals* written with the aid of his students contains numerous mistakes; for example—the function of the brain is to cool the blood; blood flows from the liver to other parts of the body; food is cooked in a person's intestinal tube; flat-footed people are treacherous; species of eels, worms and insects come into being in grime by spontaneous generation; mice die if they drink in the summer; goats breathe through their ears; elephants suffer from only two diseases—excessive accumulation of gas and the post-nasal drip; vultures can be made pregnant by the wind; horses and men are the most salacious animals. One of Aristotle's students, Theophrastus, became the leading botanist of antiquity, famous for his observations, description and classification of plants. His scientific treatises were considered the definitive works in the field until the sixteenth century.

As in Egypt and Mesopotamia medical practice in Greece evolved from religion and the priest; Apollo the sun god was the original mythologic god of healing. Historically, however, it seems that the first real physician was Aesculapius, who had fought in the Trojan war. He was so admired by the Greeks that they deified him; the priests proclaimed him the son of Apollo and erected temples of healing and for his worship. These ecclesiastical sanitariums were visited by people seeking relief for various kinds of diseases and it was said the remedies were often miraculously effective. Aesculapius had two daughters named Hygeia and Panacea whose task was to take care of the snakes kept in the temples as symbols of the god of medicine. This divine physician was eminently successful, curing so many people that Pluto the god of Hades, complained to Zeus about the tremendous decline in the number of immigrants arriving in his subterranean realm. Fearing that the children of earth might become immortal and desirous of reestablishing a more conservative balance between the living and the dead, Zeus had Aesculapius slain by a thunderbolt. The people however continued to worship the god of medicine, sacrificing roosters and offering to him images of the part of the body that was ailing—the heart, lung, limbs, intestines or the generative organs. The great medical work of Aesculapius was carried on by his vicars, the priests, in the temples or sacred resorts which were always situated where the surroundings were beautiful and salutary—near mountains, forests, and springs where the water was pure and contained healthful minerals. Treatment consisted of baths, massage and diet followed by prayer and sacrifice, and according to the priests the gift of a rooster was not sufficient, as Aesculapius demanded fees for his services, preferably in the form of gold and silver. There were doctors during the prescientific days who recommended physical therapy or the use of force as efficacious treatment of many ailments; for example, violent blows on the forehead or on the front or side of the neck or the back of the leg. Hippocrates' teacher prescribed walking or wrestling to reduce a fever. Even in the highly advanced fifth century B.C. the temple priests still practiced medicine and thrived from the fees and offerings of numerous gullible patients who were entranced and intoxicated by the power of divine medicine.

The first secular physician of whom there is authentic historical information was Democedes, a skillful practitioner who was employed by a Greek city government and once cured the Persian king and queen. The monarch had been suffering from a dislocated ankle and his royal spouse had a painful growth on her breast. However, it was Alcmaeon, the most famous Greek physician before Hippocrates, who started the scientific investigation of medicine by dissecting animals and describing his anatomical observations. He recognized man's brain as the organ of thought, explained the origin of the nerves, located the optic nerve and the Eustachian tube, and explained the physiology of sleep. Other Greek medicos described the blood vascular system, the respiratory system, discovered the labyrinth in the inner ear, black and yellow bile in blood, and explained pleurisy as a disease of the lungs. Empedocles was the first to believe that the blood flows to and from the heart. Also a leading authority on sanitation, he once had a hill cut down allowing the north wind to blow fresh air into his home town which was afflicted with a plague. He rendered a similar service to another city by draining a local swamp. A clever and felicitous conversationalist, Empedocles often employed psychology in treating his patients, particularly those whose ailments were psychosomatic, and he advised all people seeking health and happiness to abstain from marriage and beans.

The most notable of all Greek doctors was Hippocrates, who separated medicine from religion. He declared that every illness has a natural cause and advocated therapy that is based on experiment and experience instead of superstition and the supernatural. He believed in the healing power of nature and stated that the function of the physician is to assist nature in removing obstacles to recovery by employing such remedies as massage, ointments, emetics, suppositories, enemas, purgatives, cupping, cutting, cauterizing and blood-letting. Hippocrates seldom prescribed drugs, but instead stressed the importance of hygiene, diet, rest; he frequently urged his patients to get plenty of fresh air and to fast occasionally and always to eat little—once a day is adequate for most people. The most prevalent ailments in Greece were colds, pneumonia and malaria. Hippocrates observed that in most cases a disease in developing usually reaches a crisis, in which either the illness or the patient comes to an end. Doctors should try to have their patients die young—as late as possible. Hippocrates however subscribed to the mistaken doctrine of the four humors, that is; illness results from a surplus or a shortage of one of the four bodily fluids—blood, phlegm, yellow bile and black bile. To correct the disturbance and restore the natural blend of the fluids or the harmony of the body the physician must prescribe a hot diet for a deficiency and blood-letting for an excess of one of the elements. The Hippocratic oath, containing the highest ideals of the profession and which the father of medicine administered to his students in the fifth century B.C., is still the accepted summary of medical ethics today. In Hellenistic times the physicians began to dissect human bodies, learning more about the eye, the brain, nerves, liver, pancreas, intestines and the sexual organs. They discovered the significance of the pulse, distinguished arteries from veins and discovered the true circulation of the blood.

From about 600 to 450 B.C. the Greek scientists were also philosophers. They were cosmologists, that is; they inquired into the nature of things—the origin, the processes, and the structure of the universe, what changes and what remains unchanged, and they formed conclusions based on logical reasoning and hypothesizing. Only in Greece, where the priests were not very influential, were men allowed to speculate freely about earthly phenomena without attributing creation and causation to one or more gods.

The first Greek philosopher was Thales, the scientist who stated that water is the stuff from which all things are derived and that everything including man ultimately returns to water. Although he was a materialist Thales believed that every particle of metal, plant, animal, or man possesses vitality or an immortal soul which changes form but does not become void, for water can solidify or evaporate but it never dies. Therefore the living and what appears to be dead are essentially and constitutionally the same. Anaximander maintained that the primary substance is an infinite and boundless mass, alive and always in motion. From this body of matter all things have broken off and that someday all the pieces will return to the endless original cosmic substance. Anaximines chose air as the original stuff from which, by rarefaction or by condensation, all other material things are produced. Air when inhaled makes flesh, bone and blood, when rarefied becomes wind, cloud or fire and when condensed changes to water, earth or stone.

Xenophanes, another monist, declared that the ultimate substance in the universe is God. He rejected the popular belief in many deities and the practice of making gods look like people. If animals could paint or carve images they would make their gods look like animals. Ethiopians make their gods black and snub-nosed, Thracians give them blue eyes and red hair. There is only one god—a material cosmic substance, who can see, hear and think. He rules the world through the power of his mind and He should receive religious reverence. Pythagoras believed that the fundamental principle in nature is not physical—it is metaphysical and mathematical—the harmonious relationship between substance and number; the secrets of the universe and the destiny of man are revealed by numbers, which possess a mystic significance. A point is 1, a line is 2; feminine is 2, masculine is 3 and so 5 is the essence of marriage. And in music, since the harmonious octave reaches over 8 notes, 8 must be friendship. The perfect figure of the Pythagoreans is an equal-sided triangle of 10 dots which contains 4 dots on each side and one in the center. Everything is really made of numbers or are reflections of number forms. Pythagoras established a religious school and community which practiced the collectivistic sharing of goods and prohibited the eating of meat, eggs, or beans. A religious reformer, the philosopher inculcated upon his followers the qualities of simplicity, modesty, abstinence, moral discipline and self-control. He believed that after death the soul leaves the body and undergoes a period of purgation in Hades, then it enters another body in a chain of transmigration. To break this seemingly endless peregrination of the soul one must lead a completely virtuous life, like the Brahmans of India. Pythagoras recalled that at one time he had been incarnated as a strumpet, at another time his soul had resided in the body of a hero at the battle of Troy and he also alleged that he had detected the voice of his late friend in the cry of a dog. When one eats meat he might be eating the flesh of an ancestor, which is cannibalism. The Pythagoreans also introduced into philosophy the dualistic notion of contrasts or opposites, for example, good and evil, light and darkness, left and right, straight and crooked, odd and even, perfect and imperfect, male and female, rest and motion.

Heraclitus asserted that change is the basic principle of the universe. Fire is forever moving and changing, it is never still, it is kinetic energy. Like the water of a river it always flows, it is in a constant state of flux, always in motion, never the same. Fire, like electrons, is therefore the essence of all material things. Air, water, metal, stone, everything in the universe is made of fire and everything changes. The soul of man is pure fire and the finest soul is made of cosmic fire; it is dry and warm and cannot be destroyed. Life is full of antithesis—change and counterchange. The result of conflict is creation, the result of discord is harmony and all things have their birth in strife. The universe had no beginning and will have no end.

Parmenides upheld on opposite view. He proclaimed that the world was not only finite but it is always at rest. Stability and permanence are the real nature of things. "There is no motion. Empty space is simply nothing and as nothing can hardly be said to exist, space is an illusion. An object could not move without occupying first one space and then another; therefore there is no such thing as motion." The seat of reality is eternal and immovable.

Zeno defended Parmenides. "The flying arrow does not really move at all because at any one particular instant it must be in one particular place. Now, if an object is in one place it is at rest, and if the arrow is at rest during each moment of its flight, when does it move? Change is an illusion". A rebel against tyranny and a leader of a revolution, Zeno was threatened with torture. He bit off a piece of his tongue and spat it in the tyrant's face, for which he was pounded to death in a stone mortar.

Melissus argued cleverly: "Either things exist or they do not exist. If they do not exist then further discussion is unprofitable, but if they do, we may proceed to the conclusion that they have always existed or else contend that they have been produced. If things were produced then they must have come either from being or from non-being. Nothing can possibly come from non-being, and if we say that being arose from being, we must admit that being was before being came to be, which is nonsense. Therefore we must conclude that all being is eternal—everything that is has always been and always will be".

Empedocles was a pluralist who maintained that there are four basic indestructible elements: earth, air, fire and water. Each of these elements is composed of tiny particles which are separated by strife or hate and united by love to form the numerous things in the universe. All things are alive and never die. He believed in transmigration and claimed that in the past he had been a girl, a flowering plant, a bird, a fish, and a god. His erstwhile divinity was never advertised. Eating meat, he said, was a form of cannibalism and as a physician he advised people to be vegetarians. One day Empedocles disappeared leaving his shoes at the crater of Mt. Aetna.

Leucippus and Democritus held that everything in the universe is composed of atoms, even fire, mind and soul. Atoms vary in size and shape, are indestructible and indivisible, infinite in form and number, they move freely and continuously in empty space. They combine and they separate; convergence leads to the production of an object—a complex of atoms; disunion results in the dissolution of the complex of atoms. The number of atoms in the world always remains the same; they may change their position but are never destroyed. Democritus was a thorough materialist: there is no such thing as spirituality; there is no ruler in control of the universe; there is no one directing the movement of atoms; necessity or natural law governs everything. In spite of his materialism Democritus offered men worthy ethical principles. Happiness is the goal of life. One must not seek riches but peace and serenity of soul. Sensual pleasures are brief and transitory but a life devoted to reflection, reason and culture brings a more durable happiness. The offender is more unhappy than the victim. It is better to abstain from sin yourself than to find fault with others. The righteous man not only refrains from evil, he does not desire to do wrong.

In the middle of the fifth century B.C. there arose in Athens a group of teachers called Sophists who gave instructions on a variety of subjects including general culture, rhetoric, politics and debating. They also trained young men how to succeed in the world by learning to speak well, develop their intellectual power, to become intelligent, wise and clever. Traditional religion and conventional morals were omitted from their curriculum and the philosophical notions which they introduced and disseminated came to be known as sophism or adroit, subtle reasoning. They asserted that all the early philosophers of Greece had been wasting their time, serving no useful purpose, in searching for the origin and nature of the universe, seeking knowledge for the sake of knowledge, seeking facts that cannot be verified by evidence. Nothing exists which cannot be perceived by the senses. Furthermore everything is relative to time, place, and to the individual person involved; there are no absolute truths or eternal, universal standards of right, justice, truth, beauty and morality for all cases. Man in his particular situation or environment, at any particular time, must decide what is wise for him to think or do; man is the judge of right conduct; man is the measure of all things; man is the center of the universe. There is no fate, no predetermined course of events; man's will is free and belief in the gods is unreasonable. Some Sophists were pragmatic, others were utilitarian, some advocated the pursuit of pleasure and others maintained that in actual practice might is always right. In spite of their individualism, skepticism and relativism the Sophists were generally progressive in their point of view as they condemned war, slavery, and racial discrimination and favored freedom of speech and the rights of the common man. Above all they stimulated thought. The conservatives, however, were afraid that widespread liberalism and superficial sophistication among the callow Greek youth would undermine traditional morals and beliefs and lead to atheism, anarchy and chaos. They insisted that the masses and the immature must have absolute standards or organized society would perish.

The conflict between conservatives and progressives resulted in a new philosophic movement with the restoration of absolute standards but with new goals, purposes and motivation. Thinking, generalizing and philosophizing became popular and three very famous individuals in the history of thought would appear in the following order—Socrates, Plato and Aristotle.

Socrates lived in Athens in the second half of the fifth century B.C. He was trained to be a stone mason and a sculptor but his ambition and proficiency in the field of stone were only mediocre. His primary interests in life were thinking, talking, and rationalizing, not about cosmic matters but about human beings. Socrates wanted to make people think, acquire knowledge, reason logically and be wise and virtuous. He wanted people to free themselves from their prejudices, their biased opinions and their dependence on myths and superstitions. In spite of his apparent skepticism he was not averse to consulting Apollo's oracle occasionally and he might even sacrifice a rooster to Aesculapius. Socrates believed in a God, in the spirituality and the immortality of the soul and that everyone is cognizant of the good and possesses a conscience which is acquired at birth from God. The Socratic method of teaching was questions and answers and he would not permit the use of a word the meaning of which was not made perfectly clear, particularly such words as, truth, justice, virtue or beauty. The following are some of his maxims and aphorisms: the beginning of wisdom is to know one's self; if one knows what is right he will do what is right; no man is voluntarily bad; knowledge is the highest good; right is not relative to time or condition; it is absolute, eternal and holds equally well for all times and all places; knowledge must be separated from opinion; the good man will not return evil for evil, for then he is no longer good, but no better than the evil man; the good man will return good for evil, for good is always the same, does not change with conditions. To be happy is to be virtuous and to be virtuous is to be wise. Happiness is to want as little as possible. Socrates believed that aristocracy is the best form of government but the officials of such a state should be men of knowledge and ability and they should be trained for the job. However he recognized the advantage of democracy and appreciated the liberties and opportunities it afforded him.

Physically Socrates was a very unattractive man. He was short, stout with a prominent paunch, slovenly dressed and always barefooted; baldheaded with bulging eyes, flat nose, upturned nostrils and an unkempt beard. But as a person he was charming and amiable, beloved by numerous devoted followers and greatly admired by all his intimate associates except his wife, Xantippe, who was very unhappy over the philosopher's failure to support his family. Socrates loved the streets of Athens, loved to talk to the people, to spread ideas, to debate, to dialogue and to ventilate questions, to get at the truth of all problems. He never wrote anything but his influence on human thought was enormous.

As a politician he was uncommonly faithful to the state and as a soldier in the Peloponnesian War he was courageous, valorous, a self-sacrificing hero. But not everybody liked Socrates. The orthodox, the reactionaries and conservative political incumbents were alarmed by his exposure of fraud and hypocrisy, they were disturbed by the effectiveness of his criticism of popular beliefs, and were fearful of the influence of his teachings. So they arrested him and accused him of impiety and of corrupting the youth. He affirmed the charges against him and when asked what punishment he deserved he told the court that since he had only tried to make Athenians think, the judges should really regard him as a public benefactor and that he should be rewarded with a pension and be supported by the government for the rest of his life. The court disagreed and condemned him to death—to drink a cup of poisonous hemlock. He had opportunities to go into exile and to escape from prison but he refused to leave his home town. Furthermore, he had always been patriotic, law abiding and punctilious in his civic duties—the order of the court must be respected and obeyed, he insisted. Now 70 years of age, he told the jury: "Thus we part and go our separate ways, you to live and I to die; which is better God only knows". Death, he once said, was either sleep without dreams or a change of residence.

Socrates' most famous disciple was Aristocles, known in history as Plato, which was a nickname given him because he had a broad frame. A rich Athenian of noble ancestry, he established a coeducational university called the Academy from which the word academic is derived; it specialized in the teaching of mathematics and philosophy. According to Plato the universe is divided into two realms—the material and the spiritual. The material world is what we perceive with our senses, where everything is transient, changing, imperfect and unreal. The spiritual realm is composed of ideas that are immutable, eternal, real and perfect. When a person is born his soul passes from a previous living body into a new one but he is already in possession of the perfect, eternal concepts. Upon the death of a person the individual soul returns to its spiritual home where it awaits another assignment by the supreme universal soul or the creative force which Plato called the demiurge. In the interval of transmigration from one body to another the soul gets a glimpse of the ideal realm and although he henceforth dwells in an imperfect world of changing things he may through training of the mind recall the innate spiritual concepts. Whatever man apprehends with his physical faculties in the material world is a copy or representation of a pattern or model. A tangible table is just an imitation of the universal concept, table, which embraces the tables of all sizes and shapes in existence. The individual table is faulty and fleeting, it comes and goes but the mental idea, the class or category of table is the standard, archetype, unchanging and eternal. The same Platonic reasoning could be applied to radio, bicycle, dog or horse or to the difference between particular cases or examples of justice, beauty, or virtue as compared with abstract, perfect and ideal justice, beauty or virtue.

In the *Republic*, one of Plato's great books, the philosopher described what he regarded as the perfect political organization, an ideal state for human beings. The people would be divided into three classes—first, the intellectual aristocracy, second, soldiers, and third, the masses. All children, regardless of social rank, male and female, must attend school until the age of 20 when the state will give them physical, mental and moral tests. Those that fail will become members of the largest class in society—farmers, laborers, and business men or those who desire wealth, private property, material things. Those who passed the examination would receive ten more years of schooling and when they reached the age of 30 they would be tested again. Those that fail must become soldiers and live in military communism where possessions, property, love and wives would be shared equally, free for all warriors. Their function in life was to maintain law and order and defend their country. Those that passed the second test must study five more years and if they pass the final examination they will become the members of the ruling class—governors and administrators of the state. These intellectuals too will share with one another all their possessions—their property, their physical comforts and their wives. The materialistic majority would devote their time and effort to economic production and distribution and provide society with all the physical needs but were taught to be temperate, to curb their appetites and selfishness in their pursuit of wealth. The soldiers, the protectors or guardians of the commonwealth were instilled with courage, honor and devotion to duty, while the intellectual rulers were imbued with philosophy, wisdom, justice and altruism. Plato's utopian republic would establish government by the most intelligent, qualified few, with state censorship and regulation of literature, music and education; but the acquisitive class, which was most of the people, were allowed to enjoy private ownership, freedom of competition, and the amassing of wealth based upon or limited by personal ability. The rulers would forbid slavery, give women the same rights as men and provide free education for all persons in the community.

The most brilliant student in Plato's Academy was Aristotle whose college nickname was "the brain." He descended from a long line of physicians that traced their origin to Aesculapius. Aristotle did not become a practicing doctor of medicine but he was one of the great Greek scientists and his learning included the entire range of human knowledge. His father was the court physician in Macedonia and sometime after his graduation from Plato's Academy Aristotle was summoned by King Philip to become the tutor of Alexander, the crown prince. Many years later after conquering much of the then known world Alexander the Great acknowledged his indebtedness to the teaching of the famous philosopher. In 334 B.C. Aristotle founded a school called the Lyceum in which he introduced learning through research and emphasized its importance in the study and teaching of natural science.

Aristotle disagreed with Plato in the belief that only universals are real. As a scientist he preferred concrete facts to abstract notions and declared that general terms such as, flower, horse, man, table are just words, names, and exist only in thought for the purpose of distinguishing one category or class from another. These Platonic concepts or transcendental ideas are necessary and convenient, but true reality exists in individual or particular, tangible, perceptive things or objects. However concepts and precepts both are in essence fundamental and indispensable; form and matter are related and linked to each other in the world of reality. Aristotle formulated a body of rules for correct thinking which was based on the principle of the syllogism or deductive logic which consists of a major and minor premise and a conclusion. The classic example was: all men are mortal. Socrates is a man. Therefore Socrates is mortal. To establish the probability of a premise one must presuppose the existence of ample facts derived from experience and observation.

Aristotle taught that the chief objective in life is to find happiness and the best and wisest way to obtain happiness is to be guided always by reason and virtue, and to be rational and virtuous is to follow the middle road. Always balance one extreme over against another; cultivate moderation and you will attain harmony and tranquillity. Excess and deficiency are both bad qualities but a happy medium between the two is moderation, which is good. Thus, courage is a sensible compromise between cowardice and rashness; modesty is better than extreme pride or excessive humility; liberality is the middle ground between stinginess and extravagance. Avoid extremes—do nothing too much or too little. Don't be brusque and don't be obsequious, but be friendly. He advised the cultivation of the golden mean; neither irrational indulgence nor ascetic abnegation is virtuous. Don't be licentious but don't shun all pleasure. The noblest quality of man is rationality. Aristotle's ethic had no relation to his concept of God or of individual immortality. God is not a personal being, has no human characteristics but is a mysterious, vital force—the source and the goal of all motion and power—the first and final cause—the Prime Mover of all things, who started the universe on its career. Aristotle also believed that every human soul has a divine spark which at death returns to God.

As for politics Aristotle held the opinion that since men are by nature imperfect and often wicked, a government without defects is impossible. Evils, errors and moral decline will inevitably appear in every state. There are, he said, three forms of government in the world—government by one, which is monarchy, government by a few, which is aristocracy, and government by the many, which he called polity. Each of these can be good but unfortunately each tends to degenerate and become bad. Monarchy becomes tyranny where one man seizes and holds power by force; aristocracy becomes oligarchy where a clique of plutocrats or militarists or insidious politicians gain control; and polity becomes democracy, or government by the least intelligent, the amoral demos, the undisciplined common mass. Which type of government is likely to exist in any country would depend upon the particular conditions of time, environment and character of its citizens. Acceptable to Aristotle was a constitutional republic based on popular government, legal equality for all, with a large middle class not too rich and a fairly virtuous citizenry. A good political organization would be a combination of a strong executive, an aristocratic council and a democratic assembly. Writing on democracy Aristotle cautioned that if you give people equal rights they will in due time want equal possessions. And he opposed socialism and communism, maintaining that when all property belongs to everybody, nobody takes care of it. Without monetary reward there would be no incentive and no ambition for laborers and business men. Private property is indispensable. To become prosperous and comfortable is not evil but money-grubbing, excessive, greedy profiteering or ostentatious living is wrong and the government should prevent the concentration of wealth. He also believed that government should help the poor by providing them with small farms to enable them to support themselves and maintain their self-respect. But the sharing of property and women and their offspring, as Plato recommended in his utopia, was according to Aristotle, unwise and impractical. If possessions are to be the same for all there is no reason for exertion and if wives and children are not one's own there will be no real love and affection.

Toward the end of the 4th century B.C. the Greeks began to lose much of their self-confidence, their pride, their patriotism, their faith in their gods and in their leaders. This was the Hellenistic age when Greek and Oriental cultures began to fuse, pure Hellenism declined, political strife and dissension became rampant, and the eastern Mediterranean world gradually grew ripe for conquest by the Romans. New thoughts and new guides were now necessary and to meet this demand among the educated, the wealthy and more sophisticated Greeks and Hellenized Easterners there arose many popular philosophies offering their respective precepts for personal happiness. Skeptics asserted that real truth or real knowledge is unattainable, it can never be known. It is a waste of time to try to find out the origin and the nature of the universe and one must be agnostic about the existence of a God. Since truth and knowledge are always relative to the individual and to particular circumstances, and since the opposite of any opinion is equally plausible, then it is wise to suspend all judgment and repudiate all dogmas and doctrines. All we can know is what we can experience or perceive in the world around us through our senses.

Cyrenaics advocated hedonism, the pursuit of bodily pleasures or complete sensual indulgence. The value of physical satisfactions is determined by the intensity of a sensation rather than its duration. The wise man is lord of his appetites and since the future is uncertain he will take immediate advantage of choice physical delights. Cynics believed that the essence of virtue is a quest for knowledge and the practice of self-control. One must reduce his desires, for the less one wants the more likely is he to get it. And he must renounce physical pleasures and social conventions, such as; religion, family, patriotism and civic duties. Cynics were satisfied with bare animal needs, just enough to subsist on and they wanted to return to nature. The most renowned member of the group was Diogenes, a banker who went bankrupt, made counterfeit money, had to beg for a living but had a brilliant mind. He wanted to lead a simple, natural, virtuous life and so he lived in a tub, wore a single garment, slept on the ground and was often seen carrying a candle or a lantern in search of an honest man.

He was envious of the dog and wanted to live like one and saw no reason for being ashamed of relieving himself of all physiological pressures in public whether it was urinating, defecating or copulating. He ate coarse food and sometimes natural raw meat did not agree with him. One day when he was 90 years old he ate a bull's foot raw and he died. Diogenes was admired for his intellectual acuteness by many Greeks including Alexander the Great.

Epicureans prescribed pleasure as a means of attaining happiness but they graded their pleasures. Although the moderate enjoyment of food, wine and sex were not shunned mental experiences were considered the highest form of pleasure because they are most durable and permanent. Men are free to do as they will and they will do that which promotes their happiness, which Epicurus defined as absence of pain or the equanimity of mind. Good conduct and friendship are motivated by self-interest, that is; measured by the amount of happiness that virtue and friends can bring to an individual. A person will be lawabiding, civic-minded, loyal and patriotic only if it is to his advantage to do so. Man's goal is engendered and cultivated by self-interest and so the most enlightened government would be the one that promotes the welfare of the individual. The Epicureans urged people to shed their fears—the fear of death, hell and the gods. Pain and fear must be eliminated if one is to attain happiness. Epicurus believed that life originated fortuitously by spontaneous generation and developed through natural selection. And man, like everything else in the universe, is composed of atoms, though the particles that make up the soul are extremely fine and thin. When a person dies his body and soul disintegrate and the atoms are scattered throughout the world. There is no such thing as life after death. Though gods do exist they are also atomic aggregates and have no concern with human beings or their conduct. A person should seek no more than tranquillity of body and mind—simple food, modest shelter and devoted friendship.

Stoicism was founded by Zeno, a Phoenician Greek, who lectured and held discussions from a porch or stoa in the market place of Athens. Zeno taught that man should be indifferent to both pleasure and pain, joy and grief, and should accept things as they are, because it's impossible for man to change the world. He should repress his emotions for all things as all events are governed by the laws of nature and are predetermined. One day Zeno was beating his slave for stealing and the slave protested that according to the stoic philosophy he was not responsible for committing the offence and Zeno replied: "And according to my philosophy I cannot help beating you."

Disagreeing with the Epicureans, the Stoics believed that the universe did not come into being through chance but that it was a planned system, created and controlled by a Divine Power and it is the duty for every man to be resigned, to accept his fate, suppress all feelings, and submit to the will of God. Only in one area does man have free will and that is in the realm of ethics. Man must exalt reason, practice abstinence and self-control. There is one God, He has a purpose, a plan for the world; He loves mankind and He knows all that is going to happen. The human soul is a divine spark emitted by the universal soul and is the source or the instrument of all our feeling and thinking. From the universal soul or God who permeates the universe, stems all life, all movement and all knowledge. The Stoics did not agree on the question of immortality; some believed that all souls lived until the end of the world, while others, recognizing the need of incentives and motivation, contended that only the good and wise souls exist after the death of the body. Going out of his school one day Zeno tripped and broke one of his toes. Suspecting that this was a hint from the hereafter or the call of fate, he struck the ground with his hand and cried, "I am coming, but why must you rush me." Then he strangled himself and died. In spite of man's apparent helplessness to control his destiny Stoics did hope that someday there would be no more oppression, no more wars, and no more conflict between rich and poor, aristocrats and commoners, masters and slaves. There will emerge a society of united mankind ruled with justice and benevolence by philosophers—a world where all people regardless of race or nationality would be brothers—all children of one God.

After a brief spell of prosperity, toward the end of the fourth century B.C., mainland Greece began to decline economically and so in government and culture. Incessant strife between rich and poor gave rise to radicalism; excessive individualism produced constant political discord, while self-interest and ultrasophistication led to the loss of patriotism. Athens was losing its economic and intellectual leadership and the young, energetic Greeks, responding to Alexander's invitation, began to migrate to Alexandria, Antioch, Rhodes, Pergamum and scores of other cities—old ones that were being rebuilt or new ones that were being established. These Greeks usually became the leaders in trade and industry, in government administration and in various cultural fields. Joining and cooperating with them were thousands of enterprising and industrious colonials—Egyptians, Jews, and Arabs. Throughout the Near East all urbanite literates learned to speak Greek, which became an international language modified by diverse localisms. The Orientals also adopted Hellenic customs and manners and the Greeks in turn were influenced by the Eastern usages, conventions and especially religious beliefs. The Hebrew Bible was translated into Greek by Jewish scholars in Alexandria, and Greeks, disillusioned with their own religion, began to show keen interest in Oriental mystic cults that promised salvation in a future life.

The Hellenistic cities were splendidly laid out according to plans of engineers, with wide, paved streets, boulevards, parks and squares, aqueducts, water supplies for homes, drainage systems, and all sorts of public buildings including libraries, museums, temples, theatres, concert halls. There were fine harbors, lighthouses, bazaars, stadiums, zoos, hippodromes for chariot races, and houses several stories high. All this was made possible by thriving industry and commerce which extended as far as the British and Baltic peoples in the northwest and to the Chinese and Hindus in the east. The Hellenistic Age (323 B.C. to 133 B.C.) was characterized by a tremendous increase in wealth and by sumptuous living in superb palaces and mansions abounding in objects of art and in comforts and conveniences provided by servants and slaves. Laborers and peasants did not share in the prosperity of big business and there were no statesmen or philosophers who championed their cause, though the government occasionally distributed relief to prevent starvation among the slum dwellers. The impoverished masses throughout the Near East were never enthusiastic about Greek culture but continued to speak their own languages and to follow their old customs, worshipping their traditional gods and living a wretched life of ignorance and poverty. Educated and affluent Greek and Oriental residents of the Hellenistic cities considered themselves cosmopolitans, citizens of the world, and generally looked upon patriotism as narrow and parochial and regarded religion as synonymous with superstition. There were serious and thoughtful, rich persons who became devoted members of

Oriental mystic cults or found tranquillity of mind in Stoicism; but many more were skeptical or cynical or they turned to their own distorted version of Epicureanism and urbanely offered hedonistic rationales for their amorality and self-indulgence, their acquisitive pursuits, and their passion for food, drink and voluptuous women.

The Greeks intermarried with the natives and were eventually absorbed by the Egyptians and the Arabs, but the Jews remained substantially unmixed owing to their religious law which forbade marriage with heathens. Alexander the Great and some of his successors in Egypt had urged Hebrews to come to Alexandria and by the beginning of the Christian era there were about one million Jews in Egypt. Residents of the metropolitan areas, they engaged in commerce, industry and the professions and like the other urbanites became greatly imbued with the culture of the Greeks. In due time many thousands of them lost their ethnic and religious identity, joined the trend toward Epicureanism, and became assimilated in the cosmopolitan Hellenistic society. The majority of the Jews however remained faithful to the Mosaic law and to their unique culture.

Hellenistic culture was very productive in literature and the arts but their works and compositions were not as creative nor as profound as the Hellenic. Unlike the classic architecture their buildings were massive and elaborately adorned and their sculpture was extremely realistic and dramatic but often displayed exaggerated emotion and sentimentality. Their literature included romantic love stories, bucolic tales, and simple, charming episodes in prose and poetry. They were fond of clever epigrams and witty, salacious comedies of life and manners. They produced a number of keen literary critics, a few historians and erudite scholars who compiled a vast amount of information which helped preserve the great work of the classical Hellenes. The greatest achievements of the Hellenistic Greeks were in the various fields of science and mechanics, as described in detail above.

CHAPTER VIII

(PART 1)

The Roman World
From Its Beginning to Its Pinnacle

About 3500 years ago the Italici, like their kinsmen, the Hellenes, decided to migrate south from central Europe in search of more fertile soil and a warmer climate. The Hellenes moved into the southern part of the Balkan peninsula and the Italici settled in the central part of the Italian peninsula. In both cases the lands were already inhabited— Greece and the Aegean islands by a more culturally advanced Mediterranean people while Italy was occupied by primitive Africans, some brown, some white, who were still living in the stone age. Both groups of aborigines were conquered and absorbed by the invaders from the north.

In Greece the land was rugged, there were high mountains and low valleys, transportation was difficult and hazardous, communities were small, inaccessible and isolated and so little villages and small towns became independent states and the Greeks were unable to form a united nation. Italy on the other hand was topographically more favorable to union, for it was not cut up into small districts, the terrain was not so rough and rocky, it was easier to travel over the land, to conquer, to unify and to rule the villages and towns. The Greeks had numerous bays and harbors and insufficient fertile soil and therefore were compelled to become sailors and shipbuilders and seek food and raw materials in foreign lands, but the Italian soil was very productive and the people were able to raise an abundance of cereals, vegetables, grapes, olives, cattle and sheep. The Greeks therefore became substantially a nation of merchants while the Romans remained essentially a nation of farmers. It is also significant that the Greek ports faced the highly civilized East whereas the harbors of Italy were on the West coast and faced the peoples that were still barbarians. Trading and dealing sharpened the minds of the Greeks and frequent contacts with the more civilized East gave them an advantage over the Romans whose basic needs were provided by nature and who therefore could remain content, conservative and unenlightened. The Romans also differed from the Greeks in national character, temperament and capacity. The Greeks achieved fame and glory because of their great intellectual and cultural talents and contributions in art, literature, science and philosophy. On the other hand, the Romans excelled in practical matters, in government, in war and diplomacy, in engineering and in the development and use of law.

Of the several tribes of Italici who came down from the north the most important were the Latins. It was in the district of Latium where Latin was spoken, that the small town of Rome was founded in 753 B.C. Just to the north of Latium was a district known as Etruria (now called Tuscany) which was then inhabited by the Etruscans. Hailing from the more culturally advanced Aegean world or Asia Minor, they settled on the westcentral coast of Italy around 900 B.C. From their old home in the Near East they brought many advanced ideas which they imparted to their neighbors—the Romans, whom they subdued and ruled during the 6th century B.C. From the Etruscans the Romans learned how to fight in phalanx formation, how to build massive walls and gates around their cities, how to pave their streets and use underground drains and sewers. Other Etruscan contributions included the vault, the round arch, excellent metal works, fine vases, superb figures in bronze and terra cotta, bas relief, frescoes and portrait painting, the so-called Roman numerals and also valuable methods in agriculture and industry. The Etruscans participated in many games and sports including discus and javelin throwing, pole vaulting, wrestling, boxing, racing, and gladiatorial combats. They danced and played the flute and other musical instruments. Women had a relatively high station though girls were allowed to obtain their dowries by prostitution. The Etruscan gods and religion were very gloomy but the people believed in a life after death—a heaven and a hell. They sacrificed sheep, bulls and occasionally human beings, and the priests claimed the power to foretell the future by the flight of birds or by studying the liver of a sheep.

In 509 B.C. the Romans revolted against their Etruscan absolute monarch and gained their independence. Then they established a republic replacing their traditional government by a king; and since the revolution was effected by the rich landowners or patricians it was they and not the people who generally dominated the undemocratic republic. The government consisted of two executive officers or heads of state, called consuls, elected annually by the patricians, a senate composed mostly of patricians, and popular assemblies representing all the citizens but lorded over by the patricians and the rich. The consuls had equal power and alternated their control but in time of crisis or national danger one of the consuls was made dictator for six months. Executives came from the senate and generally returned to the senate at the expiration of their terms. As Rome grew and governmental functions increased they added a few magistracies or administrative branches, relieving the consuls of some of their burdens. These ministers were praetors or assistants to the consul, who took over the latter's judicial duties; quaestors, in charge of the treasury and state funds; censors who kept lists of citizens necessary for the army and for the assessment of taxes and who exercised power over the private life of the Romans by supervising the morals of all the people; and they could expel a senator for immorality and could deprive any citizen of his right to vote; and there were aediles who administered public buildings, markets, streets, police, public games, theaters and brothels. Most power, though, was possessed by the senators who numbered about three hundred, who discussed and managed all matters and served for life. Senators could speak as often and as long as they liked. Through legislation they regulated finances, public works and religious affairs, conducted war and foreign relations and governed provinces and colonies. The senators on the whole were highly competent, educated, often former much experienced ministers, statesmen or generals of noble background—old, prominent families. The people's assembly of all citizens had only the right to vote yes or no to proposals made by the magistrates or the senate; they were not permitted to frame, criticize or amend measures and were allowed very little discussion.

The distinguished patricians, who were comparatively few in

number, filled all the important offices, commanded the armies and controlled the affairs of the republican government. The great majority of the people were the commoners, known in Rome as the plebeians or the plebs. Over the years these underprivileged masses endeavored to gain civil, social and political equality with the patricians, the rich landowners, a movement often referred to as the struggle of the orders or a class conflict, which lasted from the fifth to the third century B.C. In the early years of the Republic the Roman army was all patrician, but as wars with their neighbors increased and were intensified the government found it necessary to enlist more men and to improve their military tactics by training and using hoplites or heavily-armed infantrymen. Consequently, in need of more soldiers, the patrician officers were thus forced to draft the plebeians into the army, but the plebs went on strike and refused to serve unless they were granted some political privileges. There was no violence between employer and employees as they resorted to collective bargaining which ended in a victory for the plebeian hoplites. As early as the fifth century B.C. the commoners won the right to elect officials from their own order, called tribunes, who were regarded as the champions of the people. These tribunes were given the right to veto decisions of any magistrate or minister and later of the senate; they were inviolable and a solemn curse was placed upon anyone who disturbed a tribune while he was performing his job and any person who attacked him could be put to death without a trial. After a few years there were ten such tribunes and they enjoyed an unusually strong political position.

In 449 B.C. the plebeians forced the government to give the people a code of written laws—the laws of the Twelve Tables. Essentially civil and criminal regulations, these laws were binding on all classes alike and the average citizen was pleased when the laws were engraved on twelve, impressive wooden tablets and set up in the Roman forum for all to read, even though the code was very severe and discriminatory. The right of appeal to the assembly was recognized and the people could now see for themselves what the written law was. Liberalization continued as the plebeians secured the right to become a senator, a consul or any magistrate; the assembly got the right to initiate legislation and even to make laws without the senate's approval. Plebeians were finally permitted to intermarry with patricians and were given a voice in the supernatural world, that is, allowed to enter the priesthood. The plebeians by the third century B.C. gained most of the civil, legal, and social rights they desired and in theory Rome looked like a democratic republic. In practice, however, the senate continued to rule as before, all its members as well as all other officeholders continued to be rich landowners or wealthy businessmen or professional men—aristocratic patricians or plebeian plutocrats. Furthermore, officeholders received virtually no salaries; the majority of the people were illiterate; consuls, praetors, censors and other magistrates were elected on separate days; and since all political and governmental activity took place in Rome itself very few common citizens outside of the city had the time, the money or the inclination to participate in the affairs of state. Representative government was as unknown to the Romans as it was to the Athenians. The republican government, controlled by a privileged and generally able aristocracy, lasted for about 500 years and then, around the middle of the first century B.C. the Romans returned to a monarchical or imperial type of rule.

Rome's struggle for existence did not end with its attainment of independence from the Etruscans, for the latter remained hostile and belligerent and it was not until the middle of the fourth century B.C., after a number of wars had been fought and won, that the Romans were assured of their complete freedom. The Etruscans were forced to cede as tribute, a great deal of their territory to the Romans. In the meantime, the Gauls, fierce, blond, naked warriors, came out of the north, overran and plundered the Etruscan lands, then stormed into the city of Rome and burned most of it to the ground. However, the Romans bought off the Gauls for 1000 pounds of gold and the barbarians departed. They tried three more times to capture the city but were defeated in every return bout. Other rivals of Rome in Italy were the kindred Italian tribes and states and the Greeks who lived in the southern part of the peninsula. In 338 B.C., the same year in which all the Greek city states were taken over by Philip of Macedon, all the Latin speaking people were brought by force under Roman control, and finally after a few more wars, the Greek colonies were subjugated. By 265 B.C. the Romans held dominion over the Etruscans, the Italic states, many mountain tribes and over the Greek city states in southern Italy. A tiny little town of simple peasants thus became a mighty imperial power, prepared to defend and protect its precious gains from marauding barbarians or greedy competitors.

Surrounded for centuries by hostile neighbors, the Romans found military preparedness indispensable and in this area they evidently excelled. All citizens aged 17 to 46 were liable to active service in the Roman army and the older men were employed for garrison duty. At first there was no compensation, they served for a short time and then returned to their farms. But as the campaigns increased and the soldiers were needed for longer duration, state pay was introduced. The young men, mostly hardy peasants, devoted ten years of their life in the camp and field. Their pay was meager, their food was simple— bread, cereals, vegetables, wine and seldom meat; in fact, they preferred corn to meat. For a long time the Roman army used the phalanx formation but after a while they found it to be somewhat too rigid and inflexible; and it proved to be most ineffective against elephants, first used against the Romans by the Greeks. They therefore decided to fight in open formation. The army was then divided into smaller units which were swifter and more maneuverable and could be adapted to special circumstances. The Roman weapons included darts, stones, javelins, lances, short, long and two-edged swords, catapults and battering rams, and the soldiers were protected by metal and leather armor, helmets and shields. Very helpful were their fortified camps where they intrenched in a square enclosure, protected by ditches, earthen mounds and palisades of stakes.

Army discipline was strictly enforced. A general might behead without a trial any soldier who disobeyed his commander, who refused to fight or who fell asleep on guard duty. Sometimes the condemned man was beaten or stoned to death in camp or his hand was cut off and if he managed to escape his family was forbidden to receive him. On the other hand individual soldiers were encouraged to perform deeds of valor by public praise of heroes before an assembly of the troops when the general would describe in detail the acts of bravery and patriotism and then distribute appropriate rewards and honors. Sometimes the state, deeming it prudent and politic to publicize a significant victory would have the general populace as well as the army celebrate a triumph with a grand entrance and military parade in the city of Rome. Another incentive that stirred up a passionate desire to fight was the promise to soldiers of sharing the plunders of war—money, gold and silver, land, slaves, and movable goods. The Roman war machine usually worked very efficiently but politics and religion sometimes hindered its progress. Occasionally a politician of high rank but deficient in military strategy was selected to be commander of the troops and his blunders would lead to disaster, and a priest sometimes misinterpreted the supernatural omens and the army would suffer defeat. The soldiers were blindly loyal to their generals and expected them to be competent and they also relied on their soothsayers to be accurate in their reading of the signs. When a forecast was favorable and the gods were with them the troops would fight with more confidence and enthusiasm. But in spite of drawbacks the Roman armies were invincible and although they sometimes lost a battle they always won the war.

All nations are more or less imperialistic, that is, they would all like to expand if possible. Some don't possess the requisite geographic situation or the needed appropriate qualities and character. The Romans were strategically located near and among Etruscans and Greeks and were fortunately endowed with such attributes as courage, resourcefulness, physical stamina, and they had a profound admiration for organization and iron discipline. A remarkable patriotism was inculcated through constant training in the home, the school, the temple, and the army and through the eloquent orations in the assembly and the senate—all urging and imbuing reverence for their ancestors, loyalty to the state—obedience and self-sacrifice. Because of their geographical location Rome had to fight for survival against culturally superior Etruscans and Greeks and success made them aware of their aptitude and skill in fighting. People like to do what they can do well and so they continued to fight, particularly when they learned that their investment in warfare was a very profitable enterprise. They gained land, wealth, power and prestige. Buffer states, set up to protect the homeland, tended to grow larger and were inclined to extend their territory, as turbulent neighbors became menacing. Victory boosted their pride, enhanced their patriotism, and emboldened them to challenge their most formidable antagonist Carthage, the imperial champion of the Mediterranean world.

In their policy toward the conquered states in Italy the Romans were moderate and wise. Instead of annexing the lands and crushing their former foes or selling them into slavery, as ancient conquerors frequently did, they allowed the states to retain self-government with varying degrees of privileges. Some became allies, others were granted full citizenship, some received only partial citizenship without voting rights, others were just given private rights, that is, they were permitted to marry Romans and to trade with them. The self-governing states were tactfully granted only domestic autonomy as Rome took over the foreign policy of all the members of the Roman federation. They also created a number of colonies peopled with veteran soldiers and poor plebeians who were given land to farm and develop. The colonies were established at strategic points to enable the settlers to keep an eye on the Roman allies and also to spread the Roman language and customs among the people. The policy of compromise—agreeing to mutual concessions with former enemies—proved to be wise and profitable during the long conflict with Carthage when most of the states in the Roman league demonstrated their loyalty.

Carthage was originally a Phoenician colony founded in the ninth century B.C. but with the decline of the mother country it became an independent city state. It was located in north Africa where Tunis now is. Carthage had the finest harbor in the western Mediterranean, was wealthier and twice as populous as Rome. It had a very fertile hinterland where they raised grain, cattle and a variety of tropical products. Its greatest amount of wealth, however, was derived from commerce and the lucrative mining industry that they developed—gold, silver, copper, iron and tin. Like their Phoenician forefathers the Carthaginians had a bent for commerce and navigation and they were constantly in search of more raw materials and markets. By the third century B.C. they had enlarged their territory in north Africa as their land extended from Libya to Gibraltar. Their ships sailed to west Africa to bring gold, ivory and slaves, and to Britain and the Baltics to buy tin and amber. Carthage captured a number of Spanish towns and islands, seized the valuable mines of Spain and conquered Malta, Sardinia, Corsica and the western part of Sicily.

The Carthaginians were culturally advanced in many fields but they still practiced human sacrifice and their government was dominated by an oligarchy of thirty plutocrats who believed that what was good for the wealthy was good for Carthage. Though there was a senate and an assembly the members were always controlled by the above-mentioned clique representing the commercial aristocracy. Unlike the citizen soldiers of Rome, who sometimes made demands of their government, the Carthaginian army was composed of foreign hirelings who were completely loyal to their employers so long as they received their wages. These mercenaries were officered by professional soldiers and a commander who was nominated by the senate and elected by the assembly. As a maritime power Carthage had a large navy which was reputed to be the finest in the world.

The Romans had not been very much disturbed by Carthaginian expansion in Africa but when they moved into Spain and into the islands adjacent to the Italian peninsula Rome considered it trespassing or an infringement on their area of interest. A foothold in Sicily by an aggressive imperialistic power was serious and naturally aroused fear in Italy and so the Romans decided to check the incursion before Carthage overwhelmed the entire Mediterranean world including their own homeland. Sicily is only about one mile from the Italian coast and had a very rich soil, producing an abundance of grain, oil and sulphur. Carthage was determined to expand wherever it liked and was eager to destroy a menacing rival for world power and a potential competitor in international commerce. Some Romans favored a policy of defensive isolation, others did not think they were strong enough to challenge the mighty Carthaginian navy, but the expansionists and the ardent patriots were optimistic and they persuaded the government to adopt a policy of curbing encroachment on the Roman sphere of influence and to drive the Carthaginians back to Africa. War was inevitable. During a civil imbroglio in Massena, Sicily both powers became involved when they intervened, Carthage helping one faction and Rome the opposing party. This incident precipitated the struggle known as the Punic Wars. (Punic is the Latin word for Phoenician.)

The first Punic war began in 264 B.C. and ended with victory for the Romans after twenty-three years of battling. At the beginning of the war Carthage had an advantage because the Romans had very little maritime experience. However, with the help of their Greek naval allies and after studying a beached Carthaginian galley they were able to construct a large fleet. And then they revived and improved on an old Greek nautical tactic which really turned the tide for the Romans. They invented a huge grapple that would hook or clamp their ship to the enemy's and fasten a bridge from one vessel to the other enabling Roman troops to rush aboard and fight as on land. In this method of hand-to-hand warfare they excelled and after a number of sea battles the Romans gained naval supremacy in the western Mediterranean. They took over all of Sicily and exacted a large indemnity. Sicily became Rome's first province outside of the mainland, and a short time later the islands of Corsica and Sardinia were also acquired.

As compensation for her losses Carthage conquered Spain and so the Romans decided to extend their frontier to the mountains in the north. They drove out the Gauls in northern Italy and took possession of the lands on their side of the Alps. Then the Romans demonstrated their interest in Spain too by establishing a diplomatic foothold in the Spanish town of Saguntum. But this was in the Carthaginian sphere of influence and so the north Africans seized and destroyed Saguntum. To avenge her ally Rome declared war on Carthage and so the conflict between the two imperial powers was resumed. This, the second Punic war, lasted eighteen years and was marked by the heroic exploits and adroit maneuvers of the great commander of the Carthaginian army—Hannibal. As a child he had sworn eternal enmity of Rome and intended someday to get revenge for Carthage, and at the age of 27 he was made the head of the Carthaginian military forces. Since the Romans controlled the western Mediterranean Sea Hannibal had to invade Italy by way of Spain across the Pyrenees Mountains and the Alps. It was a hazardous venture but Hannibal was persistent and intrepid. He led his huge army with supplies, equipment, horses and war elephants over steep narrow mountain passes covered with ice and snow. He also had to contend with landslides and marauding hostile tribes, while thousands of his men, horses and elephants frequently lost their footing on the steep, impassable paths and tumbled to their death in the deep ravines. The army finally got across the cold mountains and reached level ground and warm climate but they had lost about half of their 50,000 men, many horses and most of the elephants and the survivors were starved and exhausted. Some friendly Gauls joined Hannibal hoping to regain the lands they had recently lost to the Romans. After a brief rest, Hannibal, who was now blind in one eye, set forth to conquer Italy. Although vastly outnumbered the ingenious general, with boldness and military cunning, won a series of battles routing one Roman army after another, devastating the land and managing to maintain his own forces in Italy for about sixteen years. His greatest victory was the battle at Cannae where the Romans lost more than half of their soldiers, about 45,000 men, and the Carthaginians lost only 6000. The Romans tried open warfare and failed and then for a while they followed their dictator Fabius in his type of cautious guerrilla tactics but the Carthaginians still prevailed. Hannibal seemed to be invincible and a few Italian and Greek states deemed it prudent to desert and join the African conquerors.

An attack on the capital city appeared to be inevitable. The inhabitants were haunted with fear. Some Roman women were so hysterical and panic-stricken they ran weeping to the temples where they cleaned the statues of the gods with their hair and implored the supernatural spirits for help and mercy. To appease the deities, who had evidently been offended by the Romans, the government authorized human sacrifice and accordingly two Gauls and two Greeks were buried alive. The gods relented and the attack did not come. Hannibal needed more siege guns and more soldiers to capture and to hold the city of Rome. He requested aid from his government but neither supplies nor reinforcements were forthcoming from Carthage. In the meanwhile the indomitable Romans regained their strength, rallied and determined to protect their city, to defend every inch of ground. Moreover, they decided that since they still controlled the sea, they would send an army to invade Carthage hoping Hannibal would be recalled to Africa. The plan worked. Now the Carthaginians became alarmed and Hannibal was summoned home to save his country.

At the battle of Zama Hannibal met his first and only defeat. The Romans were led by a very able general—Scipio, who after this victory became known as Scipio Africanus. The Roman commander respected Hannibal and the two generals held a conference and politely talked things over before the battle, but could not agree. Later they actually met in a personal encounter and Scipio was wounded. After the war Scipio, a highly civilized general, was inclined to be generous and even interceded in behalf of Hannibal though to no avail. The chief reason for Roman success was probably the superior morale of free citizen soldiers as opposed to a professional mercenary army. The government of Carthage, beset with financial troubles, was unable to pay her soldiers, and mercenaries don't fight very well unless they are paid. Also the allies and associates of Carthage, always ruthlessly exploited, were not reliable in time of adversity and they now took advantage of an opportunity to regain their independence. On the other hand, most of the Roman allies were loyal because they had been treated comparatively well. The second Punic war ended as Carthage sued for peace. The former great power was forced to cede all her Spanish possessions, surrender all but ten of her warships and had to pay Rome about twelve million dollars indemnity. Carthage also was not allowed to wage war outside of Africa and even to fight in Africa she had to get permission from Rome. After the war Hannibal tried to democratize the government of Carthage but the controlling wealthy oligarchy was too strong and with the cooperation of the Roman patricians, who also were averse to liberalism, the old warrior was overthrown. He fled to Syria where he persuaded the latter country to go to war against the Romans, which facilitated and hastened the latter's intervention in the conflicts of the east. The Syrians were defeated, Hannibal again became a fugitive and when the Romans caught up with him he committed suicide in 184 B.C.

With Carthage vanquished and Hannibal out of the way, Rome emerged as the strongest power in the Mediterranean world. The leading Hellenistic kingdoms, Egypt, Syria and Macedonia, were generally competing and fighting one another while the Greeks and the smaller eastern states were constantly in turmoil, troubled by internal dissension or harassed by hostile neighbors. The Romans now had no serious rival. The urge to power, the temptation to control the entire area was irresistible and so imperialism became the prevailing foreign policy of the Roman government. At first the paramount reason for Rome's imperial expansion was self-defense but as trade and commerce developed and economic prosperity resulted, greed and ambition became the primary motives for conquest. By the middle of the second century B.C. Rome had annexed Greece and Macedonia and made protectorates of Syria and Egypt and a number of small states in Asia Minor. About a hundred years later Syria and Egypt as well as the small states in Asia Minor were converted into provinces. And in the west the Gauls in northern Italy had been thoroughly subdued and the rebellious Spanish were brought under control.

By the second century of the Christian era the Roman empire embraced all of southern Europe, most of western Europe, including what is now Spain, France and England, parts of central Europe, the

Balkans, the lands now occupied by the Turks, the Arabs and the Israelis, and all of north Africa. The Mediterranean Sea became a Roman lake. The Romans were now the arbiters of the world and the international police who maintained law and order among the states, protected their subject peoples from the barbarians, and resolved their disputes with one another.

Very tragic and superfluous was the third Punic war, 149 to 146 B.C. Though she was deprived of all her foreign territory and rendered politically impotent, Carthage began to revive her commerce and agriculture and thereby aroused the envy and apprehension of the Roman imperialists. If not checked forthwith Carthage might recover her wealth and prosperity which would lead to her political resurrection. World conquerors could not tolerate competition. Furthermore there was a great deal of fertile land around Carthage, a lucrative field of investment for avaricious business men. On every occasion and after every speech, Senator Cato, leader of the war mongers, would cry out: "Carthage must be destroyed." Militants demanded war, a pretext was found and a Roman army landed in Africa.

Before the city was attacked Carthage agreed to the terms that Rome had apparently demanded. They surrendered all their weapons, their ships and even 300 children of prominent families as hostages, but the Roman soldiers were determined to carry out the Senate's orders. The people of Carthage were commanded to leave their city, but when they refused to go, it was besieged. After a heroic resistance which lasted about three years the Romans broke through, and for six days the inhabitants fought desperately, and furiously, street by street, and house by house, but were finally overpowered. Out of approximately 500,000 people, 55,000 remained alive and the half-starved survivors were sold as slaves. The city was burned to the ground, its site was plowed, covered with salt to destroy the fertility of its soil, and a curse was laid upon anyone who should ever live there again. The Carthaginian territory was then annexed by Rome. It was in the same year, 146 B.C., that the beautiful and prosperous Greek city of Corinth was also burned by the Romans and its inhabitants were enslaved.

Military prowess made Rome the undisputed master of the Mediterranean world and the plunder from the vanquished nations brought an economic windfall to many Romans. Those who profited from the wars and the loot were privileged senators and shrewd business men, successful generals and their friends, corrupt governors and greedy tax collectors in the conquered states and provinces. Businessmen who held contracts with the government to supply the army and build roads and public works reaped enormous profits. In the conquered territories the Senate asked tax collectors to give the government a stipulated amount and allowed them to keep for themselves all they could extort from the provincials. The publicans, as the unscrupulous contractors and tax gatherers were called, became fabulously wealthy. Governors, generals, and some senators were equally venal and unconscionable and were parties to the squeezing of the provinces of virtually all their wealth and valuables. Rich men acquired by purchase, bribery or influence, large tracts of farm land and established huge estates, called *latifundia*, where they employed thousands of slaves. Thanks to the victorious wars, the cost of farm labor was nominal since slaves were plentiful and cheap; they needed only food and clothing and they worked from sunrise to sunset. Furthermore the slaves who were regarded and treated by their owners as human machines could replace or reproduce themselves at the bidding or with the aid of their masters, which was a contributing factor in the low cost of production. Free agricultural laborers required respectable wages, and unwilling to become chattels, could no longer find jobs in the country. And the independent small farmers, the middle class who had formed the bulk of the Roman population and the backbone of the army, had been almost decimated in the numerous wars. Those who returned often found that their old farms were ruined or had been confiscated by rich landowners, or they just didn't have sufficient capital to resume cultivation. And even when they did restore their farms they could not compete with the new type of plantation with its slave labor, mass production and low prices. Also, much of the Italian land had been damaged by war or its soil had become exhausted or it was more suitable for the growing of fruit and the raising of livestock for which farmers needed money and cheap labor. Taking care of sheep, cattle and poultry requires fewer hands and so there was less work for free peasants.

Many of the war veterans who had been deeply impressed and fascinated by the magnificent cities of the east and their luxurious and sophisticated life style, found it hard to return to the dull and tedious routine of the old farm life. So the impoverished farmers and the jobless farm laborers flocked to the city of Rome where they augmented the already numerous unemployed Roman citizens and refugees from the provinces. In the cities also slaves took the place of former wage workers. Urban slaves were often skilled artisans and those from the eastern countries, particularly the Greeks, were frequently cultured, well-informed and mentally superior to their masters. The uncouth, newly rich Romans made good use of the captive Greeks—artists, physicians, teachers and engineers, intelligent office workers and refined domestic servants. The Hellenistic civilization, with its renowned achievements in art, literature, philosophy and science, brought over by the eastern slaves, would in due time rub off on the unenlightened Romans. Slaves would civilize their masters or at least train and educate their children.

Those Romans who couldn't make it in the mad rush for wealth went on relief—they received gifts of food and free entertainment at the public games. Unable to find work and completely frustrated, they were known as proletarians, people who had no property and produced nothing but children. Imperialism also begot a new opulent middle class, consisting of (1) the equites, or those who could afford horses and their army equipment and earned their money in commerce and banking during the wars; and (2) the publicans or those who held war contracts and made their millions at the expense of the government and the exploited provinces. Like all parvenus they were often inclined to be vulgar, coarse, ostentatious and frequently corrupt and fraudulent. The patricians eschewed trading and banking as inelegant occupations and piously invested their money in real estate and in large scale farming on land which they flagrantly appropriated or confiscated in Italy and in the provinces. They generally lived in villas or in the city and became absentee landowners employing agents and slaves to do their unpleasant and arduous tasks. The military also underwent a transformation. It was no longer an army of dedicated patriots defending their homes and farms but a force of professional soldiers hired to maintain order and defend the interests of the rich and the politicians who governed the Roman empire. Individual wealthy patricians and capitalists sometimes had their own private little armies, retinues of escorts and bodyguards to uphold and flaunt the prestige and power of the plutocrats.

The Romans had been predominantly a nation of simple farmers, sturdy, industrious, honest and with great respect for authority—the aristocracy was reputed to be noble in character and honorable in conduct and the government was just and moderate. But then the Romans turned imperialistic. At first the motives for Rome's expansion was self-defense but as trade and commerce developed and produced prosperity and affluence other inducements for war and conquest became apparent. The more lands they conquered, the more they wanted to conquer. Repeated success made them arrogant and greedy. They were spoiled by victory. Former innocent, scrupulous farmers and high-minded patricians changed into acquisitive capitalists; wise and conscientious rulers became ambitious self-seeking politicians, corrupt and avaricious. The average Roman was now dedicated to the pursuit of wealth, power, and extravagant pleasures.

Confronting the rulers of the Roman republic were two major problems: how to administer the conquered nations and how to resolve the class conflict between the rich and the poor. For a city-state to control and regulate the affairs of a huge heterogeneous empire was no easy task and the Romans made many mistakes. However they improvised and managed to muddle through for about a hundred years and then finally had to resort to a more effectual rule by an absolute monarch. The other problem concerned the turbulent multitude of unemployed welfare clients, the destitute urban masses. These unfortunate Roman citizens had helped win the wars and build up the empire, yet got nothing out of it but misery. Almost all the spoils of war went to the wealthy patricians and rich plebeians but the small farmer and wage worker got virtually nothing. They were lodged in filthy, disease-infested tenement houses in the slums and were given grain or bread to keep them alive and prevent grumbling. They were permitted to sell their votes to the politicians in the assembly and to relieve them from boredom they were given free tickets to the circus, the public games or the gladiatorial combats. The wealthy, on the other hand lived in sumptuous houses with costly furniture, rich fabrics, Greek statues, precious trinkets, rare and exotic foods, servants, slaves, and entertainers.

Roman society seemed to be divided into paupers and millionaires. The latter regarded the welfare recipients as parasites who deliberately abandoned their farms to sponge on public and private charity. The unemployed insisted they wanted to work—they asked for jobs or farms, not doles. They agitated for the dividing up of the large estates and the founding of colonies for ex-farmers to start their lives over again. But the great landowners in control of the senate were vehemently opposed to reform which threatened their wealth and power. In the early republic patricians and plebeians, after battling for many years, had been able to compromise on civil and political rights of Roman citizens and gradually the plebeians gained equality. But civil and political rights were easier to grant or to acquire than economic justice. The rich were more willing to share theoretical legal rights than to share tangible material wealth. Furthermore national morality had declined and avarice had increased and so compromise was no longer fashionable. The alternative was resort to violence.

Not all the aristocrats were callous conservatives opposed to reform. The Gracchi brothers, Tiberius and Gaius, were two honorable and idealistic grandsons of Scipio Africanus the famous conqueror of Hannibal. They believed that if Rome was to continue to be strong and healthy it must have a large number of independent and prosperous farmers and many free and happy, employed laborers. Tiberius was elected tribune in 133 B.C. He proposed taking some of the government owned lands, then occupied by agricultural capitalists, dividing them into small tracts and distributing them among the poor, landless citizens of Rome. These small farmers would pay the government an annual tax and would be given a generous loan to enable them to buy stock and necessary implements. Also a law would be passed to restrict the amount of public land that any Roman might possess. The assembly of citizens approved these proposals but the landowners in the senate denounced the measures as robbery and disastrous for the country and incited discord and violence. Hiring an armed band of thugs the senators provoked rioting which resulted in the death of Tiberius and about three hundred of his supporters. The senate then ordered all the bodies including Tiberius thrown into the Tiber river.

Ten years later his brother Gaius resumed the struggle to break the senatorial monopoly and relieve the destitute proletarians and landless farmers. Gaius, as Tiberius, was elected to be a tribune to help the common people and like his brother, he proposed the confiscation of public land and its redistribution among the would be small farmers. He would also establish colonies in Italy and north Africa, would provide cheap grain for the poor, encourage emigration to all parts of the empire and give employment in the building of roads and other public works. He also favored the extension of full citizenship to all Latins and to some other Italians. But again the senators resisted change, denounced Gaius as a public enemy and instigated riots and bloody battles. Thousands of liberal reformers perished by order of the senate, including the people's champion who committed suicide with the assistance of one of his slaves who also died. Gaius's mother was forbidden even to wear mourning for her son.

The senate thus set the precedent of employing violence to bring about or prevent political change and henceforth ambitious men seeking power found it most expeditious to use the sword to gain and maintain control of the government. To assure success and popularity it was necessary to win a few military victories somewhere in the empire and return to Rome as a conquering hero. The Gracchi brothers were benevolent civilian noblemen but the two prominent leaders who followed them were military men, dictatorial and brutal. Marius, son of a laborer, gained renown as a soldier and was rewarded by being elected consul six times. He was associated with the democratic faction of Rome, the populares, who were trying to wrest the power from the senatorial group or the optimates. Once in power, Marius created a voluntary, standing army of professional soldiers who would fight for money and other rewards, such as, pensions and land. These soldiers would have complete loyalty to their commander, their employer who paid them, and were not averse to committing the most savage atrocities in fighting for their boss. Marius was very popular with the masses because he was of humble origin and professed to be the champion of the oppressed. He was hailed for his military success against barbarian tribes and hostile foreigners, such as the Gauls, Germans and north Africans. However in domestic affairs he had no definite plan, no liberal reforms; he was ineffectual, a disappointment to the common people. And so for a while Marius retired and went into exile, but subsequently he returned to help suppress a revolt of the Italian allies for Roman citizenship. In the meanwhile the senate had found a very able patrician named Sulla, a zealous defender of the cause of the conservatives. He also was a successful general who had won distinction in the Italian conflict and soon became a rival of Marius for the control of Rome.

More menacing than the kindred allies was an eastern king, Mithradates, who was demanding that all Italians go home and he threatened to conquer Greece and all of Asia Minor. In fact he ordered the massacre of all Romans living in the east and about 80,000 men, women and children were slaughtered. Mithradates was the ambitious ruler of Pontus, a little nation located in what is now southern Turkey, but it hoped to expand. The king was half Persian and half Greek, handsome, athletic and highly educated but a ruthless tyrant who murdered his brother, his sister (who was also the queen), a number of allies, friends, and several of his illegitimate children. Either Marius or Sulla was to be put in command of an army to thwart the state of Pontus and to eliminate the bloodthirsty, vainglorious Mithradates. The senate appointed Sulla to conduct the war but the people's assembly wanted their friend Marius to have that honor, whereupon Sulla led his army into the city and drove Marius into exile. Sulla then departed on his military mission. While Sulla was away Marius returned to Rome and was chosen consul for a seventh term, but he died three weeks after his election. Later, having pacified the rebellious eastern states, Sulla came back home, defeated the son of Marius and became the dictator.

Both Marius and Sulla were military despots who could not tolerate opposition and so they exiled or tried to murder as many of their political adversaries and their friends as possible. They regarded the slaying of potential rivals and dissidents as necessary and proper as the killing of foreign enemies in time of war and so commoners slaughtered aristocrats and patricians slaughtered plebeians. Marius introduced a reign of terror when thousands were summarily executed by order of the dictator. Then his followers paraded through the streets with the severed heads of noblemen on their pikes and adorned the Roman Forum with the heads of senators. Dead bodies were left in the streets to be devoured by birds and dogs. At one time Marius freed thousands of slaves who then went berserk finding release in indiscriminate plundering, raping and killing. Then the rampaging slaves were put to death. When Sulla came to power he set up a patrician reign of terror as hideous as the plebeian carnage which preceded it. After defeating the followers of Marius, Sulla took 8000 prisoners and had them shot down with arrows and then had the heads of the captured generals placed on pikes and exhibited to the people. Marius' son committed suicide and his head was conspicuously displayed in the Forum along with many others. Among the enemy soldiers Sulla's men picked up a youngster, named Julius Caesar, a cousin of Marius junior, but they let him go free because he was too young to execute. About 5000 civilian followers of Marius were butchered by the conservatives. Leaving the government in the hands of the anti-democratic faction, Sulla retired in 80 B.C. and devoted the rest of his life to pleasure.

Sulla had succeeded in curbing the assembly and the tribunes and had restored authority to the senate, but the senate was still dominated by corrupt and reactionary patricians who were concerned only with their own welfare. The poor were still jobless, landless, restive and riotous. Rome was replete with politically-minded generals— demagogues and dictators were in the offing. After the departure of Sulla the most likely military politician was Pompey. He achieved fame and popularity by crushing a dangerous uprising of slaves, by ferreting out the troublesome pirates and by suppressing a rebellion in Spain. His most notable accomplishment was rectifying the disturbing eastern situation where he succeeded in conquering Syria, Phoenicia, Palestine, Pontus and other states. Mithradates, who was now completely subdued, avoided humiliation and execution by committing suicide before his capture. Pompey brought home many prominent prisoners and also millions of dollars in plunder for the government as well as for himself and his friends, and was given a triumphant procession. Enormously popular, Pompey could have taken over the government but he was hesitant and unwisely disbanded his army. Whereupon the senate declined to approve the treaties the general had negotiated with eastern rulers and refused to grant the veterans the bonus of land they had expected after the wars. Instead the fabulous booty was divided among the generals, politicians and tax collectors.

Pompey though a highly successful army commander was no political strong man, for a prospective military dictator does not discharge his soldiers before a coup d'etat and always purges the capital and his entourage of potential rivals by assassination, incarceration or exile. Instead of seizing the government for himself he made a deal with two aspiring politicians, Julius Caesar and Marcus Crassus, to form a triumvirate or a ruling group of three of which Pompey was to be the leader. Crassus, the richest man in Rome, made his millions by supplying the army with necessary materiel, by land speculation, by acquiring and renting houses and tenements and by the manipulation of crafty financial schemes. He owned so much property in Rome that he found it necessary to establish his own fire department to protect it.

Julius Caesar was a very capable young man born of aristocratic but impoverished parents. He was highly talented in many areas and was also brave, adventurous and dissolute. As a young man he was once kidnapped by a group of pirates and was ransomed for a huge sum of money. Shortly after being freed, he chartered a few vessels and crews, captured the pirates and ordered their execution, but being a compassionate fellow, he had their throats cut before they were crucified. Then he returned to Rhodes where he was a scholar majoring in rhetoric and philosophy. Often in need of money, Caesar cultivated the friendship of Crassus, accepted his loans and patronage and in return helped him secure assignments and opportunities which would bring glory and provide challenging diversions for the great plutocrat. The triumvirate agreement was made personally more binding when Caesar presented his daughter Julia to Pompey in marriage—an unusual arrangement as the husband was six years older than his father-in-law. Pompey had recently divorced his third wife because of her intimacies with Caesar.

These were riotous times in Rome as lawlessness, turmoil and mob violence were widespread. Politicians employed armed slaves and gladiators or hired gangs of hoodlums and ruffians to terrorize the city and burn down buildings; to guide and protect the voters at the polls, to attack obstinate opponents and fight pitched battles in the streets when necessary. Mercenary lobbyists used bribes and brawn to influence legislators, and prominent politicians needed bodyguards to protect them from physical intimidation and assault. When Cato, a courageous and highly respectable statesman, criticized the policies of Julius Caesar he was beaten almost to death. One of the more zealous followers of the popular trio reduced the effectiveness of senatorial opposition by dumping a pot of dung on the head of the leader of the conservatives. The members of the triarchy apparently had the support of a majority of the people, since Pompey could get the vote of the veterans and the middle class businessmen, Crassus had connections among the rich and Caesar was a high born democrat well endowed with charisma, a born leader of the masses. Consequently the senate soon found it expedient and prudent to ratify Pompey's treaties and to grant bonuses to his veterans.

To complete the requirements for their jobs as rulers of Rome the members of the triumvirate also had to exhibit their military prowess. Pompey had already established an enviable reputation in that field and so the other two were now given their opportunities to obliterate troublesome spots in the empire. Crassus and his troops were sent to the east where violent disturbances were chronic and perennial, while Caesar was appointed governor of Gaul and provided with an army which he could utilize to enlarge the empire and win laurels for himself in combat. Crassus unfortunately lost his life in Mesopotamia where his conqueror having heard of the Roman nabob's passion for money had his head cut off and poured molten gold into his mouth. Caesar was more fortunate and more talented. He remained in Gaul for nine years and displayed extraordinary brilliance by subjugating the entire country (modern France), by also crossing the Rhine and invading Germany and by making two military expeditions to Britain. A gifted writer, he was his own war correspondent and public relations agency, making and writing history at the same time and incidentally building up his fame and esteem among the highly impressionable citizens of Rome. Caesar's reports, *Commentaries on the Gallic Wars*, was given wide circulation and helped to establish his reputation as a military genius and as a worthy author of lucid, vigorous prose. He also had considerable experience as an administrator and politician, having served as national quaestor, aedile, praetor and consul as well as the provincial governor of Spain and of France. An eloquent speaker, he had been a demagogue, had won popular allegiance through his eloquence, and gained thousands of votes among the poor by giving them bribes, free bread, and free admissions to public games and races in exchange for their political support.

While Caesar was away the triumvirate came to an end. Pompey's wife died in 54 B.C. and Crassus was killed the following year and so with the death of his daughter and of his friend, Caesar lost all personal ties with Pompey. Now, competing for leadership, the two men became enemies. With conditions as they were, with turbulence and turmoil obtaining at Rome, strong, central government was needed and either Pompey or Caesar would become commander-in-chief of the military forces and probably the dictator of the country. The senate preferred Pompey because he was inclined to be more tractable and would compromise; in fact he was already considered a conservative while Caesar was regarded by the upper classes as a very ambitious and dangerous radical, a despotic man. Consequently Pompey, supported by most of the senators, was elected to be the sole consul or chief ruler of the land. Caesar was then informed that if he wanted to return to Rome he would have to give up his command of the army in Gaul, that he would be denounced as an outlaw if he came home with his legions. But Caesar suspected that he would be banished anyway even if he arrived without his troops, so he addressed his veterans, his "fellow soldiers," who admired him not only for his phenomenal military success but also for his personal bravery and his humanity and graciousness in the treatment of his rank and file soldiers. They were thoroughly loyal and so Caesar defied Pompey and the senate, crossed the Rubicon river, the boundary between Gaul and Italy, and marched toward Rome. Everywhere Caesar was welcomed as a friend of the common man and within two months all of Italy was occupied; Pompey fled to Greece, many aristocrats likewise left the capital, though the majority of the senators remained in Rome.

Caesar pursued Pompey and decisively defeated him in central Greece after which the latter fled to Egypt where he also had an army and Caesar followed his former son-in-law. Forced to make a choice between the two Romans Ptolemy wagered on a Caesarian victory and therefore had Pompey murdered. However, Egypt was in the midst of a conflict of its own. Ptolemy and his brilliant young sister, Cleopatra, were having a battle over who was to sit on the throne and Caesar decided to intervene. His motives were twofold—imperialistic and sexual. First, he believed that the Roman empire ought to embrace the immensely rich land of Egypt and second, he became profoundly enamored of the seductive Ptolemaic queen. Caesar had already established a reputation for being very enterprising with the ladies. After a military triumph his soldiers would often sing a song warning husbands to keep their women under lock and key for Julius Caesar was in town. Now concealed in bedding, the charming Cleopatra was secretly brought to Caesar's headquarters by one of her faithful servants and presented to the great philandering general. Utilizing her melodious voice and her graceful wiles, the Macedonian Greek princess convinced Caesar that she was more desirable and was better equipped and qualified than her brother to govern a Roman province. Immediately afterwards the Roman commander drove the Egyptian army into the Nile, drowned King Ptolemy, and made Cleopatra ruler of Egypt. So impressed and so embedded was Caesar with his latest acquisition that he remained in Alexandria for nine months when a son was born to the queen of Egypt. The child was named Caesarion after his father. Then the invincible general left his honeymoon and rushed over to Asia Minor where a son of the great Mithradates was leading a serious revolt against Roman rule. Caesar crushed the rebellion in five days and then sent to Rome his famous brief and pithy report of the victory—"I came, I saw, I conquered." In the year 47 B.C. he returned home accompanied by Cleopatra, her young brother, and her baby, Caesarion.

After two mopping-up operations in Spain and north Africa, after four victory parades and a glowing account of his numerous conquests, Caesar was made dictator for one year, then for ten years and finally for life. Various and copious reforms followed his assumption of power. He converted the senate into an advisory council, he controlled the assemblies, consuls, tribunes, censors, praetors and all the other magistrates, and although he was an agnostic, he was made the high priest or manager of religious affairs; in fact, he was deified, a temple was dedicated in his honor and in the new calendar July was named after him because he was born in that month. Caesar was magnanimous, tolerant and benevolent. Being a man of clemency, he forgave his former foes but his enactments were more pleasing to his progressive friends. He extended citizenship to many provincials, put an end to the practice of extorting excessive taxes from the provinces by swindling publicans and governors and substituted a direct tax collected by government agents, and he promised to grant citizenship to all free men in the empire. He provided an elaborate program of colonization in the provinces, opened up unused farm lands for veterans and the urban poor, and rebuilt and repeopled the cities of Carthage and Corinth. He reduced the number of citizens eligible for public welfare, created many new jobs for the unemployed by instituting public works, reduced the number of slaves, ordered the employment of more free men, abolished imprisonment for debt and had the bankruptcy law changed to relieve debtors. Other economic reforms included the forbidding of excessive interest rates, improvement of coinage, and the stabilization of the currency by the use of the gold standard. Law and order prevailed in Rome as the dictator reduced crime and gangsterism and he prohibited downtown parking to relieve traffic congestion. With the aid of Greek astronomers he had the old Egyptian calendar changed into what was to be called the Julian calendar, which with minor alterations made in the sixteenth century, is in use today. Caesar initiated or made plans for many more reforms and projects including the codification of Roman law, the building of libraries, theaters and temples, more roads and canals, the draining of marshes and the reclaiming of more land; the reform of local governments, and a general census and survey of all the people and resources in the empire. He introduced the custom of issuing reports regularly, informing the public of important news or events. These communications would be posted on bulletin boards on the walls of the Forum and reporters would copy the information and broadcast it all over the empire.

Caesar proposed to do much more but his career was cut short. The senators remained conservative, opposing the dictator's many enactments, and were jealous of his power and success. They preferred government by an aristocratic oligarchy to enlightened despotism, and so they organized a plot to assassinate Caesar, the patrician friend and benefactor of the common people. Some participants in the conspiracy, which was led by Brutus and Cassius, had served with Caesar for many years, some had been pardoned after opposing him, and others had recently been appointed to office by him. On the fifteenth of March, 44 B.C., Caesar was surrounded by a group of the conspirators and stabbed to death in front of Pompey's statue in the Senate house. The body of the great statesman was taken to the Forum, burned on a pyre, and Antony, Caesar's most trusted lieutenant, delivered the funeral eulogy. Believing they had liberated the country from tyranny, the assassins expected wide public approval, but they were mistaken. Caesar's soldiers and the populace were outraged and furious and demanded revenge while Antony's eloquent and stirring funeral oration conduced to the outbreak of riots and civil conflict in which thousands of Romans were slaughtered. Defeated in battle, Cassius and Brutus committed suicide, and among the many who were murdered during the blood bath was the distinguished author of magnificent orations, the conservative senator, Cicero.

Emerging as new leaders were Antony, Caesar's favorite officer, a competent soldier, enthusiastic about war, women and pleasure;

Lepidus, another capable commander under Caesar; and Octavian, a very intelligent and serious young man of eighteen, a grand-nephew and adopted son of Caesar's and heir to his estate. Like the first triumvirate the members of this triarchy separated—Antony went east, Lepidus went south to north Africa, and Octavian, who was not a soldier and had no military chores to take care of, stayed home. Lepidus was later forced to resign and the empire was divided into the eastern and the western part, the latter going to Octavian and the former to Antony.

During his campaigns in the east Antony became more intimately acquainted with Cleopatra, the fascinating queen of Egypt. She had first crossed his vision many years before when Julius Caesar held his passionate summit meetings in Alexandria, but now Antony was the master and he too became infatuated with the beguiling vampire, who was usually clothed in a transparent silk dress to reveal her attractive architecture. For a short time he did manage to break away from Cleopatra's clutches, returned to Rome and renewed his alliance with Octavian and as an earnest of his sincerity he married Octavian's sister, Octavia, and then they went off to live in Greece for rest and inspiration. However, he soon lost interest in his new wife; he found her inadequate and boring, and so he hurried back to the open arms of Cleopatra. The queen had been married to her younger brother but as in the case of the older sibling Cleopatra had him ousted from office and put to death in order to remove political competition and to make room for prestigious paramours or celebrated consorts. This time Antony made his attachment in Egypt official and legitimate by divorcing Octavia and marrying the royal siren. Caesarion was now designated as the true heir of the late dictator—Caesar, and was proclaimed the joint ruler with Cleopatra in the east. Antony assigned Syria, Crete and parts of Asia Minor to Egypt and when his fertile and crafty consort bore him two children, he graciously allotted them some rich Roman provinces also.

Antony's conduct generated alarming rumors and aroused widespread indignation in Italy. Octavian who had grown to be an astute and ambitious politician and was eager to become the exclusive ruler of Rome, incited the public and persuaded the senate to declare war on Cleopatra. Antony was deprived of all his political powers and denounced as a traitor. In 31 B.C. at Actium off the west coast of

Greece the Roman fleet decisively defeated the naval forces of Antony and Cleopatra. Several months later Alexandria was taken by the Romans and Antony committed suicide, dying in the arms of his beloved queen. Undaunted Cleopatra offered her services to the victor, but Octavian, unlike his uncle Julius and his more recent associate, Antony, was no playboy and furthermore the queen was now close to forty and her erotic allure had perceptibly diminished. He accordingly rejected her overture and instead proposed to display her in a grand Roman triumphal procession as an infamous prisoner. Cleopatra preferred death to such humiliation. Enrobed and adorned in her royal finery, she had a poisonous serpent inject its venom in her breast, and the Ptolemaic dynasty came to a close. The Queen was buried beside Antony. Her son by Caesar was slain but her two children, fathered by Antony, were spared to be mothered by one of his early wives. The former kingdom of Egypt was annexed by Octavian who made the ancient country his private estate.

CHAPTER VIII

(PART 2)

Pax Romana and Prosperity
Emperors: Good, Bad and Eccentric

The era of civil strife now came to an end and concomitantly the Roman republic ceased to exist. In its place they created the Principate where Octavian was known as the princeps or the chief citizen of Rome. In the year 27 B.C. the senate conferred upon him the exalted title of Augustus which was a mark of divine distinction implying majesty and sovereignty. The name Caesar would eventually come to mean emperor whereas the title Augustus became Octavian's new name. The head of state was also commander of the army or the imperator and also the highest priest or pontifex maximus, head of the Roman religion. All the Republican forms were retained. They still had a senate and a popular assembly, consuls, tribunes, praetors, quaestors, aediles, but all legislation and all magistrates were persons recommended and selected by Augustus before they were formally elected or appointed to office and they were not permitted to enact measures or take any important steps without his approval and guidance. Augustus was capable, industrious, conscientious and tactful. He showed respect for the senate, for its dignity and its opinions and the senators reciprocated. Although he was the richest man in Rome and had enormous power, he shunned all pomp and luxury and led a simple, modest life never flaunting his wealth, which pleased the poor, and never flouting Roman traditions, which pleased the conservatives. Caesar had shown how much could be accomplished by one-man rule and Augustus wanted to follow in his great-uncle's footsteps but without Caesar's political indiscretions and without his haste; for the new ruler was a young man with a great deal of time and patience.

Augustus brought peace and prosperity to the Roman world after a century of civil conflict in which the people had lost almost all confidence in government. He increased trade with the provinces, planted many new colonies, paid the soldiers pensions with his own money, reformed the tax laws, made them just, and he abolished the practice of farming out tax collecting. Business improved as the government gave jobs to numerous workers by building roads, repairing highways and by the construction of many architectural works. He established a system of police and fire protection, improved the water supply, suppressed piracy and brigandage, reformed the courts, made the laws more humane, reduced exploitation and corruption in the provinces, extended postal service to many parts of the empire, encouraged literature, sponsored amusements for the masses, and reestablished a large standing army and a permanent navy. Augustus desired to restore the old family life, and the ideals of morality and reverence for the gods. Religion was made important again, temples were rebuilt, sacrifices were revived, Augustus was worshipped as a god and they named the month of August after him.

The first Roman emperor was not a brilliant man, was not a soldier and was not healthy. He did not live dangerously but carefully, did not govern arbitrarily but cautiously, hence he lasted a long time; he ruled for about forty-five years and lived to be seventy-six. He gave the people what they wanted—order, security, food and entertainment and they loved him. But dictatorship no matter how benevolent had one serious flaw and that was the problem of succession. In theory the senate had the right to elect the ruler but the senators didn't have the courage to do anything about it and so the incumbent or sometimes the army would select the new emperor. From 14-68 A.D. there were four rulers—Tiberius, Gaius, Claudius and Nero, all descendants of the Julius and Augustus family. Tiberius was an able and honest administrator and his policies were constructive and peaceful. But in the year 37 when Tiberius died the imperial bodyguard placed in power a very whimsical character named Gaius, popularly called Caligula. He started his reign with liberal intentions and beneficent policies but in a short time power went to his head and he became ludicrous and mentally deranged. Following are a few of Caligula's oddities. He bathed in perfume, senators were compelled to kiss his feet, he levied a sales tax on prostitutes, he forced his grandmother to commit suicide, proclaimed himself a major god equal to Jupiter, enjoyed watching people tortured to death and told persons he had the power to kill anyone, to cut off their heads. He was also crazy about horses, appointing one to be a priest and another to be a consul. One of his best friends was a horse who attended formal state dinners at the imperial table and ate choice foods from very expensive dishes. On one occasion when there was a shortage of meat for the animals used in the gladiatorial games Caligula ordered all baldheaded prisoners be fed to the beasts. Such grotesque deportment became intolerable and plots were arranged to end Caligula's incumbency. In the year 41 the Praetorian Guard, the emperor's private army, which had put him in power four years earlier, murdered the mad monarch and replaced him with his very shy and reluctant uncle, Claudius. Claudius was well read and well informed especially in history but he was weak, dull and easily managed. Nevertheless the empire was equitably administered, a number of public works were undertaken, transportation was improved, he granted full citizenship to the Gauls and his armies conquered Britain. However his reign was marred by female intrigues and scandals, as he was dominated by his five successive wives who took advantage of his docile nature. His last wife Agrippina, who was also his niece, spent her days and nights trying to secure the succession to power for her son, Nero, an offspring of a former marriage. Beautiful but immoderately ambitious, she could not brook female competition at court and sought to eliminate all potential rivals of Nero for the throne. When Claudius eventually became aware of her machinations he hurriedly announced that his son Britannicus, would be his heir and the next emperor. Whereupon Agrippina, tenacious and indomitable, decided to murder her uncle, the emperor. She fed Claudius poisonous mushrooms, which proved lethally effective, and Nero, with the aid of his mother, preempted the throne. Burrus, a close friend of Agrippina's and an authoritative officer of the imperial guard, was most instrumental in procuring military support.

Very influential and highly competent as an adviser in the government was Nero's tutor, the distinguished stoic philosopher, Seneca. The queen mother, Agrippina enjoyed the glamour of her position and exulted at seeing her image alongside her son's, engraved on the imperial coins. But Seneca and Burrus, the praetorian prefect, advised Nero to reign without his mother's aid and intimated that she was politically superfluous. This infuriated the matriarch and she let it be known that she was capable of replacing her son with his stepbrother, Britannicus, who was the true heir to the throne. This threat so provoked Nero that he had his potential rival murdered, and so his mother Agrippina retired to her country villa. Burrus and Seneca continued to administer the government remarkably well and Nero was popular with the masses as he provided the public with spectacular games and gladiatorial combats and distributed money generously among the poor. The emperor's counselors, aware of his limitations and real interests, encouraged him to refrain from participation in the affairs of state and devote his time to hobbies and other extracurricular activities. About five years after he became ruler he began to pass his life in excessive lust, lechery, gluttony and rowdyism. Sometimes he would disguise himself and with friends rove through the streets, rob a few shops, kill someone occasionally, accost and insult women, and visit taverns and brothels. In spite of his scandalous behavior, and his horrid crimes, he had a passion for music, poetry, art, acting and athletics, and tried to emulate the culture of Greece. He professed an aptitude in all these fields, dabbled in painting and sculpturing, writing poetry, composing music, singing, and playing various instruments, performing in plays at leading theatres, competing in races, games and sporting events. Nero tried to keep his voice in trim by syringing his throat, by vomiting and by eating garlic and olive oil. His talent was infinitesimal and he was woefully amateurish and deficient in all his artistic and athletic endeavors. However his performances at stadiums and theaters were always wildly applauded and he was thrilled and proud.

Enlightened Romans thought these performances and exhibitions were ludicrous and disgraceful and some patricians began to make plans for Nero's removal. However, his spies discovered the plot and a reign of terror ensued, in which all persons suspected of opposition to the emperor or critical of his affected and exaggerated artistic and athletic proficiency were put to death. Many prominent persons including senators were also executed to enable Nero to confiscate their estates. The treasury had become exhausted because of his elaborate, expensive shows, spectacles and games and because he gave away so much money—perquisites to soldiers and financial rewards, a gift of about forty dollars each, to every Roman citizen. Nero lost both of his great ministers when Burrus died and Seneca was dismissed for criticizing the emperor's poetry and conduct. Three years later after the great fire when another conspiracy to depose the emperor was discovered, Seneca and other intellectuals were forced to commit suicide. Nero's new advisers also encouraged him to indulge in all his appetites and leave the governing of Rome to them. Greatly in need of money Nero appropriated the people's gifts consecrated and offered to the gods, as well as the gold and silver images in the temples. He once demonstrated his contempt for the Roman religion by voiding his bladder on the statue of the fertility and mother goddess, Cybele. Yet he was delighted a few years later when he himself, a cruel, vicious and degenerate man of only twenty-five was deified by the people and was worshipped as a god.

Besides his mother Nero had another woman who exercised a great deal of influence on his life. She was Poppaea Sabina, an aristocratic, immensely wealthy, charming but unprincipled Roman beauty. When they first met both he and she were already married and though the young emperor fell madly in love with her, she was unwilling to be just a mistress. So Nero forthwith appointed her husband governor of Portugal and divorced his own wife. That made the two lovers conveniently available to each other. However Nero's mother, having recovered and resurged from her recent retirement, expressed vehement objection to both his divorce and to his new matrimonial alliance. Octavia, the emperor's first wife, was a respectable and obedient young lady while Poppaea was an ambitious, selfish and beguiling woman, not unlike Nero's mother. She reproached Nero for being a slave to his mother and finally convinced him that Agrippina was conspiring to dethrone him. Poppaea, like her mother-in-law, could not endure female competition and Nero was so infatuated with his new seductive queen that he finally consented to have his mother put to death. She was brutally murdered and when he viewed her dead body he remarked that he never knew that his mother was so beautiful. Octavia, his first wife, was also slain with the emperor's connivance and her head was brought to Poppaea who amply rewarded the murderer. One evening in the year 65 Nero came home from the races and when Poppaea reproached him for being so late he brutally kicked his pregnant wife—a blow from which she died. The funeral was very pompous and Nero delivered the eulogy.

A person of manifold interests, this extraordinary monarch once spoke dispargingly about the layout of Rome's streets and buildings, he deplored its many ugly spots and its lack of scientific city planning. He thought it ought to be rebuilt, modeled preferably after the Greek cities and renamed Neropolis. Shortly after he made these strictures about Rome's architecture a great fire broke out, burning down two-thirds of the buildings, killing thousands of people and making hundreds of thousands homeless. Rumors spread that the emperor had started the fire and then watched it from a tower while he sang and fiddled on his harp. Now needing a scapegoat he blamed the disaster on the members of a peculiar and unpopular sect called Christians and had a number of them very cruelly executed. The city was declared a disaster area and funds were provided to take care of the needy and to rebuild the burned out metropolis.

When the situation in Rome cooled down Nero went to Greece to participate in the Olympics. He wanted to display his skill as an athlete, charioteer, actor, and especially as a singer and harpist because the Greeks knew more about music than any other people in the world. Immense crowds greeted him and applauded his performances enthusiastically and thunderously at the stadiums, the theater, and concert halls. He was so overcome by the people's appreciation and recognition of his remarkable talent that he promised the Greeks future immunity from the payment of tribute to Rome. The judges prudently awarded the emperor numerous crowns of victory in the contests and Nero returned home and proudly flaunted his prizes and trophies.

But a few months later disaffection and revolts broke out in Gaul, Spain, the Rhineland and in the eastern provinces. Galba, commander of the army stationed in Spain, marched toward Rome and was proclaimed emperor by the senate; and when the imperial guard, the army, and even his best friends refused to defend him, Nero deemed it more healthful to make his exit and leave town. Then when he was declared a public enemy and he envisioned a torturous execution he decided to commit suicide. He considered poison, the Tiber river, and a dagger but he lacked the courage to kill himself and so he had to enlist the aid of a servant for the final thrust of the knife. His last words in paraphrase were: Here dies a great artist.

Galba's program for Rome was the strict administration of justice and rigid economy in the distribution of government funds in the form of gifts and pensions. Such policies were immediately and vehemently denounced by the army and by the proletarians and so the imperial guards decapitated Galba and placed Senator Otho on the throne. But the Roman armies in Germany preferred a General Vitellius, who moved into Italy and removed Otho. However Vitellius was more interested in feasts and banquets than in government and in 69 he was ousted by the army that had been stationed in Egypt and Syria under the command of Vespasian. The soldiers wanted their commander to take over the throne and the submissive senate quickly agreed to their choice.

The Flavian dynasty consisted of Vespasian and his two sons— Titus and Domitian. The Flavians were of plebeian stock; Vespasian was the son of a tax collector and the grandson of a debt collector, and as emperor frequently consorted with commoners. Important administrative positions were now given to members of the middle class and the financial policy was moderation in government spending and a balanced budget. He undertook the construction of a number of public buildings including the famous Colosseum and provided plenty of food and jobs for the poor. The provinces enjoyed prosperity and were fairly well governed, although there were uprisings in Gaul, the Rhine district, in Britain and in Palestine. The revolt of the Jews was suppressed with the capture and the burning of Jerusalem in the year 70, which was followed by the dispersal of many Jews throughout the Roman empire.

Titus was a generous and popular ruler but he died two years after his accession. During his brief reign the Colosseum was completed but in the year 79 an enormous fire in Rome destroyed many important buildings and the city of Pompeii was buried by the eruption of Vesuvius, and in the year 80 Rome was stricken by a deadly plague. The third Flavian emperor, Domitian, was an extravagant ruler but he provided employment to many by instituting a prodigious program of public works, he tried to revive the old faith, including emperor worship, encouraged art and literature and gave the people ample but expensive games. He also administered the provinces ably and some additions to the empire were made. However he was very despotic and became suspicious and cruel. This begot enmity, plots and intrigues and the emperor was assassinated.

Since Domitian had no son and had not named a candidate to succeed him the senate selected a man named Nerva, a mild, elderly politician to be the monarch. It was also decided that henceforth the adoptive principle would supersede the hereditary method of choosing a new ruler. Nerva, who was not in good health, selected as his understudy, the best warrior in the empire, and then after a reign of only two years he passed away and the great general Trajan became the chief executive.

Nerva was the first of the so-called "five good emperors," or the Antonines who ruled from 96 to 180. His successor Trajan was a conservative who respected the dignity of the senate and pleased the business classes by his efficiency in managing the government finances. A great soldier, he pursued a policy of imperial aggrandizement enlarging the Roman world to its widest limits. He conquered Dacia or modern Rumania where they still speak a Latin language, he annexed Armenia and Mesopotamia and led his army as far as the Indian Ocean. Trajan also built many roads, bridges, aqueducts and amphitheaters.

Following Trajan came Hadrian, a cultured, learned and brilliant man, one of the ablest and most beneficent of the Roman rulers. He could converse intelligently and intellectually on numerous topics and unlike Nero, he really possessed some artistic talent. Trajan had pursued an aggressive foreign policy—continuous conquest of more and more territory but Hadrian preferred to curtail further expansion, to consolidate and set up strong defensive frontiers and erect huge secure walls where the border contained no high mountains or wide bodies of water. Such strengthened fortifications were the chain of forts linking the Rhine and Danube rivers, built by previous emperors, and the Hadrian wall in northern Britain. He would even sacrifice a bit of Roman real estate if it strengthened the line of defense. His aim was to keep out the barbarians and so the army was reorganized with appropriate defensive equipment and well-trained cavalry for efficient mobile patrol duty. Desirous of helping the people everywhere he gathered together a number of experts of all sorts—artists, city planners, builders, and engineers and they visited and made a study of the needs of each province in the empire. In Rome he rebuilt the Pantheon and had many other public buildings constructed and in his travels he ordered the resurrection of the architectural charm and grandeur of Athens, Antioch and Alexandria and the erection of handsome edifices in numerous other places of the eastern provinces. All cities must have schools, temples, aqueducts, public baths, theaters, libraries and stadiums. For Jerusalem Hadrian proposed to build a temple to be dedicated to Jupiter on the site of the Jewish temple of Jehovah. The Holy City of the Jews would thus become a sacred center for the supreme deity of Roman pagans. This plan was considered so sacrilegious and mortifying by the Jews that for the third time they revolted against the Romans, fighting a suicidal war for freedom. It took the Romans three years to subjugate the tiny province and both sides suffered a tremendous loss of lives. Hadrian also reformed the government of Rome and of the provincial cities, reorganized the administrative system by forming a new bureaucracy of expert civil service workers, and he encouraged the study of law and the judicial system. The senate was no longer a legislative body, it was just an order of nobility.

Antoninus who had been adopted by Hadrian to be his successor, took over the throne when the latter died in 138. The ruler for twenty-three years, he was inclined to be liberal and humanitarian, building many hospitals, evincing great philanthropy toward orphans, slaves and the jobless. He encouraged education even for poor children, and tolerated the religious minorities—Jews and Christians. The senate was so impressed by the emperor's magnanimity and moral excellence that they bestowed upon him the title "Pius." His predecessor had been an habitual traveler visiting virtually every province in the Roman world; Antoninus Pius, on the other hand, never left the city of Rome, yet peace and prosperity prevailed throughout the empire. His choice of a successor was his son-in-law, Marcus Aurelius, a highly educated man who became famous as a stoic philosopher. An idealist of saintly character, his most troublesome problem was war—revolts in the east and barbarian attacks in the north. German tribes made frequent forays across the border and threatened a general invasion. The revolts in the east were finally suppressed and the barbarians were driven back, though the emperor was forced to allow many of the German invaders to settle peacefully and permanently within the Roman borders. The frontiers were now secure again but the fighting was very costly in men and money. Very calamitous too was the plague that came in from the east with the returning soldiers, bringing misery and death to thousands of people all over the empire.

Marcus unwittingly committed two serious errors. One was permitting German soldiers to settle on the Roman side of the frontier and allowing them to join the empire's defense forces, which in time would lead to a decline in the army's patriotism. The other mistake was naming his son Commodus the heir to the throne instead of choosing the best qualified person for the job. Commodus proved to be the worthless son of a noble man. He was not only incompetent but debauched and cruel and was enthusiastic mostly about sports. He participated in chariot racing and gladiatorial combats and enjoyed fighting and killing animals and men in the arena. His indoor passions included gambling, crapulous eating and drinking and sexual dissipation both natural and unnatural. The prosaic tasks of government were left to executive assistants who were generally corrupt, suspicious and merciless. After twelve years of misrule Commodus was assassinated by his wrestling trainer with the assistance of the emperor's Christian mistress.

CHAPTER VIII

(PART 3)

Roman Culture From Its Prime to Its Decline
Social Customs and Intellectual Achievements

The Roman empire was a universal state composed of a group of former independent nations that were subjugated, united and dominated by the emperor. Around the time of Marcus Aurelius in the second century of the Christian era, the empire was about the size of the United States of today and contained about 60 to 70 million people of diverse ethnic background. It was divided into over forty provinces each headed by a governor who was appointed by and was responsible to the emperor. The governor was assisted by a staff of well trained and intelligent administrators and civil service workers. The provinces were required to pay Rome tribute and taxes and provide an allotment of soldiers for the imperial army which numbered about 400,000 men. In return the Romans assured the provincials security, law, order, peace and prosperity. Not everybody was rich and happy, there were still many slaves, paupers and destitute freemen, but the wealth was no longer in the hands of a few affluent families in Rome and Italy, as was the case when the government was still a republic. Now there were also many provincials who were educated, successful landowners and business men and some of them too were exploiters and parasites.

Not all the nations that were subjugated were assimilated. The Orientals and the Greeks, who were considered more culturally advanced than their conquerors retained their own customs and languages and some were even allowed a little political autonomy. But of course all subject states must remain loyal to the emperor, observe religious ceremonies in his honor, contribute their share of money to the Roman treasury, and provide soldiers for the empire's defense. On the other hand in the west where the conquered provinces were less advanced culturally than the Romans the people voluntarily adopted the Latin language, followed the Roman social and political customs and were governed by Roman administrators. These nations became thoroughly absorbed; Spain, for example, contributed two of the greatest Roman emperors—Trajan and Hadrian. Other territories besides Italy and Spain that were more or less Romanized were Portugal, France, Belgium, Switzerland, the area near the Rhine and Danube rivers, Rumania, and England where about eighty percent of all borrowed words were derived from Latin. After the year 212 all free residents of the empire became citizens and some of the Roman senators, administrative officials, and most of the members of the army were provincials. Thanks to the diversity of ancestry of the numerous immigrants and emancipated slaves and to the probably widespread incidence of miscegenation the Roman people had become a mixture of Italians, Greeks, Semites, North Africans, and various western Europeans. Ethnically and culturally they were heterogeneous and cosmopolitan.

Throughout the empire there were many self-governing cities, about 5000 of them—modeled after the mother city, politically, socially and architecturally. They had their own senators and magistrates and their own aristocracy, who managed all municipal affairs and adorned their communities with beautiful public and private buildings. Although farming was regarded as the most honorable occupation most people in the empire were city dwellers and were inclined to be urban and cosmopolitan in their attitude and style of living. Rome was the largest city with a population of over a million inhabitants, Alexandria about 500,000 and most of them were much smaller. The unfortunate city of Pompeii, which was destroyed in the year 79, had only about 20,000 persons. The oldest cities were in the east; in the western provinces they were usually built by the Romans, often on the site of a military camp or colony. They all had their paved narrow streets, a forum, a senate house, temples, theaters, stadiums, race tracks, public baths, aqueducts and sewers. Like the affluent Roman citizens the rich provincials paid for the construction of these comforts and facilities and helped support and provide amusements for the indigent masses. A number of towns of Roman origin still exist today in Italy, Spain, France, England and in the Rhine and Danube area.

These cities were all connected with one another by a network of excellent roads all of which eventually led to Rome. These were the best highways the world had seen before the nineteenth century and many of them are still used today. A tourist could travel from England to France to Spain, Italy and Greece, Egypt and Palestine without crossing foreign frontiers, without having his baggage inspected or paying customs duties. However merchants had to pay tolls on bridges, some export and import taxes in towns, and there were twelve customs districts into which the empire was divided where the officials collected duties when their boundaries were crossed by freight-carrying wagons. But the tariffs that were levied were for revenue only and were relatively light so that the Romans virtually enjoyed free trade throughout the empire. Horse-drawn vehicles transported soldiers, couriers, travelers, merchants and all sorts of merchandise. They had first and second class tickets, sleeping carriages and free passes for privileged passengers. At about every thirty miles, along he highways were stations where the omnibuses would stop to change horses and drivers, to consult a repair man, or a blacksmith or a doctor. These roadside stopping places were also equipped with an inn, a store, a saloon and a brothel; and in the cities of course hotels provided more convenient facilities and accommodations. Occasionally the composure of the traveler was disturbed by robbers and thieves plying their trade in town or country. Nevertheless one could cover about one hundred miles a day on the Roman horse and wagon line—the fastest and most efficient transportation system before the advent of the railroad. Many Romans went on tours to Greece, Egypt and Hellenistic Asia to visit historic cities, famous buildings, art museums; to attend lectures, to learn about the customs and beliefs of other societies and they often left crude drawings, inscriptions or their names on historic monuments and walls of public buildings. Graffiti writing was a popular pastime among youthful Romans as revealed in the ruins of Pompeii.

In the early days of the principate empire Rome enjoyed prosperity in agriculture, industry and commerce. Army veterans had been granted small plots of land where they engaged in truck farming, selling their garden produce to the nearest city population. The happy days of the yeoman farmer had returned. But as before, during the time of the republic, small farms tended to grow large. The empire was still expanding, the army was still taking prisoners, slaves were cheap, and so wealthy men bought up land, employed slave labor on large estates or *latifundia* and drove small, weak competitors out of business. Successful farmers shifted to more profitable crops, such as, grapes, olives, sheep, large scale farming. By the end of the second century agricultural depression returned and the small farmer was again forced to move to the city looking for work or government relief, or food at low prices, free medical service and free entertainment. Then as the Romans ceased conquering and eradicated piracy, the sources of slavery disappeared and the cost of slave labor rose again. The owners of the latifundia then began to turn the farm land over to share-croppers or coloni as the Romans called them. These poor peasants were usually the erstwhile independent farmers who were forced to give the owner a large share of their produce and keep only a bare minimum for themselves.

Much of Rome's prosperity had been due to the tribute and taxes that they collected in the provinces and from the profits and interest they received from investments and loans they made in various parts of the empire, particularly in the western states. In addition to their banking and financial operations the Romans built up a few industries of their own, which enabled them to earn a fair amount of income through exports. Italians were proficient in the production of food-stuffs, wine, olive oil, flour, leather, textiles, pottery, hardware and various metal goods. A brisk business activity also developed over-land and overseas and they traded with all parts of the then known world, importing lead and tin from Spain, amber from northern Europe, copper from Cyprus, slaves, animals and ivory from Africa, spices, perfume, ointments, precious stones, cotton and silk from China and India. The Romans never became highly industrial but exports from Italy commenced to decline and an economic slump set in as Roman skills in farming and manufacturing began to spread to the provinces who before long became economically more self-reliant.

The Romans were not well versed in political economy nor were they enthusiastic about scientific inquiry and their emperor and politicians were generally averse to mechanical improvements, especially if they produced technological unemployment. So long as slavery was plentiful labor-saving devices were rejected by the authorities, as for example, when ingenious artisans and engineers offered plans for a hoisting machine in the construction industry or suggested the use of water mills and water power. Even when the quantity of slavery decreased there were enough unemployed proletarians to handle the required manufacturing jobs. The Romans did not conceive the necessity of invention and so they never experienced a technical or industrial revolution.

Most historians agree that Rome's greatest gift to the western world was its system of law. Like all primitive legal principles the early Roman laws were regulations and precepts based on unwritten social and religious customs and were inclined to be severe and merciless. A crime was not only a violation of social mores it was also a sin or an offense against the gods, and the priests were the legal authorities, the counselors and interpreters of the law. But the Roman law did not remain rigid—after a while it was modified as new principles and precedents were established. By the middle of the fifth century B.C. law was divorced from religion and in the early years of the republic the laws were written down in the Twelve Tables and published in the forum. Roman law was still very harsh, for example; fathers still had absolute control over their children; they were permitted to beat, chain, imprison, sell or kill them. Creditors were allowed to confine bankrupt debtors in jail or in a private dungeon, to enslave them or even put them to death. Penalties against ordinary criminals included fines, exile, enslavement or execution and were usually discriminative, that is; they varied with the social rank of the victim. A person who broke the bones of a freeman would be fined 300 asses or 18 dollars and if the victim was a slave he would pay only 150 asses or 9 dollars. A thief caught in the act had to become a slave to the man he had robbed. Capital crimes included murder, arson, bribery, perjury, attending a nocturnal revolutionary meeting, and damaging or stealing a farmer's crops at night. Any person convicted of killing his father might be tied in a sack with a rooster, a dog, a monkey or a poisonous snake and then thrown into a river. The right of appeal to a higher court was allowed and sometimes the prisoner would commute his own sentence by just leaving town, that is; he would go into exile voluntarily.

As the stoic philosophy was disseminated among the Romans law became more humane, more liberal, especially in the second and third centuries. For example, enlightened emperors who had read the philosophers proclaimed the general precepts that law should always accord with morality, that confessions obtained by torture are not valid, that guilt lies in the intention of a deed rather than in its result, that a man should be held innocent until he's been proved guilty, and that it is better for a guilty person to go unpunished than for an innocent man to be condemned. They also reduced the power the father had over his family. They took from him the right of life and death and transferred it to the courts. He was now forbidden to maltreat, to imprison, or to sell his children into slavery. A husband no longer had the right to kill his wife when she was caught committing adultery—he would now just discard her. He was also legally permitted to have only one concubine at a time. Even slaves now had their rights and were protected against cruel masters. In protecting life and property law aimed to give every man his due and from the stoics the Romans learned that all men are by nature equal, that they are entitled to certain basic rights which no one may violate. The sources of Roman law were the primitive tribal laws, the Twelve Tables, the statutes of the assemblies, decrees of the senate, edicts of emperors, decisions and interpretations of jurists and judges, the philosophy of the Greeks, particularly stoicism, and the customs and laws of the many various eastern nations in the empire. As conditions and problems changed, the laws were accordingly modified. From time to time there were deletions and amendments of the obsolete and classifications and compilations of the revised ideas until they culminated into the famous Justinian Code formulated between the years 528 to 534. This code contained all that the Romans knew about civil rights and the principles of justice and it influenced every system of law in the western world as well as a few in Africa and the Orient.

Roman civilization lasted over a thousand years and its most prosperous and peaceful age was during the first two centuries of the Christian era. By this time the people of Rome were no longer the same simple and patriotic farmers who had fought against the Etruscans and Carthaginians, they were now a heterogeneous and polygenetic but more or less Romanized race, consisting of Italians, Greeks, Spaniards, Gauls, Britons, Germans, Jews, Syrians, Egyptians and other north Africans. They all spoke Latin, though in their homelands the common people continued to use their native languages.

At the top of the social order were aristocrats, affluent business men, important government officials and successful professional men who lived in great comfort and luxury in private palaces, town houses and country villas. These homes were extravagantly decorated with splendid marble columns, marble mosaic floors, brilliantly colored tapestries, vivid murals painted on stone walls, ceilings adorned with gold and plate glass panels. They were sumptuously furnished with tables and stands made of fine wood, some with ivory legs, divans and beds of wood and bronze, statues, vases, and numerous and varied objects of art, all of which made the rooms look like museums. Outside of the opulent mansions were flower gardens, game preserves, fish ponds and swimming pools. Their food too was often sumptuous and exotic and was served in gold and silver dishes by a large retinue of servants. Besides the usual meat, fish and fowl they ate rare and foreign foods, such as, peacocks, cranes, songbirds, humming birds and strange sea food brought in from all parts of the empire and from the Orient. Romans enjoyed their meals and banquets as the men reclined on comfortable couches and sometimes they even set up crude air conditioners that sprinkled drops of cool water on the diners. Some homes were also provided with a vomitorium or a room where gluttonous gourmands could retire and administer an emetic or gag themselves and throw up all they had eaten and then start all over again with their favorite viands and wine.

The aristocratic privileged few held in contempt all other classes of people—small shopkeepers and traders who were considered ignobly mercenary, no better than peddlers, hucksters and hawkers who constantly lie, cheat and deceive their customers; and laborers whose work was regarded as dirty, vulgar and demeaning. The prevalence of slave labor kept wages low; free workers received about twenty to thirty cents a day but since rent, clothing and essential foods were commensurately cheap the laborers managed to subsist. Although the Romans did not have a weekly day of rest they did have numerous regular holidays besides special days to celebrate prominent victories. During the reign of Augustus there were 66 holidays every year. By the time of Marcus Aurelius there were 135 and in the fourth century almost half of the days of the year were days of rest. On these holidays the people were allowed free admission to the circus for exhibitions and spectacles—shows, wild animal hunts, chariot races, games and gladiatorial combats. Many workers of the lower middle class were hired by the army but work in industry was not steady and these people suffered from frequent periods of unemployment when the government had to take care of them. Although agriculture was looked upon as the most respectable occupation peasants or farm workers were just as indigent and wretched as the urban proletarians. The majority of the common people organized themselves into guilds or trade and occupational associations. These, however, were not unions but sort of social clubs formed to provide artisans and tradesmen with recreation, amusements, medical aid and in due time a decent burial for every member.

The Roman masses lived in drab, dirty, jerry-built apartment houses three to six storys high that often collapsed with tragic results to the inmates. They were miserable dwellings constructed of cement and brick but with wooden beams; were subject to frequent fires and many tenants were often burned to death. The streets in the slums were narrow and unpaved, filthy, noisy and malodorous and at night they were infested with robbers and thugs. Food for the lower classes consisted mostly of hot wheat cereal, dairy products, beans, onions and a few other vegetables, and occasionally a piece of pork. Impoverished masses sometimes more, sometimes less, always existed alongside the wealthy upper classes even during the most glorious age, the first and second centuries. Fortunately many of the emperors at that time were enlightened individuals possessed of a sensitive social conscience who used their power to alleviate the lot of the poor; and there were aristocrats with noblesse oblige inclined to be humane and philanthropic, besides prudent politicians who knew that a contented herd is preferable to a grumbling rabble. Hence they distributed free bread and provided entertainment and recreation.

At the bottom of the social ladder were the slaves, or persons converted by circumstances into human chattels of other persons, a universal ancient practice. During the days of the republic when the

Romans were fighting aggressive wars of conquest, they took great numbers of prisoners. As enemy soldiers they could have been killed but out of kindness of heart and because there was a demand for cheap labor the Roman army officers spared the lives of their captives. Bankrupt debtors were enslaved, pirates engaged in the lucrative practice of seizing and selling human beings, and sometimes slave dealers and slave owners aided and abetted the procreation of these living machines. The condition of slaves depended tn the master's character and on the kind of work the slave was capable of doing. Those who toiled in mines, on plantations, or rowed the galleys and labored long hours, with little food or rest, were looked upon as two-legged animals. They were whipped brutally, pitilessly, driven like herds of cattle, and sometimes chained, tortured and left to die of starvation in dirty dungeons. But in dealing with domestic servants the masters were usually humane and were especially considerate in their relations with intelligent and educated slaves who came from the cultivated eastern lands and who were employed as managers of property and of businesses, clerks, secretaries, teachers, artists, musicians, doctors and other professional men, and even as independent businessmen. Slaves were also allowed to buy their freedom and occasionally a kind master would emancipate some as a reward for their loyalty or efficiency. Numerous freedmen of various nationalities became successful and prominent Roman citizens and were absorbed in the population.

Most of the nation's food supply and most of the manufactured goods were produced by slaves and former slaves. When prisoners were plentiful, slaves were cheap and every gentleman was expected to have at least ten. Some had hundreds and even thousands while emperors usually possessed over 20,000. Around the beginning of the first century the city of Rome alone contained about 400,000 slaves, approximately one-third of the population, and sometimes they were sold for as little as one dollar a head. Among the wealthy they were needed as doorkeepers, valets, masseurs, cosmeticians litter bearers, who were sometimes preferred to horse and vehicle, and as couriers who provided private postal service. They also trained slaves to be gladiators and then rented them out.

Slaves possessed no legal rights. They were not permitted to own, inherit or bequeath property; they could not marry legally, their children were considered illegitimate and their family life was nonexistent. Slaves might be seduced by their master without legal redress. The master was allowed to beat, imprison, brand a slave with a red hot iron, or crucify him if he ran away, condemn him to fight beasts in the arena, or to kill him without cause. If a slave killed his master all the slaves possessed by the master might be put to death. When slaves became old and useless they were released from servitude and usually the government would keep them alive. There were several slave revolts but they were all ruthlessly suppressed. The greatest of the uprisings took place in 73 B.C. and was led by a brave and intelligent gladiator named Spartacus who recruited over 100,000 fighters. They held out for about three years but were finally crushed by a huge army commanded by General Crassus. Spartacus was cut to pieces and six thousand of his followers were crucified and left hanging on the crosses for months to discourage slaves who might still be obdurate.

In the first and second centuries Roman wars became defensive and not many prisoners were taken; piracy was exterminated and so the supply of slaves diminished. The scarcity of human chattels increased their value and so the owners became more concerned about the welfare of their precious possessions. Furthermore, in the first and second centuries the emperors were much more humane and enlightened, hence new and more civilized laws were enacted. The practice of killing a slave when he became useless was prohibited; others were forbidden to condemn slaves to fight in the arena, abused slaves might take sanctuary in a temple and could sometimes change masters. By the third century Ulpian, the great jurist, proclaimed that by the law of nature all men are equal.

In the early years of the republic the family was completely dominated by the father; his legal authority, his power of discipline was unlimited. He owned his wife and children as well as all the property and he could treat them, punish them or dispose of them as he pleased. Any Roman man could divorce his spouse for any reason but under no circumstances could a wife divorce her husband and if he discovered his wife or daughter committing adultery in her own home he might kill her and the paramour or accomplice. The husband on the other hand was permitted to commit adultery with impunity and his wife was not even allowed to accuse him of the act. It had been decreed that a female must always be protected and counseled by a male—father, brother, husband, son or guardian. A wife was allowed to eat with her husband though she had to sit on a stool while he reclined on a sofa, yet the Roman matrons were honored and they enjoyed a dignified position in their homes directing the work of the slaves in the household. Mutual devotion and affection between husband and wife and children were not absent. Unlike the Greeks respectable Roman women were frequently seen in public at the games, the theaters, in the streets or visiting friends. There were priestesses in the temples and women also often showed considerable interest in government and assisted their husbands in business and politics.

It was customary for parents to arrange a marriage; seldom was there courtship or sentimental attachment. Girls were not allowed to marry until they reached the age of twelve and boys had to be at least fourteen. As a result an unmarried woman above 19 was considered an old maid. Weddings featured much music, feasting and folk ceremony, including the placing of an iron ring on the bride's fourth finger of her left hand and the carrying of the young wife over the threshold. As a symbol of the marriage agreement the bride and groom would break a straw. When the Romans became wealthy and worldly, marriage began to lose its significance and among many in the upper classes the nuptial conventions were completely abandoned. Love became free and many couples began to lend and swap their mates with one another. Sexual morality declined, birth control became more prevalent and the number of offspring among the affluent decreased. Children were for the mindless proletarians who couldn't afford them, not for the prosperous and the sophisticated. The Roman poet, Juvenal, observed that rich women preferred lap dogs to children. Family discipline broke down and the women began to move toward emancipation and equality. They were granted the right to own and dispose of property, they could now eat in a reclining position like their husbands and they were given the right of divorce. Many wives took advantage of their new freedom, for almost every wealthy woman had at least one divorce and some could boast of six or seven. Opponents of feminine liberation feared that total equality would lead to female superiority and women would lose their charm and grace. Seeking equality they worked in shops and factories, studied philosophy, music, and dancing, wrote poetry and became actresses, athletes and gladiators. They fought lions and other wild beasts in the arena and some died in combat before thousands of spectators. Married and unmarried women appeared in public unchaperoned with male friends; they kissed each other and dined together while their husbands were away. Many Romans regarded marriage as a superfluous, antiquated custom and avoided it altogether, substituting concubines and prostitutes for wives.

The Roman cities were replete with the meretricious traffic in harlotry. It was such a flourishing business that they found it necessary to form a guild of brothel keepers and since the women wanted a single standard for the sexes male prostitutes were available as were homosexuals and sodomites. All prostitutes were required to register with the government and their business was regulated. The brothels were located outside the city walls and were open only at night though there was generally an ample supply of women of easy persuasion that could be procured at the temples, games or theaters. There were 32,000 strumpets registered in the city of Rome during the reign of Trajan and they all were required to pay a sales tax. Fees for prostitutes varied; the cheapest was five cents. Educated courtesans charged much more for their service as they catered to wealthy and intellectual patrons and offered them many delightful supplementary pleasures in addition to the piece de resistance. They sang, danced, played the flute or lyre, recited poetry and engaged in cultural conversation. Married women guilty of adultery would sometimes enroll as prostitutes and thereby gain immunity from punishment. Augustus tried to restore the simple, sober, moral life of the early republic. Laws were enacted curbing extravagant spending on houses, servants, banquets, weddings, jewels and dress. They reduced some of the powers of the father over his family but allowed him to retain the right to execute an adulterous daughter and her accomplice and provided permanent banishment instead of death for an adulterous wife. Married men seeking extramural sexual release were still permitted to have intimate relations with registered prostitutes, but senators were not allowed to marry actresses, harlots or freed women. Actors and freed slaves were forbidden to marry a senator's daughter. Women were usually excluded from participating in athletic exhibitions and female spectators were restricted to the upper seats at the gladiatorial games.

Even though women were being emancipated and were acquiring

equal rights they still acknowledged the ineradicable sexual differences from men and the physical attraction between the opposite sexes. They wanted to be loved and admired by men and so they endeavored to make themselves as fetching and desirable as possible. Where nature was not very kind to them in face or body contour they applied cosmetics, such as, rouge, paint, black dye for eyelashes, perfume, jewelry, diaphanous silk garments and other artifices. A popular remedy for inelegant complexion was a mixture of dough and the milk of an ass. Most Roman women were brunettes but occasionally where blondes were preferred they were obliged to buy wigs or import German slave girls. After 300 B.C. men generally shaved and had their hair cut short though there were whiskers and long hair fads. In the second century Emperor Hadrian grew a full beard to cover a few ugly facial blemishes and so as a demonstration of their loyalty and affection for their monarch Roman men began to wear beards but usually close cut hair was the rule. Both men and women wore tunics, loosely fitting sleeveless blouses that hung down to the calves and held in by a belt. A businessman's tunic had a narrow purple stripe and a senator's had a broad purple stripe. Over the tunic they wore a very long wrap around, measuring about 18 by 7 feet, made of white wool, called a toga. Footwear was made of soft leather or cloth; the women added jewels and gold trim to their shoes and senators wore red sandals.

The Romans devoted a good deal of their time to recreation and sports. Bathing and swimming were popular and as a result the Romans must have had clean bodies. Rich folks had their private baths and pools with hot, tepid or cold water and a separate room for massaging the master. Plebeians flocked daily to the great state-owned public baths—huge and luxurious, also equipped with hot, warm and cold water and also with balconies, restaurants, art galleries, libraries and club rooms. They had places to bowl, play ball games, a gymnasium, rooms for an olive oil rub-down, and halls where one might listen to music or the reading of poetry, participate in cultural discussions, play chess or just shoot dice. The morning hours were for women while the men came in the afternoon or evening, though mixed bathing in the nude was permitted frequently, and at the social and cultural gatherings both sexes mingled freely. These mammoth bath houses accommodated almost 3000 bathers and swimmers and the entrance fee was less than one cent with no charge for children.

Like the Greeks the Romans admired athletic prowess, but unlike their more cultivated predecessors, the Romans had a propensity for violence and they added blood and iron to their games and sports to make them more thrilling. The games were considered a form of religious celebration. They were opened with solemn processions and were generally attended by the priests, the vestal virgins and the emperor, the high priest, all of whom were given conspicuous seats of honor. They held the usual track meets, and jumping, wrestling, javelin and discus throwing contests; for their prize fighters the boxing gloves were too soft, so they reinforced them at the knuckles with iron, lead or brass bands, three-fourths of an inch thick so that punches would be more painful and bloody. The pugilists pummeled each other until one became covered with blood and was knocked senseless. But the people were more enthusiastic about races and gladiatorial combats. The races were sometimes a contest of jockeys on horseback but mostly they were a long run of chariots drawn by one, two, three or even four horses handled by a single driver. These chariots would usually make seven circuits around a five mile, oval shaped arena and they would continue for several hours. The stadium had enough seats to accommodate over 200,000 spectators and both on and off track betting abounded among all people who had a little money.

More savage and bloody were the combats of wild beasts and of professional human killers. All kinds of animals were made to fight one another or they were hunted in the arena, covered with rocks and bushes and killed by skilled hunters. At other times hungry lions, tigers, panthers, bears or other wild animals fought men armed with spears or daggers, and occasionally unarmed men and women condemned to death were pushed into the arena to fight frantically for their lives with the ferocious beasts. Another type of contest was a duel between two gladiators armed with short swords or knives or a battle between one group of armed fighters against another group— even with hundreds of men on each side, and they all fought to the death. There was one combat after another. The butchery continued for many hours while thousands of spectators shouted, cheered and yelled with delight as men were stabbed by opponents or as a person was gnawed and mangled by a wild beast. Hundreds of dead animals and many human bodies had to be dragged from the stage, and when the arena became soaked with blood it would be covered with sand. In the duels when one of the combatants went down the spectators or the emperor, who often attended, decided whether the loser should be spared or whether he should be given the final death blow. They would signify their preference by waving handkerchiefs or by pointing their thumbs upward. Thumbs down indicated the death wish for the victim and in this case a band of musicians played an appropriate crescendo to intensify the thrill of the kill. To further amuse the populace there was a gruesome sideshow where they crucified criminals at the colosseum and sent in hungry bears to tear the suspended victims to pieces while they were still alive. Before the bloody duels and battles began there was a ceremony when the participating gladiators would march before the crowd and then stand in front of the emperor's gold and ivory box seat and exclaim: "We who are about to die salute you." There were also intervals of relief from the sanguinary pastime when people would betake themselves to the stands that sold food, candy and drinks and listen to the bands of musicians who made melody and blared away incessantly.

Gladiators were generally criminals or slaves but there were also free citizens who loved notoriety, enjoyed danger and adventure, and had a passion for applause, who sometimes volunteered to enter the ring to face any fierce animal or any armed man and fight to the death. Commodus, the son of Marcus Aurelius, was one of these volunteers. Not all criminals were qualified to be gladiators. They were required to be convicted murderers, robbers or arsonists or they must be guilty of mutiny or sacrilege. Then they were obliged to get special training at gladiatorial schools in the use of swords, knives and daggers and they were taught how to overwhelm and kill a wild animal and how to slay a human opponent in a fight. When there was a shortage of contestants they would lower the entrance requirements and permit perpetrators of lesser crimes to enroll at the schools and learn the art of wielding deadly weapons. As a reward the victorious gladiator could become a slave, prisoners of war who had shown extraordinary skill in fighting would be freed, and slaves who had shown exceptional bravery were emancipated; and all gladiators who survived the combat were permitted to make a professional career of the sport if they so desired. Many of these successful killers earned a great deal of money and glory and like athletes and actors of today they became popular heroes, idolized by the masses. Many other cities imitated Rome and built their own stadiums and colosseums and produced their own races, circuses and savage combats but Rome of course had the most famous athletes and contests and it was there that the staging of the great shows was the most elaborate and spectacular. Some Romans were opposed to the atrocious exhibitions but most people thought they were socially salutary. The latter argued that in view of the fact that nearly all the victims were condemned convicts the vivid horrors might deter future potential criminals; also that persons with sadistic instincts would find vicarious release in viewing the bloody, truculent fighting; and some thought that the cruel sport would eventually tend to lessen the spectators' fear of death and as they became inured to human horrors and suffering they would become better conditioned for the traumas of war. On the other hand, Seneca, the stoic philosopher believed that the murderous amusements tended to barbarize cultivated onlookers.

Family instruction was the first form of education Roman children received. Parents would train them to perform domestic chores and inculcate upon them the prevailing personal and civic virtues. About the end of the third century B.C. private schools were opened to the public but only the wealthy youngsters could afford to attend them; as each pupil had to pay his teacher eight asses (48 cents) every month. The child had to be about six or seven years of age to begin his elementary education and most, though not all of the pupils were boys. They learned to read, write and reckon. They also were taught to sing, to declaim and to recite and memorize the laws of the Twelve Tables and to always display a proper frame of mind and to behave in accordance with the conventional rules and regulations of the school. Patriotism and morals were fundamental; flogging for misconduct was frequently resorted to. Arithmetic was the most difficult subject because of the cumbersome Roman numerals, the letters of the Latin alphabet, and because they had no sign for zero. The practice of finger counting was most popular in figuring out simple bills and accounts but when computing large sums involving thousands they would point to or touch various parts of the body. They also used a counting board or abacus and each pupil had to bring his own bag of reckoning stones.

For the very wealthy children aged 12 to 16 there were secondary or high schools where they studied grammar, the Greek language, Latin and Greek literature, music, mythology, history, astronomy and philosophy. There were also finishing schools where young men and women were taught to sing, to play the lyre, and to always move about in a graceful and flexible manner. For girls there were additional music and dancing classes. In the secondary schools the teachers were generally Greeks, either slaves or freedmen, and they emphasized Hellenic history and literature and stressed the importance of creative composition, of using correct words in speech and writing. The Romans also had their colleges where they featured rhetoric, oratory, physical science and philosophy, legal training, and how to be eloquent and articulate, and the science of speaking well. Many students traveled to Greek universities for graduate studies particularly to Athens, Rhodes and Alexandria. In the second century the enlightened emperors established a great university at Rome known as the Atheneum where they offered advanced courses in philosophy, law, medicine, mathematics, architecture and mechanics.

The Romans excelled in war, in governing huge empires, in engineering, in the building of roads and in the formulation of a highly civilized code of laws, but the Greeks far surpassed them in literature, the fine arts, in pure science, in philosophy and in abstract thought. However, Roman aesthetic and intellectual attainments, although derived from the Greeks, were highly significant and noteworthy. The greatest Roman authors lived in the last period of the republic and in the early years of the empire, which was known as the Golden Age of Roman literature. Most of the early writers were from the Greek districts of southern Italy and Sicily.

It was in the third century B.C. in the Greek territory of the Italian peninsula that cultural contacts commenced between writers of the two kindred peoples. Andronicus a Greek slave translated part of the *Odyssey* into Latin. Shortly afterwards a Roman named Naevius wrote a satirical, political comedy which landed him in jail, though he was later forgiven; and he then composed a patriotic epic poem about the first Punic War, using the style of Homer. In the same century Ennius, who was half Greek, wrote numerous tragedies and comedies in the manner of Greek dramatists and then published an epic about the second Punic War, modeling it after Homer's *Iliad*. Plautus and

Terence composed comedies that resembled the Hellenistic plays of current manners and customs. The works of Plautus were vivacious, lusty comedies with hackneyed plots about seduction, illicit love and other banal affairs, abounding in puns, broad banter and boisterous raillery—productions that were very popular with the common people. Terence, a Carthaginian, also wrote comedies about every day life but he was more restrained and polished in his style; his wit was more subtle and he had more skill in delineating character. His audiences were more sophisticated and aristocratic.

The Romans were not ardent playgoers like the Greeks. They could take the comedies which teemed with mirth and ribaldry but the serious tragic dramas were for Greeks and intellectuals only, and even many educated Romans preferred to read the tragedies rather than see them enacted. The general public considered serious drama dull and tedious, preferring the spectacles of the arena, the circus, trained animals performing tricks, acrobats, rope dancers, mimes or farce comedies and strip-teasing burlesque shows. Mimicking which was exceedingly popular was at times carried too far, especially in the ridiculing of prominent persons, and actors were sometimes put to death for it. Caligula once had a comedian burned alive in the crowded amphitheater for making a disparaging pun about the eccentric emperor.

The Roman theater was built by the government and was an open air semicircular structure made of wood. Stone theaters first appeared in 52 B.C. Admission was free but the crowds compared to those at the arenas, were relatively small; women and slaves were allowed to attend but the women sat in the rear rows and the slaves were forced to stand. Most of the actors were Greek slaves who also took many of the female parts. Roman citizens who became actors had to forfeit their civic rights and females who chose the stage for their career were classed as prostitutes. At first the actors used paint and wigs but later they substituted masks for their make-up. The Romans believed that acting debased one's character, that the profession required the actors to always pretend to be what they were not and constant feigning makes a person morally inferior—one loses his candor and becomes unstable; it weakens his personality. Audiences were often very noisy and it was necessary for the management to warn the people that they must be quiet and polite during the performance, that unruly customers might be summarily ejected. Mothers, unless they were pregnant, were urged to leave their babies at home and all women were admonished to keep their habitual chatting to a minimum. Whenever the audience failed to laugh at and applaud a comedian's humor or if they exhibited no reaction to an actor's platitudinous remark they would repeat the joke or the cliché. Some members of the audience finding the play devoid of interest would hurriedly repair to a prize fight, a burlesque show or the circus. Finally, it was customary for an official of the theater to inform the audience when the play was ended, and then to declare that applause was appropriate and decorous.

Among the early important prose writers in the second century B.C. was Polybius, a Greek hostage, who was the first great historian of Rome. An admirer of the republican constitution, his work was accurate and profound, a scientific analysis of Roman history. He hoped the book would have a healthful influence on politicians and aspiring statesmen. In the first century B.C. Sallust, imbued with the works of Thucydides, wrote splendid scientific history. Democratically inclined with a penchant for philosophical comment, he became famous for his trenchant epigrams and keen biographical analyses. Julius Caesar, a contemporary of Sallust, wrote a creditable account of the conquest of Gaul and of the civil wars including the part he played in the conflicts. His prose is terse, plain, forceful and effective, that is, it contributed greatly to his popularity. Cicero, in contrast to the great soldier-statesman, was dedicated to the study of Hellenic thought and the art and science of prose and oratory. He became a famous author of letters, orations and treatises on ethics, government and philosophy. An extremely influential author, Cicero had an ornamental and highly polished style of writing. He was a supreme artist in the use of words, a complete master of the Latin language, and his writings abound in bits of wisdom.

The Golden Age of Literature produced many great poets. In the last century before the Christian era Lucretius combined his knowledge of science, philosophy and verse to create a remarkable, didactic poem, *On the Nature of Things*. Using artistic language in magnificent manner he expounds the atomic theory, the biological doctrine of survival of the fittest and the tenets of epicureanism, deriding superstition and the fear of death. He also wrote beautiful descriptions of animate and inanimate beings and depicted superb scenes of nature.

Catullus wrote graceful lyrics of passion and personal feeling, with occasional bits of wit and obscenity. He was also the author of many epigrams but he is best known for his amorous and satiric poetry.

The reign of Augustus produced three great poets—Vergil, Horace and Ovid and one eminent historian—Livy. Vergil was the poet laureate in the court of Augustus and was liberally patronized by the emperor and the minister for cultural affairs. With a strong penchant for agriculture Vergil wrote many delightful poems about cows, horses, bees and other charming creatures. He portrayed the fascinating features of rural society hoping thereby to arouse a return to nature, to dignify farm labor, revive the ancient virtues, and to stimulate public nostalgia for Roman rustic life. Vergil's masterpiece, however, was the *Aeneid*, an epic poem that recounts the legend of the founding of Rome. This romantic and sublime work glorifies Roman imperialism, it is full of patriotic fervor and is very sincere, moral and lofty in tone and style. Horace, the son of a freed slave, was another great poet of the Golden Age. His literary talent was also recognized by Augustus and he too became a poet laureate and was sponsored and handsomely rewarded by the government. His poems were light and graceful but sometimes contained deep and melancholy descriptions of daily life and pieces about current manners. He wrote odes, didactic epistles and was one of the first authors of satires in verse. Imbued with Greek philosophy, he was a favorite among the sophisticates who enjoyed his wit, urbanity and his ironic comments and shrewd observations on life. In accordance with the prevailing policy of the emperor, Horace fervently extolled the old Roman virtues of simplicity, courage, firmness and reverence. Ovid, the third of the three great Augustan poets, was not as friendly with the emperor as the other two because his works were often morally frivolous. He had written an immensely popular collection of poems, called *The Art of Love*, a witty and salacious handbook on the art of adultery containing detailed advice on the effectual technique of sexual seduction. Unfortunately for Ovid the current policy of the government was restoration of pristine moral discipline with the purity and sanctity of traditional family life. Furthermore, Augustus was very much concerned and embarrassed about the lascivious conduct of his granddaughter, Julia, who was attaining notoriety because of her immoderate, promiscuous sexual intimacies. Suspecting correlation between his granddaughter and Ovid's sex manual the emperor banished the poet from Rome for writing harmful pornography and exiled Julia for being a too avid illustrator of the amatorial arts. Ovid's most important poem was *Metamorphoses*, the chief source of knowledge of classical mythology, containing the fascinating Greek tales transmitted to the modern world. Ovid wrote frivolous short stories in crisp verse with great facility and with a predilection for the erotic. Another superb literary artist of the Golden Age was the pious and patriotic historian, Livy. His *History of Rome* covers the period from its rise to the attainment of world supremacy. The work is dramatic and picturesque and was evidently intended to prove that the Roman people were honorable in action and character and that the republican form of government is the best that mankind had devised. Livy has nothing but praise and glorification for the Roman traditions—religion, family life, patrician virtues and qualities. Elegant and artistic, the book is a literary masterpiece, but it is neither scientific nor philosophical.

The Silver Age of Roman writers, the first and early second century, was not the most brilliant literary era but it did produce a number of authors of considerable merit. Of these the most talented were writers of prose, particularly history and biography. The well known Tacitus wrote a history of Rome from the year 14 to the year 96 depicting a depressive picture of political chaos and social corruption; and by way of contrast he eulogizes the primitive Germans—their simplicity, honesty and sexual purity. Tacitus discourses impetuously on the evils and delinquencies of the emperors and the immorality and sumptuous living of the rich, he deplores the profusion of uncouth alien residents in Rome, and he yearns for the traditional patrician virtues, for the euphoria of the past. He manifests a greater interest in morals than in politics and asserts that the greatness of a nation is determined not by the laws of the government but by the quality and character of its leaders. Tacitus wrote felicitous, dignified prose with occasional wit, sarcasm and aphorismic allusions. Another historian was the Jewish Roman, Josephus. He very proudly boasted of Hebrew achievements but advised his people to be realistic, to surrender and become a province of the invincible Roman conquerors. Even though he finally joined the enemy he remained a Jewish chauvinist and rejoiced immensely when he learned that the leading anti-Semite in the empire was compelled to be circumcized by the appearance of a godsent, significantly located ulcer. Plutarch, a Greek biographer in his charming *Parallel Lives*, compares the leading heroes of Greece and Rome. Utilizing all pertinent details available, he composed vivid verbal portraits and an excellent account of the careers and character of the most eminent Greek and Roman personalities. It is a fascinating book interspersed with delightful anecdotes, lively episodes and wise comments on morality, virtue and heroism. Suetonius, a popular Roman biographer, wrote the lives of Julius Caesar and the emperors from Augustus to Domitian. His style was sensational and risque and his writings abound in anecdotes, gossip and scandal.

Other eminent authors of the Silver Age were Pliny the Elder, famous for his voluminous erudition, who compiled a scholarly work of his scientific knowledge, his renowned *Natural History*. A nephew, Pliny the Younger, steeped in the classics, was the author of graceful, elegant letters, full of information about private and public events, such as the vivid story of the eruption of Vesuvius and the covered towns of Herculaneum and Pompeii. Quintilian was the most outstanding authority on rhetoric; Martial, a Spaniard, was a caustic and witty composer of epigrams in poetry; and Lucian who was a Syrian critic and humorist, ridiculed all the famous Greek heroes and traditions. A realistic novel without a plot was the creation of Petronius, who narrates numerous vivid episodes dealing with life in the underworld. Among the persons Petronius cynically caricatures are vagabonds, parvenus, philosophers and prostitutes. Apuleius also wrote satirical novels mocking mankind, but he had a penchant for fantasy and for mystic, pseudo-philosophical tales, both credible and incredible. One of the superior poetic satirists was Juvenal who deplored the vices and follies, the sexual excesses and perversions, the moral degeneracy of Rome. He disliked dandies, their manners, perfumes and desires which tended to make them unmanly and feminine. He was not opposed to the liberation of the women but he hoped their emancipation would not change their basic enchantment and convert them into men. Juvenal also inveighed against the excessive influx of foreigners into Rome with their strange customs, attire, smells and gods. He regarded Greeks as culturally brilliant but found them often to be greedy and dishonest, and he thought Jews were inclined to be overly clannish.

The early Romans looked upon all the arts as unmanly, degenerate and disgraceful. Cicero thought dancing was for drunkards and lunatics and for a while the teaching of both music and dancing was forbidden in the schools. However, the attitude toward the arts changed as the Romans became rich and after their contacts with the Etruscans and the Greeks. Very early in their history the Romans were familiar with choral singing and a few musical instruments which they found in Etruria. They favored the flute and the lyre and along with those two instruments choral singing became popular at religious ceremonies and at weddings. Funeral processions were always accompanied by song, a hired band of wailing women and a group of mournful flute players. In 115 B.C. a law was passed ordering musicians to use only short Italian flutes. The lyre increased in popularity when the Romans began to write verse, the lyric poem always preceding the musical composition as among the Greeks. The singing was secondary to the words of the poetry and the lyre accompanied the singing or the reading. Now finishing schools began to teach boys and girls how to play the lyre, and talented slaves from various lands introduced the playing of horns, trumpets, clarions, cymbals, tubas, bag pipes, organs and other instruments. They even had musical contests, concerts and orchestras. As pantomimes became popular dancing too was regarded with more favor and wealthy families would sometimes hire dancing masters and build their own dancing platforms. The Romans soon learned to love good music, although occasionally an uncouth, obstreperous audience might become bored and change the orchestra's performance into a boxing match.

The Romans learned about art from the people they conquered, particularly, the Etruscans and the Greeks. The Etruscans ardently believed in a future life and exhibited a profound reverence for their ancestors and so the Roman artists imitated them by also showing great respect for the dead by making beautiful cinerary urns, sculptured coffins and realistic busts of their ancestors. In the beginning they worked with clay and sometimes with bronze but later they used stone. Roman artists improved with experience and before long excelled in portrait sculpture concentrating on secular themes, such as, emperors and national heroes. They produced not only busts but full statues, even equestrian portraits, they made columns, which they borrowed from the Greeks, and then they became expert in creating triumphal arches with their realistic narrative bas reliefs containing details about the victories of their armies. In technique the Roman reliefs were superior to the Greek because Roman sculptors carved more in depth and thereby produced a more naturalistic effect. However, with the advent of the empire their sculpture became more ornate and ostentatious as the Romans became more proud and boastful of their nation's military achievements and exulted over their opulence.

When the Romans conquered Greece and the Hellenistic world their armies plundered and brought home ship loads of artistic works—marble and bronze statues, reliefs, marble columns and many paintings too. The artistic taste of the victors was modified and they were induced to embellish their palaces, mansions and villas with the numerous pillaged art pieces. When the supply was exhausted of originals, copies were made or Greek artists were employed to create new ones. Paintings found in Pompeii evince Hellenistic influence though Roman artists excelled in creating the illusion of perspective. There were many murals, panel painting and some portraits and almost all were inclined to be realistic or naturalistic in style. They frequently and effectively used color combinations, such as, elegant greens and tans, striking red and black, as well as delicate light and shadow, creamy white and patches of light and color. Roman painters were very fond of bucolic scenes and had a tendency to introduce as ornamental background, birds, cupids and other real and fanciful figures. Secular painting was most prevalent among the Romans but there were also pictures of religious figures and one artist became widely known for employing prostitutes to pose as his goddesses. In the minor arts the Romans displayed their technical excellence in the making of vases, table ware, furniture, in the designing of jewelry, the cutting of gems and the production of objects made of precious metals.

The most significant Roman legacy in the field of art was their achievement in architecture. Here also the Romans learned from their neighbors whom they conquered and imitated, as all nations do more or less. The Etruscans, who probably originated in the Near East, were familiar with the principle of the arch, the vault and the dome and used stone and brick as their building material. The Greek influence was evident in the columns, Doric, Ionic and especially the ornate Corinthian, which the Romans preferred. Roman architects and engineers went far beyond the Etruscans and others in solving the problem of spanning a great area by means of cylindrical vaulting and of enclosing and roofing a vast space with a hemispheric dome. In the second century B.C. the Romans introduced the use of powerful cement—a concrete mixed with volcanic earth, lava, lime, small stones and broken brick, all covered with an outer layer of marble in many colors. The Romans built great monuments, triumphal arches, temples, theaters, amphitheaters, columns, basilicas, libraries, courthouses, public baths and aqueducts and bridges. Temples and theaters were inspired by Greek models but the arena, such as, the remarkable Colosseum that could seat about 65,000 spectators, was an original Roman structure and the ancestor of the modern football stadium. The magnificent Pantheon, a temple built to honor the divine ancestors of Augustus and then dedicated to all the gods, was far larger than the Greek temples. The Romans liked their buildings large and spacious, solidly constructed of massive proportions, they wanted to express power and grandeur, the glory of the empire. Roman architecture was primarily utilitarian and secular in motivation, though ornamentation was often excessive for they loved lavish display. Nevertheless harmony and grace were not lacking in many of their public buildings and in their private mansions. Roman aesthetic accomplishments were meager but their excellence and genius in architecture and engineering were far superior to all their predecessors and, until recent times, to all their successors. The main Roman legacy in the area of art was architecture rather than sculpture and painting.

When the Romans were taking over the Hellenistic world Greek scholars were at work in various fields of science and were making considerable progress. But the Romans did not take advantage of their Hellenistic inheritance and did not elaborate on their findings or create new ideas. Instead of developing or adding to the numerous Greek discoveries they absorbed them, made use of the knowledge acquired, taught it in the Roman schools and then diffused it over the world they conquered. Sensitive and intelligent Romans were aware of the beauty and the wonders of nature but they lacked intellectual curiosity about pure science and failed to conceive of a universe governed by complex scientific laws, principles and processes. However, they were gifted in the practical application of science to the mundane problems and affairs. Their extraordinary ability in engineering and technology is evidenced by their remarkable aqueducts, excellent roads, magnificent public buildings, and an extensive system of sewers and drainage. They installed latrines and sometimes made them of marble. Expert city planners, the Romans provided all sorts of amenities including an abundant supply of water, hot and cold and maintained the highest sanitary standards that Europe knew before the nineteenth century. Vetruvius, who was Rome's greatest authority on the physical and technical aspects of architecture, analyzed the principle of acoustics and advised plumbers never to use lead pipes for drinking water because the water will become poisonous. Others recommended the boiling of suspicious water before drinking it. Vetruvius introduced new building materials, pigments and a natural cement made with lime and rubble that would set under water. Mary the Jewess, a chemist, invented a double boiler, a percolator, copper tubing, and a distilling apparatus. The Romans established medical schools, hospitals, military and civilian, public and private infirmaries for poorer patients, free state hospitals for the very poor; and every city had public doctors to take care of the welfare patients. In Nero's palace the engineers constructed a bronze hydraulic engine, a mechanical pipe organ, an elevator 160 feet high and a circular dining room that would revolve like an astronomical dome. The Romans were also preeminent in the area of agriculture—farming, gardening and horticulture.

Some new miscellaneous scientific knowledge was introduced in Rome. Julius Caesar during his many amatory sojourns in Cleopatra's Alexandria became fond also of the Egyptian solar calendar and he decided that the Romans ought to use it instead of their old one. The traditional lunar calendar which contained 355 days was replaced by the Egyptian Julian calendar of 365 days and the year would start in January instead of March. Water clocks and sun dials were still being used to tell time and when Augustus became ruler he brought the great obelisk from Egypt and set it up on the Field of Mars. It became the town clock in Rome as the shadow it cast fell on the pavement which was marked off in brass and indicated the hour and the season. The Hellenistic Greek geographer and geologist, Strabo, a contemporary of Augustus, believed and taught that islands and even continents have sunk and risen, that mountains are the result of volcanic eruptions, that these outbursts are safety valves for pent-up vapors. He observed land being corroded by water forming alluvial deposits and wrote on methods of mining salt at salt springs. Strabo also made a study of plagues and believed that they were transmitted by fleas of rats. The Roman Seneca taught that earthquakes were generally caused by the expansion of gases accumulating within the earth and sometimes by the collapse of subterranean cavities. He also wrote about solid rocks ultimately dissolving, and how streams deposit the residue in the form of deltas. Seneca thought that originally the world was a watery chaos. Most people believed in the pseudo-science of astrology, that is, that man's destiny was determined by the star under which he was born and one's fate and character were the result of celestial conditions.

The Romans had an aptitude for writing compilations of knowledge, general treatises on a variety of subjects. The most famous encyclopedia was Pliny the Elder's *Natural History* which appeared in the year 77 and which is supposed to contain all the scientifii information known in classical antiquity. An amateur scientist with extraordinary curiosity, Pliny gave the reader a general description of almost everything that was known to exist but he included fables and fanciful notions as well as fact and truth. His thirty-seven volumes of information were a popular reference for scholars for over a thousand years. Pliny believed that Nature or the sum of natural forces is God but he doesn't concern himself with mundane affairs.

Following are some examples of Pliny's so-called scientific disclosures, putative facts and curious beliefs. The earth is round since the masts of ships are seen before their hulls. Islands have risen from the Mediterranean Sea. There is some kind of stone that burns (coal) and fireproof articles can be made with asbestos. Sometimes it rains milk and even blood. The sex of animals can be predetermined. For example, among quadrupeds during copulation if the potential mother faces the north a female offspring is inevitable. In Portugal mares could be made pregnant by the west wind. There are some drugs and foods that arouse sexual desire. If a woman sneezes after coitus she will most likely have an immediate miscarriage. Pliny writes of men and women changing their sexes. A man fasting can kill a snake by spitting into its mouth. The learned author also describes some strange kind of human—a savage race of people whose feet all turned backwards, a tribe in India who have heads like dogs, a race in Albania whose hair is white from birth, and another group of humans whose females conceive in their fifth year and die at the age of eight, a tribe of people who have no neck but have eyes in their shoulders. Pliny narrates extraordinary events, feats and stories about a Greek woman who gave birth to quintuplets four successive times; a man who supported a whole wagonload of wine on his back until the casks were emptied; another strong man who would pick up his mule and carry him to work; a famous gladiator who fought 120 battles and was wounded forty-five times in the front of his body but never in his back; one man had such acute eyesight that he copied the entire story of Homer's *Iliad* on a piece of parchment so small that it could be enclosed in a nutshell; another man had such acuity of vision that he could distinguish objects at a distance of 135 miles. The great Pliny met his death in the eruption of Vesuvius in the year 79. His scientific curiosity led him to approach too near to the volcano and he perished. There were other so-called compilers of scientific knowledge, some of whom specialized in zoology and medicine. One of them moralized on the habits of animals and compared them with humans. He commented on the chastity of doves and declared that they never divorce each other, contrasting to people and to partridges who were notorious for their sexual incontinence. Another amateur scientist told the story of how Alexander the Great's mother tried desperately to have sexual intercourse with a dragon in order that her son would have a father who was more noble and formidable than King Philip.

Before the influence of the Greeks the science of medicine was nonexistent in Rome, since religion and magic were relied on for the cure of all ailments. The first secular doctors in Rome were Greek slaves who were employed to treat wounded gladiators and even after some of the medical practitioners became eminently successful the people still distrusted them. They accused Greek physicians of learning through trial and error of experimenting and killing suffering Romans; they suspected the alien doctors of seducing female patients, of poisoning invalids with their strange medicines and charged the Greek medical practitioners with being mercenary—getting rich at the expense of the Romans. Nevertheless surgeons were regularly attached to the Roman legions and without the aid of a doctor, Julius Caesar would never have been born, for midwives were only familiar with normal nonsurgical delivery of babies. Thus the Caesarian operation was innovated and became prevalent around the middle of the first century B.C. Caesar demonstrated his gratitude and respect for scientific medicine by conferring citizenship on all physicians practicing in Rome. Asclepiades, who studied medicine in Alexandria and Athens, achieved phenomenal success, curing many Romans by employing simple Hippocratic remedies. He believed the heart pumps blood and air through the body and his favorite treatment and cures included baths, warm applications, massaging, sunshine, exercise, diet, fasting and abstinence from meat. Celsus, who lived in the first century of the Christian era, was a leading Roman doctor and author who compiled all that was known about Hellenistic medicine and prepared a manual for surgeons. His treatises on anatomy and surgery are considered quite competent. He discusses heart disease, appendicitis, and dentistry and describes such operations as removing tonsils, goiters, cataracts and stones from the urinary and gall bladder. In his chapter on plastic surgery he mentions physicians performing reparative work for Jews who desired to have their prepuce restored in order to become eligible for public office, because Roman law did not permit circumcized persons to work for the government.

In the second century the most talented and most influential physician was the renowned Greek doctor, Galen, whose work was highly respected for hundreds of years. He also wrote an authoritative medical encyclopedia which was widely used. Galen bemoaned the fact that anyone who intended to study osteology had to go to Africa, that is, Alexandria, for in Rome there was a superstitious custom that human skeletons must never be exhibited and for a scientist to examine a murdered corpse was considered horrible and sinful. Yet the Romans were then egregiously bloodthirsty as on every holiday hundreds of thousands of persons would gather at their stadiums to cheer on the bloody butchering of countless gladiators in the savage sporting events. Eventually dissection of dying gladiators was allowed. Galen was well educated in both anatomy and physiology and made more contributions to those fields than any other ancient doctor. In discussing anatomy and birth he made the statement that human beings are born between urine and feces. As a physiologist he was the first to observe that the arteries contain and carry blood. An epidemic drove Galen out of Rome but he returned later when invited by the emperor, Marcus Aurelius, to become the imperial family physician and especially to take care of his sick son, Commodus. The latter young man would become one of the most hideous and most infamous of the Roman rulers. Galen stayed on and had three emperors as his patients.

After a while doctors began to specialize and we read of urologists, gynecologists, obstetricians, authorities on the eye and the ear and of dentists. There were also different kinds of surgeons; they devised ingenius forceps, tweezers, and other instruments and they generally used mandragora juice or atropin as an anesthetic. They were familiar with malignant tumors and operated on cancer of the breast. There were also a few female physicians and a very unconventional or unique pediatrician, who if an infant had diarrhea, gave astringents to the nurse instead of the baby and if it suffered from constipation the nurse had to take the laxatives.

Roman therapeutics was still mixed with traditional superstition, quackery abounded and even Galen employed some astrology and a little magic on his patients—perhaps as a form of psychotherapy. A doctor Cato offered two remedies for dislocated joints—one relied on repeating a weird formula and the other advised eating cabbage, which was Cato's panacea for indigestion, ulcers, dysentery, drunkenness and warts. Other doctors recommended wax of the ear, hair, blood and excretions of human beings and woman's milk as remedies against poisons, baldness, toothache, tonsilitis, stomach and liver complaints, tapeworm, asthma, dropsy, ulcers, broken bones, foul breath, and sundry pains in the neck. A prevalent purgative was offal of lizards and a cure for angina was the excreta of dogs. Galen applied a boy's dung to swellings of the throat and another healer claimed he could cure any ailment with wine. One dentist always advised his patients to eat mouse meat for severe toothache. Galen believed in the humoral theory of Hippocrates, made much use of diet, exercise and massage; yet he recommended dried cicadas for colic, goat dung for tumors, and he introduced snake flesh as an efficacious ingredient in many of his medical concoctions. Coitus was also recommended by doctors as a cure for physical weariness, for pains in the loins, for hoarseness, dim eyesight, melancholy and alienation of the mental faculties. Some types of fever were also considered curable by sexual intercourse, provided the woman was just beginning her monthly period. A menstruating woman, according to Pliny's great encyclopedia, was possessed of miraculous power. By just looking at a swarm of bees they will all die immediately, grape juice will turn sour if she approached it, fruit will fall from a tree if she sits under it, and seeds touched by her become sterile. Sharp steel will become blunt, a mirror will lose its brightness, and ivory will lose its polish if these objects cross the vision of a woman undergoing menstruation. During this period a woman can scare away all tempestuous weather—lightning, hailstorms, and whirlwinds, provided she uncovers her body. If when menstruating she strips herself naked and walks through a field of wheat all insects will be killed. However, if she does this at sunrise the entire crop will wither and dry up. Sometimes these miracles would occur if the woman only removed all garments worn below the waist and walked through the wheatfield.

For hundreds of years there was no philosophy among the Romans because these people were so active and practical minded that they had neither time nor interest in speculation, metaphysics and abstruse thinking. But by the end of the second century B.C. Greek philosophical ideas began to filter into the land and gradually were being accepted by the educated classes. New questions about life had begun to appear and the old Roman religion was becoming sterile among many of the thinking people. Abstract thought still did not concern them much but they were interested in new codes of ethics and pragmatic rules of social relationship. They therefore passed over most of Plato and Aristotle and selected as their favorite philosophers the ones who wrote on morality and conduct. Conservatives were alarmed; they suspected that Greek philosophy would corrupt the minds of the young and so they began to drive the subversive alien teachers out of the city. The conservative Cato, who delighted in the annihilation of Carthage, wanted to displace Greek textbooks with Latin; he was afraid the Greeks would ruin Roman religion and demoralize the virtuous people. As censor, he once expelled a senator for kissing his spouse in public declaring that he never embraced his wife except when it thundered, though he confessed that he had a passion for thunder. However, many intellectuals steadfastly persisted and soon educated businessmen and aristocrats began to show a propensity for Epicureanism and by the middle of the first century B.C. the three great poets Lucretius, Virgil and Horace espoused the popular philosophy. The principal Roman disciple of Epicurus was Lucretius, whose erudite masterpiece *On the Nature of Things*, had become an indispensable book among the literati. The brilliant Latin poet, learned in science and philosophy, had concluded that happiness is what we all seek; happiness is synonymous with pleasure and pleasure is acquired through mental tranquillity or intellectual contentment. The main obstacle to one's peace of mind is fear—the superstitious fear of the gods and the fear of death. Lucretius believed that actually the gods have nothing to do with fate or the acts of human beings, and as for death, it is like an endless sleep. He also taught that every thing—tangible and intangible, animate and inanimate, are random combinations of atoms, and at death both body and soul disintegrate into their constituent particles—the atoms just separate and scatter. Atoms may come together again to form new objects and living things, but we don't know when, where and how. Many Romans mistook Epicureanism for hedonism distorting the teachings of Lucretius who rejected sensual, ephemeral pleasures as futile and declared that mental and spiritual pleasures are the ones that endure and are more gratifying. The Epicurean poet Horace wrote that one might eat, drink, and be merry but he must always remember that temperance is an essential element of happiness.

More suitable to the Roman leaders of thought and more in harmony with the traditional virtues of early Rome was Stoicism, the philosophy of Zeno, the Phoenician Greek of the fourth and third centuries B.C. Stoicism influenced many of the educated Romans—particularly the lawyers, eminent politicians, and rulers of the Empire. The Stoics believed in peace and serenity of mind attained through resignation and self-sufficiency. They urged people to avoid pain and fear and to seek intellectual pleasure but to recognize the inevitability of fate—good or bad. It is everyone's duty to be indifferent to the externals of life and death, prosperity and poverty, health and disease; for the universe was planned and a man's fate is not the result of chance as the Epicureans maintained. Life functions according to universal law, the law of Providence, Divine Reason or God. Fate and God's will are the same. Man's duty is to be virtuous, to shun luxury, to accept things without complaint, to suppress his feelings, to ignore difficulties and disappointments. Stoicism appealed strongly to the aristocrats and the wealthy, to the advocates of law and order, the proponents of social discipline, but the poor commoners could find neither comfort nor solace in the Stoic emphasis on self-control, duty and the suppression of all feeling. Some of the Stoics were idealistic and hopeful, speaking of a god, the father, who was the world soul and that all men are brothers and equal. These teachings may have helped to free some slaves and mitigated the lives of others, but they never promised a better life for all the poor and oppressed either here or in a heaven. The Stoic god was impersonal, devoid of kindness, sentiment, warmth, color or emotion. The social discipline of the Stoics meant to the masses—harden yourself, learn to endure life while you can for tomorrow you may still be alive to suffer.

The three outstanding Stoics in Rome were Seneca, Epictetus and Marcus Aurelius. Seneca lived in the first century, served as a teacher and then for a time as a prime minister to the notorious Emperor Nero. In his many writings he advised people to associate with those who excel in wisdom and virtue and once remarked that men are often brutalized by power, so clearly exemplified by his former employer. Although his private morality was not always perfect he had a high concept of ethical values and exhorted honesty, justice, forbearance, and kindliness. The goal of man should be happiness rather than pleasure, though pleasure is not bad if it is consistent with virtue. He accepted Stoic fatalism but he also yearned for a benevolent God and dwelt repeatedly on conscience, duty, righteousness and frequent self-examination. As for a future life, Seneca believed that the day a person dies is the birthday of his eternity—a prelude to a longer and better life. Epictetus also lived in the first century and was a former Greek slave. He too advised people to always accept misfortune with equanimity—pain, poverty, slavery, bereavement, humiliation, imprisonment or death. But he denounced slavery, condemned capital punishment and wanted to treat criminals as sick men. One must examine his conscience every day, one must learn to bear and forbear. Some of his moral precepts were: Don't make others suffer what you would shun to suffer. If you hear that someone has spoken ill of you don't waste time defending yourself but say you have other faults that the accuser failed to mention. Epictetus urged men to return good for evil and submit to any verbal abuse with calm detachment. As for death, it may be complete extinction or it may be the beginning of something else, only God knows. Marcus Aurelius was one of the good emperors of the second century and the last of the great Stoic sages. He was a singular rarity in history—a real philosopher king, a meditative student of thought as well as a statesman. Unlike most of the Stoics he was an agnostic—that is, he believed that certainty or absolute truth cannot be attained. Nature is responsible for everything that happens and nature is never evil. The learned emperor urged people to be just and kind and benevolent—be willing to forgive—to love thy neighbor, for man was created to be of service to others, to promote the general welfare. We should resign ourselves to the fact that men come and go—that after death we may be happy in a state of transmutation or we become nonexistent; we return to the universal soul whence we came or we become extinct. Cicero, the great orator and prose writer, was inclined to be philosophical and hortatory. His philosophy was borrowed from the various Greek masters of thought and so he called himself an eclectic. However, he frequently manifests a preference for the Stoics because of their belief in a divine providence, their advocacy of calm detachment, rigid morality, asceticism and duty. Yet he admired the practical advice of all the great Greek philosophers. The eclectic could be both stoic and epicurean and say: I repress my sensibilities so that life will hurt me as little as possible or I can cultivate my sensibilities so as to enjoy life as much as possible. The Romans were inclined to be pragmatic.

CHAPTER VIII

(Part 4)

Religious Faith Replaces Decadent Imperial Power

In early times the Romans, like all primitive peoples, believed that there existed an impersonal supernatural force, a kind of world spirit that animated the universe. Later they believed that in addition to this universal power there are specific spirits who dwell in every natural object and are in charge of specialized human interests and activities. Since everything happens by the will of these deities it was prudent to propitiate them. The center and source of the early Roman religion was the family and so they directed their prayers and libations first to the gods of the household, whose little images were appropriately displayed in the home. The father was the first family priest and originally he performed the rites and ceremonies, consisting of prayers and offerings of food, milk and wine; and occasionally an animal was sacrificed and there were special rites in veneration of the family ancestors. The Lares were the divine guardians of the entire house; Janus was the spirit of the doorway and opened the door only to benign beings. These deities guarded the family from the evil spirits who might seek to bring misfortune into the house. The spirits of Penates kept watch over and preserved the food and other supplies placed in the cupboard, the storeroom, and the barn. The goddess Vesta was the spirit of the hearth where a fire was lighted, a flame never to be extinguished. The family meal was a religious ceremony as the images of Lares and Penates were placed on the table, a little food was cast into the eternal flame of Vesta, the fire goddess and a portion of wine was poured out as an offering to the divine spirits. The worshipers sought protection from the malevolent spirits and ghosts and asked for good health and prosperity, fertility for their farm land and fecundity for their animals. As official communicant the father priest spoke thus to the gods: We are generous to you, we give you cake and wine won't you please be kind and benevolent to us and our household.

There were special rites and ceremonies at important crises, such as birth, marriage and death in the family. When a child was born they prayed for its safety, for its protection from evil spirits and during the second week the infant was purified and adopted into the family. Many deities participated in the rearing of the child—they helped to bring him up, to train him. The goddess Cuba watched over the baby's sleep, others taught him to walk and to talk. The reception of a bride by her husband involved many ceremonial rites, as for example, entering the magic doorway. When one died it was important to remember that the person must be carried out of the door of the house feet forward so that his ghost could not find its way back. They must appease the departed or the ghost would wander about with evil designs. The Romans also had their public worship and religious festivals which were connected with the seasons of the year. In April and May the festivals were concerned with germination, the growth of the seed that had been planted and they must bless the flocks and the herds. The summer celebration was for the purpose of assuring success in the gathering and storing of the grain and to express their gratitude for the harvest. In the autumn and early winter they prepared the ground and sowed the seed for the next crop and so there were pertinent prayers and festivities. The Roman calendar contained about forty-five farm and field festivals and over a hundred holy days.

Most festivals were joyous celebrations but the feast of the dead souls inspired terror as they commemorated and propitiated the fearsome dead. The father would spit black beans from his mouth and then would give utterance to the following supplication: "Shades of my ancestors, depart; with these beans I redeem myself and mine." Very significant too were the many happy religious holidays that recurred at regular intervals and usually provided occasion for fun and revelry. The Saturnalia was held between the seventeenth and the twenty-third of December in honor of Saturn, the god of agriculture and vegetation. This god had introduced farming among the Romans, was the first organizer of the original tribes and had established a communist society. During his reign there was peace and all property was held in common, no one sought to accumulate money or to acquire personal wealth, there was no slavery and all men were happy and equal. Then this legendary age came to an end, its kind king vanished suddenly and became a god, whose memory was cherished and many places were named after him. For seven days every year the Romans commemorated their god Saturn in the streets, in public squares and in their homes. During the week of the festival all work ceased, schools closed, there were no political assemblies, no battles and no war, and no punishment was inflicted. Celebration was characterized by unrestrained sensual merry-making, feasting, drinking and licentious orgies. The people were given the liberty of eating what they liked and of loving whom they desired with the understanding that the men would refrain from making love to married women, widows, virgins and free boys. The remaining females were still sufficiently numerous, bounteous and legally and morally available. It was customary for people to give and exchange objects, parents purchased gifts and pictures for their children and friends gave presents to one another. Since Saturn favored a classless society all ordinary distinctions between masters and their slaves and servants were dispensed with for the duration. Feasts were given when masters and slaves all sat at the same table and they all dressed alike, slaves and servants were allowed to give orders to their masters and they could yell and complain to them, without being reproved. Masters waited upon their slaves and servants and did not eat until their slaves were full. These holidays survived on into the fourth and fifth centuries of the Christian era.

The liturgical duties of the Roman religion were left to the priests who performed the sacrifices necessary to appease the spirits. In the Roman state religion the worshipers themselves did not participate in the ceremonies but only watched them. Public sacrifice was an elaborate ceremony entailing sacramental formalities, such as, the offering of the first fruits of the crops or a sheep, dog or pig and on great occasions, a horse, a hog or an ox, accompanied by the solemn pronouncing of holy formulas. These magic words would turn the victim, the slain animal, into the god who was to receive it and the people believed that the god himself was thus sacrificed; he died for their welfare. The viscera was burned on the altar while the priests and the communicants consumed the rest of the body. The strength and glory of the god, it was believed, thus passed into the bodies of the worshipers at the sacred meal. Human beings had many times been offered in sacrifice but in 97 B.C. a law had to be passed forbidding the practice. Some of the household deities and the various Italian tribal gods were nationalized. Janus, for example became the guardian of the gateway of Rome, open in time of war, closed when the nation was at peace. Vesta became the hearth of the state, whose eternal flame was tended by government appointed virgins. The Lares and the Penates also became part of the nation's cult.

As the problems of life began to grow more complex and as the national government superseded the father of the family and the tribal chiefs a priesthood became imperative. Pontiffs, as the state's religious officials were called, became professionals, trained and specialized in conveying messages and serving as the media from the Roman government to the spiritual world in communicating with the deities. There was also a board of augurs or unscientific forecasters to interpret signs, omens, symbols, natural and unusual manifestations and to promulgate the wishes and intentions of the gods. These soothsayers would be consulted before undertaking a military or political campaign or a new business enterprise to find out if the gods approved, that is, whether the project was destined to be a success or a failure. The Romans like all other peoples had their beliefs in the efficacy of charms, magic, amulets, talismans and in the various ways of prognosticating the future by the stars, the flight and behavior of birds and other creatures or by divination, that is, the examination of the entrails of animals, particularly the liver. Faith in the gods was important enough for the emperor's government to create in his cabinet a special department of religion headed by the pontifex maximus, or chief priest but the latter of course was subordinate to the emperor who was eventually worshiped as a god also.

The Romans had conquered every nation they fought with but they were unable to overcome the supernatural powers and so they made a deal with them. A contract was arranged whereby the Roman empire would become a humble satellite of the gods; they would pay tribute—homage and sacrifice and in return the gods would protect the Romans from the evil and hostile spirits and bring their subjects health, happiness and prosperity. The Roman gods were not concerned about man's morals and human conduct; that was for the philosophers to contemplate and expound. Nevertheless, many admirable virtues were traditionally developed through their pagan faith and generally prevailed among the Romans. Such commendable principles included honor, bravery, self-discipline, duty, respect and loyalty to the gods, the family, their ancestors, and the state. Above all individual values was devotion to the state or the welfare of the country for which one must always be ready to sacrifice his life.

The Romans were inclined to be tolerant of foreign religions so long as the latter were non-political and the adherents were loyal to the secular government. As a result many new faiths were brought into the country by captives, by returning soldiers and by the many immigrants and merchants from other lands. Romans readily identified their traditional deities with those of Greece wherever there was some similarity in function and character. Most of the Greek gods were given Latin names; for example, Zeus became Jupiter or Jove (the supreme deity), Hera-Juno (the queen of heaven, marriage and maternity and for whom the month of June was named), Athena-Minerva (goddess of wisdom and the arts), Demeter-Ceres (goddess of the cereal harvest), Aphrodite-Venus (goddess of love, beauty, desire), Ares-Mars (god of war, March was named in his honor), Hermes-Mercury (god of travel), Poseidon-Neptune (god of the sea), Hephaestus-Vulcan (god of fire and craftsmanship). They also borrowed Apollo, the very versatile god who controlled light, healing, music, poetry, prophecy, and youthful manly beauty, and the very important physician's god, Aesculapius, who governed the spiritual province of medicine and healing. The Greeks were more spontaneous than the Romans in their worship, the ritual in their temples was more dignified and they permitted more mass participation. Anthropomorphism was now introduced among the Romans and they followed the Greeks in ascribing human form and human attributes to their gods. They also deified the emperor and for a while they were sun worshippers. In addition to Greek influence many oriental mysterious beliefs began to fascinate the Roman people and consequently more deities were added to their already populous Pantheon which now numbered about 30,000 gods. In many towns there were more gods than people.

In its pristine days the religion of Rome was a warm and tender relationship between the simple peasants and mysterious gods; they made cordial, intimate agreements with their hidden deities and the people were grateful to their masters who brought them good luck and they prayed for protection from misfortune and for continued happiness. However when the Empire became greater and more powerful and the religion was taken over by the state and its pontiffs, it became well organized; but worship became mechanical, cold and impersonal; the old faith lost its emotional satisfaction. The traditional deities began to lose their appeal because they were no longer adequate in resolving the people's troubles, economic, emotional and spiritual. The old time religion had lost its intimacy; the ritual and ceremonies as conducted by the stiff pontiffs were too formal, they were meaningless and futile. Life was cruel and there was nothing to compensate them for their wretched existence; they couldn't even look forward to a decent afterlife. The Graeco-Roman Hades was a dark, gloomy subterranean abode of all departed spirits. Many of the intelligentsia abandoned the traditional faith altogether and adopted the rational philosophies of life, such as Stoicism or Epicureanism. Others believed in neo-Platonism, that is that material things are unreal and non-existent, that the soul can never be happy on earth and that the only thing real in the world is that which is spiritual. The vast majority of the people however couldn't live by philosophical precepts alone they needed a new emotional religion with pictorial symbols, intoxicating music and sympathetic gods who would answer their prayers, tranquillize their anxieties, expel their worries, and solve their problems.

    The Mediterranean world was abundantly supplied with magicians, miracle workers, oracles, sorcerers, charlatans, astrologers, ascetic saints and prophets. There were itinerant preachers claiming divine inspiration who traveled from city to city performing miraculous cures, interpreting dreams and foretelling the future. Cults and sects were organized offering their adherents immortality, asserting it is possible to overcome death and to live forever, provided one became a dedicated member of the faith and was properly initiated and participated in the mysterious ritual—ceremonies of purification, sacrifices, vicarious atonement, revelation and regeneration.

    Some Romans joined the popular Hellenistic groups—the Orphic and Eleusinian mystery cults which gave their members an emotional experience of immortality. In the Orphic ritual commemorating the death and resurrection Dionysus, the vine and tree god, a bull was sacrificed in the ceremony and the priests miraculously transformed it into the god Dionysus. After the votaries consumed a morsel of the body and a sip of its divine blood they absorbed the arcane potency of eternal life. In the Eleusinian sect the devotees joined Demeter, the goddess of grain, in mourning for the disappearance of her daughter, Persephone, held captive in Hades by Pluto, who had kidnapped her. For three days the Eleusinians had to live on a mystic mixture of flour, water and mint and then on the third night after much praying to Zeus, the supreme deity, he persuaded Pluto to release Demeter's daughter for a few months every year, and so Persephone happily returned home and a joyous festival followed. A like redemption after death was promised to all purified members of the esoteric cult. But far more appealing were the religions brought over from the Orient.

During these years of sorrow and depression and of yearning for comfort and solace there appeared among the Romans a number of Eastern mystery cults with great interest and definite ideas about life after death, offering their devotees, dramatic, enchanting services and ceremonies with all the people participating in a very colorful pageantry. These faiths were being observed and practiced by North Africans and West Asians residing in Rome, and by soldiers who had been stationed in the Middle East. As economic conditions grew worse and symptoms of national decadence began to appear, more and more Romans enrolled in these esoteric religious societies which promised to exchange a wretched mortality for a blessed immortality. Furthermore, the impressive ritual and the pageantry of the Oriental mysteries were far more seductive than the obsolete Roman ceremonials.

The two most popular foreign religions in the early centuries of the empire were the cult of the Egyptian goddess Isis and the cult of the West Asian goddess Cybele. Women were at first the most eager Roman converts because maternal deities were thought to be more compassionate and more acquainted with grief and there were millions of mourning mothers who because of wars, disease, and hunger bereaved the loss of their loved ones. But suffering males also seek to return to their mothers for comfort and solace, and so men too joined the sects of the female divinities who understood the meaning of grief and an empty heart. Both of these goddesses had lost their husbands or lovers and were in mourning—Isis for Osiris and Cybele for Attis. The poor, the suffering and the women wanted definite answers—what happens after death. And the priests provided very imaginative, plausible explanations. No other phenomenon of nature suggests so obviously the idea of death and revival, as the alternating growth and decay of vegetation, the melancholy season is inevitably followed by the joyous season year after year. The happiness of the goddesses of vegetation and fertility annually disappear and hopefully will reappear. One had to believe.

Osiris, the lover of Isis, the vegetation goddess, had been killed and the people lamented loudly and bitterly. Plaintive prayers were conducted by dignified, shaven and tonsured priests wearing white robes and surrounded by much pomp and ceremony. Morning and evening services included the burning of incense, the sprinkling of holy water and a symbolical ceremony of baptism. There were solemn processions accompanied by tinkling music and a magnificent display of splendor. But one liturgical rite required the priests to smite their breasts, to rip open their old wounds, and to cut their shoulders as an exercise of atonement. There were several days of mourning and it was believed that the tears which dropped from the eyes of Isis were so copious that they swelled the tide of the Nile River and made it overflow. Then Osiris rose from the dead, came back to life again and the jubilant worshipers celebrated with song and dance, stirring music—a symphony of sounds from cymbals, trumpets, pipes and tambourines—a gorgeous pageantry and wild rejoicing. Osiris lives again, man too will rise from the dead and be reborn. The goddess Isis was pictured in statues holding her divine child in her arms and was hailed as the Queen of Heaven, Star of the Sea, the Mother of God and the universal Mother Nature.

From Asia Minor came the other very popular goddess of fertility, Mother Cybele, also known as the Great Mother or the Goddess of Nature. It was said that Cybele's husband, Attis was born of a virgin, that his mother conceived by putting in her bosom a pomegranate that sprung from the severed reproductive organs of Attis's double. This cult also had a seasonal festival, during the spring solstice, commemorating the death and resurrection of the goddess's consort Attis which gave to the celebrants an assurance of their own salvation and immortality. Some Cybelean votaries believed that Attis was killed by a wild hog and as a result they abstained from the eating of pork. As Cybele mourned the death of her spouse and lover, the people prayed and then they fasted, and amidst frenzied lamentations the priests assembled, slashed themselves with knives and drank their own blood. Some of the male novices became so wildly fanatic that they sacrificed their sexual organs by performing self-castration. Their severed genitals were reverently wrapped up and buried in the earth or in subterranean chambers sacred to Cybele where they became instrumental in recalling Attis to life and thus hastened the general resurrection of nature's fecundity and fertility. Shortly after these rituals the streets rang with exultant shouts that God has risen from the dead—Attis lives again, salvation will come for all of you—your troubles will cease. And on the last day of the feast the image of the Great Mother was carried triumphantly through the crowds who hailed her as "Our Lady, Mother of the earth." A familiar sight in the streets of Rome was a procession of emasculated priests in Oriental costume carrying the image of the goddess, chanting hymns to the music of cymbals, tambourines, flutes and horns. People were so moved by the wild strains that they donated alms to the priests and showered the holy image with hundreds of roses and other flowers. Initiation into the Cybelean cult was a secret or mystic ceremony. The devotee was placed in a pit sometimes naked and sometimes dressed, then the pit was covered with a kind of grated or holed roof. They placed a golden crown and a ribboned wreath on a bull, adorned him with flowers and leaves, tied his legs and threw the bull on the grated roof of the pit and then stabbed the animal to death with a consecrated spear. The blood poured in torrents through the perforations and apertures of the roof drenching the worshiper red from head to foot with the sacred fluid flowing from his ears and mouth. All his sins were thus washed away in the blood of the bull and he was born again to eternal life. The genitals of the bull representing his hallowed fertility were placed in a consecrated vessel and were dedicated to the goddess.

A third cult that competed for first place among the religions of Rome was Mithraism, an importation from Persia. It was brought in mainly by soldiers who had been stationed in the eastern part of the Empire where the worship of sun gods was widely practiced. Mithraism emphasized the manly virtues of courage, endurance, loyalty, fraternity and obedience and it was organized like a secret lodge with seven degrees of initiation and its mysteries admitted men only. The sect enjoyed notable popularity during the first three centuries and by the middle of the third century it almost became the universal religion of the Roman empire. Rulers were inclined to favor Mithraism because it supported the idea of divine right of monarchs, that the Emperor governed by the grace of God and because Mithraists were not averse to war. In the year 274 Emperor Aurelian built a splendid temple dedicated to the sun god near the city of Rome and proclaimed his own reincarnation of the unconquerable sun. By this time most of the adherents of the cults of Isis and Cybele were absorbed by Mithraism and the latter's only rival was a burgeoning and emulous sect known as Christianity.

Mithraism was an outgrowth of the older Persian Zoroastrianism which had taught that there existed in the world a cosmic conflict between two gods. On one side was Ahura-Mazda, also known as Ormuzd, the creator of the world, the source of light and the embodiment of good; and on the other side was Ahriman, promoter of the corruption of men and the god of evil. Now entering the struggle, as an assistant to the spirit of light and good was an extraordinary human being named Mithra, who would tip the balance in this war, delivering victory to the righteous and he would henceforth be known as the Messiah or the Savior of mankind. The wicked Ahriman and his evil followers would be vanquished, routed and finally destroyed in a lake of fire and brimstone. But the good people, the faithful devotees of Ormuzd and Mithra would enjoy life in a world of eternal bliss. The adherents of the God of Light believed that Mithra, who was a kind of intermediary between God and man, would return to earth someday to judge all men and he would establish an everlasting reign of peace and righteousness. To many zealots assurance of immortality became more important than mundane success or the joys of earthly existence, consequently fanatics would sometimes prepare themselves for death rather than for life.

According to the Roman calendar Mithra's nativity occurred on December the 25th, at the winter equinox, when the sun returned from a long journey south of the equator. At this time of the year the people celebrated the happy home-coming of the divine sun by the display of many bright lights by buying picture cards for their children and by exchanging presents with their friends. Mithra's birth took place under a sacred tree and was witnessed by shepherds tending their sheep nearby. Possessed of all the virtues and a courageous, loyal soldier fighting in behalf of the god of goodness, he was graced at his last supper before he died, not only by the attendance of a number of his companions, but he was honored by the presence of the Sun God himself. After this final meal he fought under a standard bearing a cross of light and was killed by the diabolical Ahriman and then taken by Ahura-Mazda who carried Mithra away to the stars and to the abode of all faithful immortals—where he came to life again. It was believed by many that he would someday return to earth as a Messiah. In the meanwhile after death all men must appear before Mithra's tribunal to be judged. The wicked persons were turned over to Ahriman for eternal torment while the virtuous souls were given a celestial journey passing through seven spheres, shedding a bit of mortality at each stage until they arrived in heaven—the brilliant and radiant home of Ahura-Mazda.

The major ritual observed was the sacrifice of a bull when the believers were baptized in the consecrated blood which washed away sin, bestowed immortality on the convert and promised rewards in a future life—an actual physical restoration. This ceremony symbolized the death and resurrection of Mithra who was killed battling for the salvation of humanity. Unlike the competitive feminine deities Mithra was regarded as a real person who ultimately was identified with the sun, virtually synonomous with Ormuzd, and people prayed before images of their divine guide and protector. Mithra, as a former human was more accessible and therefore was preferred to Ahura-Mazda and so his name was used by his followers in addressing their supplications. Mithraistic ceremonies included ablutions with holy water, litanies to the sun, and the partaking of a communal meal of consecrated wine and bread, which was marked with a cross.

Still another religion, Judaism, was brought to Rome by immigrants from Judea as early as the second century B.C. Pompey in 63 B.C. conquered the Jewish homeland and in the year 70 A.D. the Roman army during a revolt destroyed Jerusalem and its famous temple, enslaved many thousands of Jews or dispersed them throughout the Empire. Most of the slaves were rapidly emancipated as they were very industrious and thrifty and were able to buy their freedom.

As a province of Rome Judea proved to be exceedingly recalcitrant and frequently tried to regain its freedom, but after the year 132 there were no more revolts and the Jews no longer had a homeland of their own, that is, not until 1948. A few remained in the old province but most of them moved to the various states around the Mediterranean world. In the first century out of approximately 100 million subjects of Rome about seven million were of the Jewish faith. They now lived in the various countries of western Asia, in Italy and Greece as well as in Egypt and Ethiopia. The largest Jewish community was found in the Egyptian city of Alexandria, where, according to the Hebrew philosopher, Philo, his coreligionists comprised about forty percent of the population. They made great contributions to the intellectual and cultural fields—in literature, history, science and philosophy.

In spite of Judea's refractory nature and its alien and unique religion, the Romans were not hostile to these strangers, so long as they paid tribute and respect to the Emperor and were willing to serve in the Roman army in time of war. But the Jews were regarded as a peculiar people because of their strange customs and ceremonies—they circumcized their male infants, they had a different kind of diet, observed Saturday as a day of worship and rest, and denounced idolatry; were averse to the use of images to represent their deity and refused to adorn a temple with statues or plastic figures either of human or divine beings. The Jews wouldn't intermarry without conversion but were not aggressive in proselyting. Nevertheless many educated Romans admired the Jews for their intelligence and their exemplary family life, abandoned their faith in idolatry—the worship of numerous gods, and began to show a predilection for ethical monotheism. A number of them even decided on formal conversion to Judaism.

The Jewish religion taught a belief in one God—a spiritual being that could not be represented by anything visible, tangible or human. Yahweh (Jehovah) wants the world to be governed by the principles of justice and righteousness. Individual morality must have a social application and charity is more important than ritual; in fact there is no difference between private and public morality. The future life would be in a perfect world—a paradise where people will receive redemption for their sufferings, and so the Jews prayed for a divine Redeemer. The Hebrew prophet Isaiah declared Yahweh to be one universal Lord, the God of all peoples. He denounced greed, treachery, brutality and idolatry but he promised that God would save the world, eradicate these evils and reward the good. Isaiah predicted the coming of a Messiah who would someday establish God's kingdom on earth, a last judgment, a heaven for the righteous and a hell for the wicked. The common people believed in Satan a personal devil, in evil spirits and in angels. The Golden Rule was stated in the Old Testament; that is, that you must do to others as you would have them do to you. It also says you must love thy neighbor as thyself—even the stranger that dwelleth among you, love him as thyself. The Jews were even commanded to do good to their enemies, to them that hate thee. Rabbi Hillel, in the first century B.C., also taught the Golden Rule; that you should not do to others what you don't want them to do to you; judge not thy neighbor until thou art in his place. He emphasized the love of man, love of peace, love of knowledge and love of God's law.

There were among the Jews in the first century A.D. about twenty-four religious sects of which the following were the most important: The Sadduces, which consisted of the upper-classes and most of the priests, were theologically conservative, that is, believed in the strict interpretation of the law. They denied personal resurrection and sought to attain happiness here on earth. The Pharisees were the middle class of people and were more flexible or liberal in their interpretation of their religious views. They generally accepted a belief in immortality and hoped it was both a physical and spiritual existence. The Essenes enrolled their members mostly from the poorer element of the population. They lived in small collectivistic communities sharing all their possessions except their wives who usually lived in town. They shunned all sensual pleasures and cohabited with their spouses only to produce children in order to perpetuate their religious faith. Very ardent and pious, they were ascetic, fasted frequently, opposed war and believed in prophecy, angels, demons, powers of magic and in baptism or cleansing of the soul with water. They looked forward to the coming of a Messiah who would establish a communistic, egalitarian kingdom of heaven on earth for the good people only. They were so strict and literal in the observance of the dogmas that they considered it a sacrilege to defecate on the Sabbath.

The Essenes made much of the ceremony called the *Agape* or the feast of unity and love, a meal of bread and wine at which they ate together in faithful communion, in prescient anticipation of the most joyous meal to come on a future great day when the Messiah would arrive and join them in the feast. Zealous and apocalyptic the Essenes believed that the early part of the first century A.D. was the auspicious time for God's Final Judgment; it would be the Great Day of the Lord—the Messiah was coming. There were many itinerant preachers, teachers and prophets predicting the certain arrival of the Messiah in the very near future when the sinners will be condemned and the righteous will be saved. John, who baptized Jesus, taught views similar to the Essenes, claiming he was sent to usher in the heavenly paradise of the Lord. The practice of baptism through immersion in water as a symbolical purification had been practiced among the Jews for centuries. John was executed by Herod, the Roman puppet king of Judea for a personal reason—John publicly accused the ruler of practicing incest.

Christianity in its beginning was also a Jewish sect which appeared with the advent of Jesus of Nazareth, but several years after the execution of their leader his devotees established an independent organization which grew rapidly and eventually developed into the prevailing religion of the western world. The word Christ meant Messiah in Greek and Jesus was the equivalent of the Hebrew name Joshua. Those who believed that Jesus was the Christ or the Messiah that the prophets had been speaking about and were expecting for many years, came to be known as Nazarenes or Christians.

Of humble origin, not formally educated but obviously well read in the holy books, Jesus traveled through Palestine helping the poor, healing the sick and teaching his interpretation of the laws and tenets of Judaism. He had a kindly and magnetic personality, was soft-spoken and an inspiring teacher who conveyed the meaning of the Jewish religion in clear graphic, simple parables. His teachings pleased the common people particularly and were very similar to those of the Essenes. He denounced the selfishness and hypocrisy of the rich and appealed to the poor, the oppressed, the lowly, the outcasts, and told them that they too will receive salvation if they repent and abide by the laws of God; they too can live in the Kingdom of Heaven. Jesus condemned the striving for material gain and declared that it is easier for a camel to go through the eye of a needle than for a rich man to enter the Kingdom of God; the meek shall inherit the earth. He advised the rich to sell their property and give the money to the poor, but he didn't recommend revolution or the forceful overthrow of either the political, social or economic institutions of Judea or of the Roman Empire. What Jesus wanted was to change human nature or the character of the individuals. His teachings followed in the tradition of the prophets—liberal, non-academic, anti-formalistic and non-conformist in attitude toward religious dogma. The following are some of his sayings: The essence of piety is the love of God and of one's fellow men. Love thy neighbor as thyself; learn to forgive, not to fight back; love your enemy and be good to those that hate you. All things that you want others to do to you, do to them. His aim was the establishment through religion a race of altruistic individuals devoid of cruelty, selfish desire, greed and lust. Revolution must take place in the heart, in the mind and soul of the individual before it occurs in society. If the teachings of Jesus could prevail there would be a brotherhood of man under a benevolent fatherhood of God. These ideas were not new, they were known to the Jews for they had already been enunciated in the Old Testament, in the sayings of the prophets and the rabbis. As a liberal interpreter of the Judaic law he favored more simplicity and opposed excessive rites and ceremonialism as the basis of religion. He also would relax the code of diet and cleanliness, omit certain fasts; he wanted the priests to be more lenient toward sinners; and he once remarked that the Sabbath was made for man and not man for the Sabbath. The progressive prophets had also advocated similar reforms long ago and had even advised the abolition of the rigidly conservative group of Sadducees. All the sects except the Essenes opposed the innovations that Jesus recommended though a number of Pharisees agreed with him that the Law should be softened and humanized. Jesus believed he was loyal to Judaism all through his life as he supported the principles traditionally taught by the prophets. He instructed his disciples to preach in the synagogues, to spread his gospel among the Jews, not the gentiles, declaring that he was sent to save the lost sheep of Israel, not the non-Jews, and he maintained that he was endeavoring to fulfill the Law of Moses not to destroy it. But he also, like Isaiah, stated that Jehovah was the God of all mankind and was concerned with all people not just the Hebrews.

About the year 30 A.D., after a very highly successful and inspiring ministry in Galilee, Jesus decided to observe the feast of Passover at the capital, in the spiritual center of Israel. Jewish pilgrims from all parts of the Roman Empire were swarming into Jerusalem. The Jews were not happy under Roman rule and revolutionary fever in Judea was chronic; it now became turbulent. Revolts against Rome had occurred before and on this festival they were celebrating their historic liberation from the Egyptians and there were reports that a popular Messiah was coming to town. Needless to say, the provincial and local authorities, political and religious, were somewhat anxious, suspicious and disturbed and the Roman administrator, Pontius Pilate ordered his soldiers to be prepared for military duties as riots and insurrection were a possibility. The followers of Jesus called him Messiah, the Christ and the Son of God though he had not acknowledged this honor except to one or two of his disciples. Though they approved and applauded his idealism and religious aims, uppermost in the minds of the masses was patriotism—independence for Judea. They hoped and prayed Jesus would lead the people in a victorious revolution against their Roman masters and restore their national sovereignty.

Upon his arrival he was greeted by enthusiastic and excited crowds who hailed him as King of the Jews, a title which he did not disavow. The people believed that the liberation of Judea should come first and then the world would recognize that Jehovah was the real and only universal God. But Jesus apparently had no interest in creating an earthly kingdom; he was interested in religious reform and in the establishment of a spiritual kingdom. He therefore immediately proceeded to the Temple where he would urge the changes that had been advocated by several of the prophets before him—the abolition of conspicuous prayers, ostentatious charities, opulent funerals and the replacement of the authoritarian Temple with the more democratic, less ritualistic synagogues; and to discontinue the practice of selling sacrificial animals and the handling of money on Temple grounds. It was customary to sell doves and pigeons in front of the building and since many buyers were foreign pilgrims their currency had to be changed into Judean coins, and so tables were set up for the purpose. Jesus denounced the practice of handling money at the Temple as sinful and he became so provoked at the sight of it that he overturned the tables of the traders, scattered their coins and drove them away with switches. Nevertheless he was allowed to teach in the Temple for almost three days without being harmed and was also permitted to eat the Passover supper with his apostles where he told his friends that he expected to be executed soon and he hoped that his death would be regarded as a sacrificial atonement for the sins of the people. They ate the Seder bread and drank the wine and sang the Hebrew ritual songs. He asked the apostles to consider the blessed bread they ate as his body and the consecrated wine as his blood, a ceremony that would inspire the development of the sacrament of the Eucharist or Communion.

Although many followers of Jesus were discouraged and disappointed in their leader's lack of political and nationalistic zeal, that he was not a military messiah, the more ardent adherents continued to speak openly and eloquently about their Savior and continued to call him King of the Jews. This aroused not only the suspicions of the Romans but also the Temple authorities and all the speeches and sermons castigating the rich and lauding the poor disturbed the conservatives, the business men who denounced Jesus as a radical agitator, a rebel and a troublemaker. The privileged priests resented his popularity and visualized the end of the Temple's control over Judaism and the destruction of its sacred traditions, while the Roman officials would certainly not tolerate an independent king of Israel set up by the common people. Jesus was therefore arrested by order of the Temple's supreme council and its tribunal found him guilty of blasphemy and then the Roman procurator, Pontius Pilate, condemned him as a revolutionist, pronounced him guilty of subversion and sedition and ordered his immediate execution. The Roman governor was a callous and unconscionable character who was later removed from office and charged with cruelty and extortion. Even though many of the masses of the people had been displeased when they learned that Jesus would not be their secular hero they didn't want him to be put to death, for they realized that he was a spiritual savior, that he was a friend of the common man and recommended the kind of reforms they favored. Hence there was much grief and there were many tears shed among the Jews who were at the scene of the execution and they considered the crucifixion a Roman atrocity for that form of punishment was never employed by the Judeans. Two kindly Jews removed the body from the cross, embalmed it and placed it in a tomb. Two days later a few Nazarenes visited the tomb and found it empty and a short time later rumors spread that Jesus had been seen alive again, that he had spoken to his disciples, had eaten with them and had even gone fishing with them as he had formerly done in the olden days. He urged them to carry on his mission and stated that he would return someday to judge all the people on earth; then he disappeared. The idea of a holy person mysteriously vanishing from the world and supposedly wafting to heaven was not new among the Jews, for the story was told of Moses, Isaiah and other prophets many years before and most Jews believed in resurrection.

The life and death of Jesus inspired the founding of Christianity but it was St. Paul who first expounded its theology and was the one who devised the discipline and government of the early church. After a brief setback the Nazarene sect began to flourish but again its growth engendered a hostile reaction among the majority of the residents of Jerusalem, who still refused to recognize Jesus as the Messiah who rose from the dead, became divine and promised to come back to earth some day. As a result some of the Nazarenes left Jerusalem and went out to win proselytes among the Jews in smaller Palestinian towns, and here they converted a few more members of the synagogues. They were now called Christians but were still considered a Jewish denomination and they still observed Passover, Pentecost and other Hebrew festivals. From Palestine they moved on to preach in the Jewish communities of Syria, Asia Minor, Egypt, Greece and Italy.

In the year 35 A.D., a Pharisee named Saul, underwent a profound conversion, adopted the Greek name Paul and before long became the outstanding leader of the Christian movement. He had been a fanatical antagonist of the Nazarenes and then one day with other agents of the high priest embarked on a journey to Damascus where they were to seize some of the converts and drag them back in chains to Jerusalem to be punished. On the way near his destination he suddenly saw a vision of Christ, the Son of God, and Jesus spoke to him, saying, "Saul, Saul, why do you persecute me." Paul was so stunned by this supernatural manifestation that he became blind and speechless. Not until three days later did he regain his eyesight and his power to speak. As a result of these occult, miraculous experiences Paul became convinced that God Himself, through Christ, had communicated with him and wanted him to spread the teachings of Jesus, the only religion that could save mankind. The Christians thus acquired a great leader, a skilled organizer as well as a very learned man who was well versed in Hebrew theology and Greek philosophy. As a result of Paul's excogitation Christianity would become a union of Jewish ethics and Greek metaphysics. He was the church's most proficient missionary but even he could not make much headway in the synagogues and so he decided to preach to the non-Jews since he believed all human beings must be saved. A few Greek-speaking pagans had shown an interest in Judaism and had already been converted, some to the traditional faith while others preferred to become Christian Jews. However, most Gentiles were reluctant to undergo the painful initiation of circumcision and were also not happy with the socially distasteful dietary requirements. But many Christian disciples, including James, the brother of Jesus, insisted that heathens must become Jews before they could become Christians. This custom was followed for about twenty years after the death of Jesus. However, Paul was wise enough to realize that Christianity would remain a small sect and might even disappear altogether unless they eliminated the two troublesome Judaic requirements. After considerable controversy among the leaders Paul's plan was adopted and as expected, enrollment in the new religious organization increased rapidly. To make Christianity even more acceptable Paul and other theologians who followed him converted the simple faith of Jesus into a syncretic religion containing doctrines and ritual, ceremonies and customs that were already very popular all over the empire and some that were endemic and indelible and so were included in an eclectic, catholic system. A sagacious organizer, Paul believed that in its early stages the growth of a movement can be greatly facilitated by compromise and amalgamation.

The fundamental doctrines in Christianity were of course common to all religions. For thousands of years in primitive times all men believed in supernatural beings—in good and evil spirits and they had tried to propitiate the good and drive off the evil ones. To attain their desires they had resorted to worship, to magic, sacrifice and baptism; they held initiation and purification rites and regarded the crises of life as spiritual mysteries and therefore priests would perform sacred ceremonies or sacraments on such critical occasions as birth, the advent of puberty, marriage, and death. These beliefs and rituals evolved and were more or less modified in the civilizations of

Babylonia, Egypt, Judea, Persia, Greece and Rome. Of these the Jews contributed most to the Christian religion as the latter was a direct offspring of Judaism. They both had the same God, "Our Father in Heaven," the omnipotent and omniscient Jahveh who was also merciful and forgiving, gracious and loving. Jesus lived and died a Jew and his teachings were the same as the ethical doctrines of the prophets in the Old Testament. The origin, the processes, the structure of the universe and world history as described in the Hebrew holy books, the belief in a Savior or Messiah, the doctrine of original sin, baptism by immersion in water, purification rites, remission of sin, asceticism and the sacramental meal of bread and wine were Jewish religious customs. In the early Christian church the features of worship were also similar to those of the synagogue; for example, prayers were recited in common, the singing of praise to the Lord were sung by the congregation, there were reading of parts of the Bible and a sermon by the minister. The Jews believed that following the word of God as revealed in the Torah was sufficient to assure one a heavenly reward whereas the Nazarenes also required faith in Christ as the Savior, the Messiah who became divine after his resurrection and was known as the Son of God.

Mithraism was the strongest and most popular sect among the mystery cults but eventually it was to be overcome and replaced by Christianity. Originally a Persian religion it was partial to the rich, the upper classes, the army and the bureaucrats, and its secret rites were expensive and were for men only. Christianity therefore would win over the masses by promising the poor, who were most of the people, a better life in the next world, that they would be compensated for their sufferings. They were assured that the poor and the lowly were preferred in the Kingdom of God, that Jesus had stated that the humble shall inherit the earth. Immortality was guaranteed and this life on earth was merely considered a testing ground for the hereafter. Heaven and hell were made vivid and realistic and Church ritual must be emotional, colorful, occult and dramatic. The Christians were also aware of the importance of women in religion, that they are more inclined to be religious, they are more emotional and more impressed by beautiful, mysterious ceremonies and they can more easily influence the children. Hence the female Romans were warmly welcomed as members of the church. However, female communicants must be careful not to arouse profane interest or attention of the male worshipers by avoiding jewelry, cosmetics and perfume; they must keep quiet and refrain from talking and singing in church. Women were required to wear veils and cover their hair while men had to leave their heads uncovered.

Mithra was a soldier, Jesus was a man of peace and by the third century war was not so popular with the people of Rome, as it once had been, for military decline of the empire had already set in. As a scholar Paul won over religious intellectuals by absorbing and introducing in his doctrines many concepts of Greek philosophy—particularly those of Plato, the Stoics, the Gnostics and of Philo, the Alexandrian Jewish philosopher who tried to reconcile Judaism with Plato. Paul came to believe such metaphysical notions as matter is inherently evil, that material things are evanescent, that the spiritual is really tangible, that one can have esoteric knowledge of spiritual things, that there is a rational principle which governs the universe and that one can mystically recognize it through meditation. The Christian God was a triad, a trinity comprising three personalities in one—Father, Son and Holy Spirit, which is the creative and guiding principle of the Lord. These ideas appealed to transcendental thinkers, neo-Platonists, metaphysicists and mystic religionists.

Osiris, Attis and Dionysus were also gods who had died to redeem mankind and Mithra, a human being, had been sacrificed to reward the good people and he too became divine and ultimately synonymous with Ormuzd, the god of light and righteousness. So now Paul declared that Christ was divine even before his birth, that he was cosubstantial with God, that Christ was the Lord. That led some rationalists to conclude that since Christ was always a spiritual being then he did not suffer on the cross and his execution was not an atrocity but a blessing to mankind because it won for all good people a happy resurrection and an eternal life in Paradise.

Mithra was also thought to have been a mythical man who had lived on earth but Jesus was an historic person known by his Christian fellowmen as an amiable father of mankind, possessed of providence and graciousness. The common people preferred such a personal, intimate god, which was another reason why Christianity found ready acceptance of the faith among the masses. Baptism and the Eucharist were also derived from the rites practiced by all the Mediterranean peoples but Paul modified, refined and Christianized them. Instead of costly rituals involving bulls and blood baths which the average Roman could not pay for, the Christian customs were simple ceremonies of purification and spiritual regeneration which the pagan convert could easily understand, afford financially and agreeably accept. Originally used to initiate adult proselytes into the Christian faith, Baptism became a rite for infants who were cleansed of original sin by the application of water and the recital of some sacred words. It was believed that every person is born with the sin of Adam which must be washed away to assure future salvation. Baptism also gave the young child admission into the Christian fold. The other basic rite commemorates Christ's Last Supper, called the Eucharist or Communion, when at a holy meal of bread and wine the food is miraculously converted into the body and blood of Jesus. By eating this consecrated bread and wine one incorporates within himself the body and blood of Christ thereby receiving redemption from sins committed after Baptism. Faith in Christ and regular periodic participation assure one a heavenly reward. Thus the suffering, the sacrifice and the vicarious atonement of Christ on the cross made possible man's salvation, his delivery from sin and its consequences, and his reception into blessed immortality—eternal life. The Mithraists worshipped the god of light and Sunday was an appropriate holiday for them and so they dedicated the first day of the week to the sun; and since Christ's resurrection, it was said, occurred on a Sunday that day was considered holy by the Christians. However it was not until the second century that the Sabbath was changed from Saturday to Sunday. Also sun worshipers in the northern hemisphere regarded the twenty-fifth of December as a holy day because the sun is nearest to the earth at that time and the Mithraists celebrated with lights and feasting and the exchange of presents. The Christians proclaimed the twenty-fifth of December as Christ's birthday, although most scholars think Jesus was born in early January. The two coincidents nevertheless facilitated the conversion of Mithraists. From the same cult the Christians acquired the use of bells, candles and the sprinkling of holy water. The Church also permitted Roman converts to replace the numerous specialized divinities with the veneration of saints and even allowed them to make statues and images of Jesus and of all holy and sanctified beings. Syncretism and compromise were significant factors in the triumph of Christianity over the pagan millions.

Other reasons for the rapid growth and great success of Christianity were the highly efficient organization set up by Paul, the discipline, zeal and proficiency of the missionaries that helped him and of those who followed, and the miserable social and economic conditions in the Roman empire. The lower classes, slaves, former slaves and laborers were finding it harder and harder to earn a living while the middle class were becoming poor as their income decreased and taxes were getting heavier and heavier. The educated people were beginning to take notice of the growing poverty and government officials were aware of increasing discontent. People were becoming discouraged and hopeless about their future and their government would not and could not do anything for them. Moreover the second and third centuries were periods of great interest in religious questions. The old gods had become disappointing and ineffectual; perhaps Christ could help them. Christians promised the Romans compensation for the present misery and injustice—a better life, eternal happiness in a perfect world in the hereafter. They offered the unfortunate masses love and equality, and in contrast to the current moral decadence, the Christians displayed a high moral conduct, as exemplified by the courage and tenacity of their martyrs. Furthermore they preached and practiced kindness, mercy, non-resistance, charity and philanthropy and above all gave the people solace and reassurance.

For about two hundred years the Roman government was fairly tolerant toward the Christians though there were occasional outbursts of persecution often instigated by insane or enraged emperors. For many years Christians were regarded as just another Jewish sect and Jews were allowed freedom of worship since they enjoyed cultural autonomy. Like all conquered nations, they paid tribute, were allowed to offer homage to the emperor without formal sacrifice in their temple, and they did not go out of their way to proselytize pagans, which pleased the rulers. But when the Christians decided to detach themselves from Judaism and become an independent religious group with no political roots, persecution of the new faith began. In the year 132 the Judeans, under the leadership of bar Kochba, whom they regarded as a Messiah, made their last attempt to break away from

Roman control. The Christians, then still considered a Jewish sect, rejected bar Kochba as their Messiah, since they already had one; they refused to participate in the revolution and henceforth became a separate religion. As Roman citizens they were expected to render the customary obeisance to the emperor who claimed to be a god also and everyone must bow or burn a pinch of incense before his statue as a person today might salute his nation's flag. Christians considered this as idolatry and refused to offer any sacrifice to the ruler in their churches. They were not nationalists for their religion would embrace the entire world; they were internationalists, universal in outlook, interested in all individuals of mankind. Unwilling to worship and pay their respects to the emperor, they also refused to serve in the military, discouraged men from joining the army, and advised people to disobey unjust laws. They preached democracy, collectivism, meekness, and non-resistance, and they denounced the rich. James, the brother of Jesus had said: "Come now you rich people, weep aloud and howl over the miseries which shall overtake you. Your wealth has rotted, your clothes are moth-eaten, your gold and silver are rusted and their rust will eat into your very flesh. The wages you have withheld from the laborers who have made you rich, cry aloud and their cries have reached the ears of the Lord. Has not God chosen the world's poor to possess the Kingdom. In that Kingdom, the rich will wither like flowers under a scorching sun."

A great majority of the Christians came from the lower orders and were not favorably regarded by the upper and ruling classes. They were enemies of the established order; they frequently met in secret, which aroused suspicion, and were looked upon as disloyal citizens and dangerous characters whose teachings seemed to aim at social revolution. They refused to co-operate in religious festivals, to support civic responsibilities and to take the customary oath in court "By Jove," which is unchristian. For a long time the common people disliked the Christians because they were aloof and clannish, shunned the society of pagans, forbade marriage with non-Christians, never attended the theater, the public games, or participated in the celebration of pagan holidays. Christians were said to dislike music, white bread, foreign wines, warm baths and shaving their beards, and were even accused of cannibalism and of drinking human blood. Nevertheless, in spite of opposition, prejudice and unpopularity the enterprising missionaries persevered in their efforts and finally succeeded in converting thousands, then millions of pagans to the new faith.

The first serious case of persecution occurred in the year 64 when Nero needed a scapegoat for the great fire that almost destroyed the city of Rome. His savage atrocities were infamous. Many Christians were seized and covered with skins of wild beasts and torn to death by hungry dogs or they were fastened on crosses and when it became dark they were burned and used as torches. He also used these lamps of human flesh to light up the games by night. It was also in Nero's notorious reign in the year 64 that St. Paul was beheaded and St. Peter was crucified head downward. After Nero's death persecution steadily decreased and was thereafter intermittent until the middle of the third century when it became more systematic, very cruel and widespread. Christians were arrested for being unpatriotic or on charges of disloyalty to the government rather than for religious misbelief. They would be freed if they were willing to offer incense to the statue of the emperor, and some did comply, but if they refused they were flogged, imprisoned, exiled or condemned to the mines. Rarely were they put to death. Only the very brutal or very religious emperors had the Christians tortured barbarously or had them burned, beheaded or fight wild animals. Some rulers destroyed the churches, confiscated church property, burned Christian books, dissolved congregations, and killed all Christians who assembled for religious worship. The rulers needed someone to blame for calamities and recurring disasters as the Romans were continually being harassed and tormented by plagues, earthquakes, hostile invaders, wars and serious defeats. But the more they persecuted the Christians the more the latter grew, for the empire was crumbling and the masses were wretched. Many people admired the strength and courage of the martyrs, their lack of fear of pain and their faith in resurrection and a future life in heaven. Membership in the churches continued to increase. In 180 there were one million Christians and in 305 they were one of the largest religious groups in the empire. Persecution ceased after the year 305 and in 311 Emperor Galerius issued a decree of toleration. His successor Constantine in 313 placed Christianity on the same legal level as the other religions and soon showed a preference toward the new faith.

One day just before a battle in which he was to fight for his throne Constantine saw a flaming cross in the sky which bore the Greek words: "In this sign thou shalt conquer." So he ordered his men to fight under a standard carrying the initials of Christ and a conspicuous Christian cross. His enemy displayed the banner of Christianity's leading rival—Mithraism, bearing the sign of the unconquerable Sun. Constantine emerged the victor in this historical battle and so henceforth displayed particular predilection to Christianity. But he didn't become a Christian formally until he reached his deathbed, when he was baptized. Later in the fourth century there was an attempt to revive paganism but in 392 Theodosius made Christianity the official church of the Roman empire and before long the church and the government themselves began to persecute pagans, heathens and non-conformists.

In the second century, during the reigns of the five good rulers, the Roman empire was a euphoriant world of peace, security, prosperity and happiness. But before his death Marcus Aurelius made a very serious mistake—he nominated his son, Commodus, 19 years of age, as his successor. In those days everything in the empire depended upon the competence and character of the emperor; if he proved to be weak, insensible and unfit for the job the entire political organization would be endangered. Unfortunately Commodus, the heir of the great Marcus Aurelius, had all these faults and deficiencies. Brilliant statesmen don't often beget equally gifted offspring and may be succeeded by dullards or vicious descendants, which was a flaw in the monarchical type of government.

A vigorous and lively fellow, Commodus was utterly devoid of morals and scruples. He was uninterested in politics, he treated the Senate with contempt and he won the support of the masses by giving each needy plebeian citizen 725 denari, which was then considered an exorbitant amount of money. Like other emperors he contributed to the barbarization of the army by enlisting many thousands of uncivilized foreign soldiers. He was an expert swordsman and a perfect bowman and his chief amusement was killing wild animals at public spectacles. Obsessed with sports, he once left the palace, attended a school for gladiators and then participated in chariot races and fought in the arena against beasts and men. He naturally won all his battles with the men and the animals may have been well fed before the combats. Commodus sometimes fought alone before breakfast with a hippopotamus, an elephant or a tiger. He was such an expert marksman and so skillful as a bowman that in one exhibition he killed one hundred tigers with one hundred arrows. One of his favorite sports was to let a panther leap upon a condemned criminal and then slay the animal with an arrow, thus saving the man to fight another day. A worthless debauchee, he drank excessively, gambled much and maintained a harem of three hundred women and three hundred boys. An obvious sadist, Commodus forced female devotees of Isis to beat their breasts with pine cones till they died. He killed men indiscriminately with a club and once had a number of cripples collected and then shot and put to death one by one with arrows. Outraged by this criminal insanity of her royal nephew, an aunt of the emperor's formed a conspiracy to assassinate him but it was discovered and so she and a number of prominent men, former associates of Marcus Aurelius, were killed. Finally the Praetorian Guard asked Marcia, a Christian mistress of the emperor's, to give him a cup of poison and when this venomous beverage seemed to work too slowly they employed a very muscular athlete, who had often trained Commodus in wrestling and he strangled the emperor in his bath. His majesty, the princeps, was only thirty-one when he expired.

After the death of Commodus the Senate took over the government and chose one of its most highly respected members, a man named Pertinax, to be the emperor. Interested in and conversant with philosophy, literature and public affairs, he was eminently qualified for the position and he immediately proceeded to reduce taxes and replenish the treasury by other means. But the Praetorian Guard disapproved of his strict discipline and plebs and freedmen disliked his economy because it would deprive them of their accustomed perquisites and doles. Soldiers forced their way into the palace severed the emperor's head and carried it upon a spear to their camp. Then the Guard decided to auction off the throne and sell it to the highest bidder. Didius Julianus offered 5000 drachmas to each soldier in return for the title. Agents of the military approached one millionaire after another encouraging higher bids until Julianus finally promised each man 6250 drachmas. Julianus was then proclaimed the emperor. Such nefarious venality aroused the decent citizens to appeal to the legions stationed in Britain, Syria and central Europe to come home and restore dignity to the position of emperor. The legions replied favorably and marched toward Rome. Of the several contending candidates who wanted to rescue the government the commander from the Danube district, Septimius Severus, emerged as the victor. He was bolder and swifter than his rivals, though he had to employ bribery also. He promised to give each of the soldiers 12000 drachmas for his support in this contest for the throne. He subdued the Praetorian Guard but punished the leaders only and thus pacified the rank and file. Julianus who had previously purchased his crown was found in the palace weeping over his failure to keep his job and his money. A follower of Septimius, the victorious general, led Julianus into a bathroom and beheaded him.

Septimius was a very strong and handsome man, well-educated, competent and clever. However he told the truth only when it was expedient to do so, and he was generally mercenary and unscrupulous, and was always cruel and ruthless to his opponents. The senate, for example, had opted for Albinus, a rival candidate for the rule of Rome. When apprised of this obviously imprudent selection, Septimius sent 600 guards to persuade the members of that august body to nullify their unwise choice and confirm his own accession. He then put a great many senators to death and confiscated their property, and before long the new emperor became the owner of about half of the real estate of the Italian peninsula. The vacancies in the senate were filled with friendly and grateful members, mainly from the eastern parts of the empire. Hereafter the senate submissively followed the emperor's orders, and he enjoyed absolute power. He assumed control of the various treasuries from which he could always extract the necessary boodle, much of which went to his military hirelings who were almost always fighting either barbarian invaders or rebellious provinces. Septimius had to enlarge his army by making military service compulsory, except in Italy; and to assure the loyalty of his provincial soldiers he increased their pay since they loved money far more than their country. The government was still referred to as a principate but it was actually a military monarchy and Septimius also made the throne despotic and hereditary. His second wife, a beautiful Syrian girl, became the mother of two sons, Caracalla and Geta. In his old age the emperor suffered severely from gout but he lingered on; in fact his departure was delayed so long that Caracalla, his older son, beseeched the physician to hasten his demise. Before he died Septimius advised his sons that to be a successful ruler in Rome one must have a loyal army well supplied with money.

Again an able emperor was succeeded by a brutal barbaric playboy. Like Commodus, Caracalla had a passion for hunting and war and a particular penchant for the capture of lions and wild hogs. He fought with lions but he also liked to have them as companions in the palace at his table and in his bed. Among humans he enjoyed the company of gladiators and military men. Suspecting that his brother was trying to share the imperial power, he had Geta assassinated. The young fellow was cut to death in his mother's arms and her clothes were covered with blood. Caracalla also had about 20,000 of Geta's followers slaughtered, and killed other citizens for sundry reasons, including four vestal virgins whom he accused of adultery. The army disapproved the killing of Geta, and so Caracalla, remembering his father's advice, restored their friendship by showering them with almost all the money in the public treasuries. His policy was always to favor the soldiers and the poor with lavish gifts and extort heavy taxes from the business classes and the aristocracy. He also spent money on building projects such as public baths and an arch to his father. Then to replenish the exchequer he doubled the inheritance tax and since the tax applied to citizens only he extended the franchise to all free male adults in the empire and thereby increased considerably the government revenue. Like so many of his predecessors he was frequently at war in the eastern lands which were continually in revolt or if aggressive independent neighbors, were attacking the empire. On one occasion before embarking on an expedition to curb troublesome Parthia, he decided to make sure that Egypt would not rebel while his army was busy in the Middle East and so he stopped over in Alexandria and supervised the massacre of all the men in the city who were capable of bearing arms. Then he proceeded to Persia but there shortly afterwards he was assassinated by a few of his associates who were unhappy with the emperor's campaign plans.

Macrimus, the prefect of the Praetorian Guard, acclaimed himself emperor, but after a brief reign he was replaced by Elagabalus, a young Syrian priest, who was a grandnephew of Caracalla's wife. He was not only a priest, he was a musician who could sing, and play several instruments. A pious man, he was also a profligate, extravagant and lecherous. He frequently gave expensive banquets at the palace when he was fond of playing jokes on the guests and of presenting his friends with costly gifts. He gave away horses, chariots, eunuchs and furnished homes; or he would tell the guests to take with them the silver goblets and plates from which they had drunk or eaten. He found it amusing to give someone a few gold pieces mixed with peas, amber mixed with beans, or onyx with lentils, pearls with rice, valuable pieces of jewelry, or just a handful of flies. Another practical joke was putting people to sleep with a great deal of wine and then letting them awaken surrounded by harmless lions, leopards and bears. When traveling this exceptional emperor required 600 chariots to carry his luggage and his courtesans. His soothsayer told him he would die a violent death and so the eccentric Elagabalus prepared himself for suicide by making available ropes, swords, and poison. However in due time, he was slain in a privy and his body was dragged through the streets, around the amphitheater and then thrown into the Tiber.

All this criminal insanity, symptomatic of Roman decay, was checked by the next emperor who gave the people a respite for thirteen years (222 to 235). Alexander Severus, selected by the Imperial Guard and confirmed by the senate, was a kind and affable man, well trained in body, mind and character. He was well educated, skilled in sports and in the military arts, and was talented in painting and in music. A modest and temperate individual, he respected the senate and recommended to everyone the morals of the Jews and Christians. He held the golden rule in such high esteem that he often quoted it and then had it engraved on the walls of his palace and on many public buildings. Tolerant of all religions he believed in one Supreme Power whom he worshiped every morning. Alexander's leading advisers were his mother and Ulpian, the renowned Roman jurist. He censored public morals by having all prostitutes arrested and by deporting homosexuals. He helped organize the workers and the tradesmen, assisted the farmers and sold most of the imperial jewelry, reduced taxes and helped the poor. There was enough in the treasury to make work by constructing libraries, municipal baths, roads, bridges and aqueducts, one of which was fourteen miles long. He also succeeded in driving back the eastern invaders though the barbarians in the north continued to be the most troublesome enemies. His mother accompanied the emperor on military campaigns which displeased the soldiers because they disapproved of women meddling in affairs of war and when she recommended negotiating with their foes instead of fighting them the army became enraged. This led to a tragic mutiny in which the soldiers killed Alexander, his mother and his friends.

The death of Alexander marked the end of the Severi dynasty after which there came a period of virtual anarchy in the empire. From 235 to 285 it sank to its lowest depth engendered by domestic troubles and barbarian invasions. Military anarchy prevailed as the soldiers were no longer amenable to discipline—only pay and booty could win their support. Civil war broke out and various factions fought one another to gain the imperial title. In one year six emperors were chosen and all six of them were assassinated. From 211 to 284 out of twenty-three emperors only two died natural deaths. In 235 the ruler was Maximinus, an utterly ignorant Thracian peasant who didn't even find it necessary to visit the city of Rome. He was a physically powerful giant over eight feet tall who could eat about forty pounds of meat and drink about eight gallons of wine in one day. In his three year reign his taxation on the wealthy and the patricians was so extortionate that it led to a revolt, but it was savagely suppressed and resulted in the impoverishment of the upper classes. There was a brief interlude in the reign of Aurelian, 270-275, when the emperor strengthened the government, improved the economy and sought to revive religion by announcing that he was the vicar of the Sun God Mithra. To strengthen the military the draft was maintained and large landowners had to provide slaves for the army in proportion to the value of their property. He also tried to restore the crumbling empire by reannexing the provinces that had seceded—Egypt, Syria, part of the Balkans in the east and Spain, Gaul and Britain in the west. But unfortunately he was mistakenly murdered by army officers. A seventy-five year old man, a descendant of the famous historian Tacitus was then placed on the throne but after six months of governing he died of exhaustion. Then the army took a chance on a younger emperor named Probus, an honest, peaceful, courageous person. He forthwith curbed the German and the Persian invaders with walls and threats and then promised his people that he could convert swords into plowshares and transform soldiers into laborers. He undertook a novel campaign of employing his troops to perform such public works as draining marshes, clearing wastelands and planting grapevines. But the soldiers had never read the Bible and preferred swords to plowshares; they refused work at jobs that were inappropriate to their area of training. As was the custom resentment forced them to murder their employer. Then in remorse they expressed their grief and sorrow over the death of such an honorable emperor and erected a monument in his memory. Governmental chaos was now restored, the empire resumed its process of decay and the barbarians returned to the borders to raid and attack the Romans.

In 284 Diocletian, a strong, qualified ruler came to the throne and directly inaugurated a number of reforms that saved the empire from complete collapse. The new emperor was the son of a former slave who rose in the army from a private soldier to commander and now to the head of the Roman empire. With the accession of this statesman, the civil war between politicians, generals and armies came to an end and an attempt was made to establish efficiency in government, economic recovery and effective defense of the frontiers. Believing that it was too large for one man to govern, he reorganized the empire by separating it into divisions and subdivisions, each headed by an agent of the chief executive and always subject to his dismissal; which made it easier to govern the huge, complex organization. This bisection into two main halves—east and west, marked the first step toward the permanent partitioning of the empire and the ultimate secession of the eastern part, which would be known as the Byzantine empire in the Middle Ages. The power of the ruler was made absolute both in theory and practice, the old principate became the dominate and it was not based on the military alone but on the aid and sanction of religion. Of course he maintained a very strong army—a professional force whose officers were no longer selected from the senatorial and equestrian orders, the privileged classes. They were now picked from the superficially Romanized barbarians and the enlisted men were the least civilized peasants, proletarians and uncouth foreign mercenaries, whose jobs were after a while made hereditary. The army was discouraged from meddling in politics because it was dependent for funds and supplies on civil administrators who were servants of the emperor. The number of bureaucrats employed in both the military department and the civil service was enormous and they formed a new privileged aristocracy. The senate now became a kind of municipal council or social club.

Diocletian moved his court to the eastern half of the divided empire and set up his headquarters near the ancient Greek city of Byzantium (modern Istanbul) which was a more strategic spot from which to deal with the most menacing enemies. His court was modeled after those of the Oriental despots, that is, he was to be regarded as both a god and a king. He was addressed as "Most Sacred Lord" and was looked upon as a Sun God, the Invincible Sun, divine and sublime, and was attended by titled chamberlains and ceremonious eunuchs. He wore silk robes of purple and gold, his shoes were decorated with precious gems, his nails were gilded and his hair was sprinkled with gold dust. He was rarely seen in public and visitors were required to prostrate themselves, kneel and kiss the hem of his robe. Elaborate and strict protocol, ceremony and etiquette enabled him to keep aloof, distant and awesome, which guarded his holy eminence against the turbulent mob or mutinous military men. The Christians suffered severely from Diocletian's religious policy. Deification of the emperor was not in consonance with Christianity but Diocletian aimed to establish the unity of religion, favoring an imperial cult which required all citizens to worship the soveriegn. The Jews who also opposed exalting a man to the rank of a god had negotiated with the Roman authorities and had been granted immunity from religious sacrifice to the emperor. But the Christians had refused to compromise and make any political arrangements with the pagan government. The latter consequently continued to maltreat and persecute them, though serious outbreaks were sporadic. The worst manifestations of violence were in the third century when several thousand Christians were put to death. They were burned at the stake, some were crucified, beheaded or thrown to hungry beasts who were waiting to devour them. Some Christians recanted but most of them stood firm under the most excruciating savage torture and martyrdom which aroused sympathy and respect among many pagans, and tended to make the church grow stronger.

Diocletian succeeded through his strengthening of the government in checking the disintegration of the Roman empire for he put an end to the anarchy, the civil wars, the devastation of the land and the provincial cities by invading hordes. But to maintain such order, safety and stability he needed a huge bureaucracy and an enormous army; and to sustain the people he had to provide jobs through public projects, welfare funds for the poor, and games and spectacles to amuse the populace and keep them happy. This presented a difficult economic problem, for Rome was in the throes of an unremitting and unresolvable economic depression—a low rate of productivity, high prices, a scarcity of hard money; and the Romans had no paper. At one time coins became so scanty that taxes and wages had to be paid in kind. Inflation was caused by the debasing of the coinage and the devaluation of Roman money, though some greedy business men, determined to increase profits, deliberately created shortages of commodities by curtailing production or by concealing or withholding merchandise from the markets. Diocletian tried to reform the currency by decreeing that it must possess an established weight and purity; and when food prices began to soar the emperor introduced the death penalty for profiteering, hoarding or for any violation of a maximum price which he set, and then extended the fixing of prices on all commodities. He also brought many industries under state control, nationalized a few vital factories and manned them with forced labor. Before long the majority of the industrial establishments and guilds in Italy were appropriated by the government and the cost of all important products and services were frozen. All shipping and all exports and imports were strictly controlled. Wages and salaries, as well as prices were regulated by the government as it saw fit. Diocletian also established the caste system for all Roman citizens as each person was tied to his job and his status and forbidden to change his work. Everyone's position was made hereditary; that is, the son of a baker had to become a baker, a stone mason's son must be a stone mason and a painter's son had to follow in his father's footsteps. Small farm owners were irrevocably tied to the soil just as the laborers and tradesmen in the city were to their work. Tenant farmers were forced to become *coloni*, forerunners of the medieval serfs, which meant they too were bound to the land they tilled, could not leave without the consent of the owner and if the land were sold they and their household went with it. Farm workers or peasants were likewise fixed to the soil. Land, factory and shops were controlled and regulated by the government; everyone was frozen to his job, even soldiers.

Such complete totalitarianism naturally created the need for an enormous bureaucracy which required a huge amount of revenue and consequently heavy taxation. Furthermore the army must be large and well equipped for the enemies were numerous and growing stronger; the laborers must be kept busy building roads, aqueducts and so forth, the hungry must be fed and the masses amused. So many taxpayers attempted to evade taxes that the government had to hire special police and then employed spies to watch the policemen. Finally it was decided to place the responsibility of assessing property and tax collecting on the *curiales* or town councillors, local landowners and business firms who were to obtain the taxes and be responsible for the town's quota. If there was a deficit they would have to make it up out of their own pockets. Being compelled to work as unpaid civil servants and often forced to pay for the privilege as well, was very repugnant to these respectable middle class gentlemen and they began to shirk and avoid the burdensome and disagreeable task. Many of them gave up their property, left town and sought employment in other fields of endeavor. But the government again intervened and forbade the *curiales* from traveling abroad or changing their type of work or profession and made their status hereditary. Nevertheless many middle class persons managed to escape, joined guilds and some even became *coloni*, and went to work for wealthy landowners—the lords of future feudalism. Everywhere artisans, peasant proprietors small business men, crushed by taxation, ran away from shops and farms they were tied to; some of them even sought refuge with the barbarians. The middle class which had been the backbone of Roman society soon began to vanish.

Much of Rome's prosperity had been derived from tribute and taxes paid by the conquered provinces and from the export of their skillfully made goods which were sold in all parts of the empire, though particularly in the less advanced colonies of the west. The Italians were expert in the manufacture of numerous commodities and were also familiar with the most productive methods of farming. But in due time the provincials acquired the Italian expertise, both industrial and agricultural, built and developed their own factories and learned to grow equally fine agricultural products themselves. They also were able to accumulate capital of their own, depending less on Italian loans and investments. The Romans could conquer no more lands and secure no more markets; in fact, they could barely defend their own territory and so they went the way of all imperialistic powers—they became decrepit, and then their empire would disintegrate. In 305 Diocletian, at the age of fifty-five, retired as emperor and devoted the remaining eight years of his life to the cultivation of his own garden raising cabbages and other plants. He had restored law and order, provided security from invasion and relative economic stability, though not prosperity. He did not resolve the crisis. Rome was a dying empire though Diocletian and later Constantine kept it alive a little longer but they could not avert its ultimate demise; they merely postponed it.

When Diocletian retired civil war broke out again—five contestants fought one another for the office of emperor. Thanks to his superior strategy and to the vision of a flaming cross in the sky, Constantine won the crucial battle and became the undisputed master of Rome. In appreciation of the assistance from heaven the new emperor issued the famous Edict of Milan in 313 by which Christianity was given the status of a legalized religion and he also restored to the Christians the church property which had been seized by Diocletian during the persecutions. Gradually, as his power grew more secure, he began to show favoritism to the Christians over the pagans, professed his belief in the faith of Jesus and gave his sons a Christian education, though he wasn't ritualistically baptized until he was near death. In 325 at the Council of Nicaea church leaders met to discuss the true nature of Christ which resulted in an ardent debate between two theologians—Arius and Athanasius. The former declared that Christ was not of a substance identical with God, He was not coeternal with Him; that God preceded or existed before Christ, that God created his Son. Athanasius espoused the view that Christ was consubstantial with God the Father and coeternal. The Trinity of Father, Son and Holy Spirit was declared to be really one substance; for mystery must prevail over reason or religion will perish. Constantine agreed with the Nicene Creed and ordered all books written by Arius be burned. Notwithstanding his devotion to Christianity the emperor didn't always practice it, for he committed at least three murders—he drowned his wife in a bath and murdered a son and a nephew.

When Constantine took over the government he reunited the two halves of the empire and ruled over both the east and west until 337. He also enjoyed the pomp and ceremony of the imperial court and he continued the policies of Diocletian—administrative, economic and social. He also encouraged education, literature, philosophy, rhetoric, law, medicine, art and architecture, and trained officials and teachers. However, Constantine hastened the decline of the importance of the old capital by constructing a new magnificent imperial seat of government at Byzantium which he called New Rome but which was later named the city of Constantine or Constantinople. The new capital site was not only elegant but it had an excellent harbor and could be made militarily impregnable, while Rome was very vulnerable to barbarian attack and invasion. Constantine's death was followed by disorder and civil strife as rival aspirants still sought the dubious glamor and prestige of being emperor. Meanwhile the land-hungry Germans continued their violent attacks on the Roman frontiers which were generally defended by inefficient, unpatriotic armies filled with barbarians who were often kinsmen of the soldiers on the enemy's side.

In 361 Julian, a nephew of Constantine's came to the throne. Although he was brought up as a Christian, he renounced the doctrines of the church deeming many of the beliefs superstitious, and aimed to replace the flourishing faith with a new form of paganism. It is said that he was also very much interested in Judaism and that he promised the Jews to help revive their homeland and rebuild their temple in Jerusalem. But he only ruled for two years and the emperors who followed Julian were Christians who resolved to extirpate paganism and establish one uniform religion for all the people. They forbade sacrifices to the many Asian and Egyptian Gods, closed or destroyed pagan temples and confiscated the revenue of their priests. The government also abolished the Olympic games, the Greek oracles and the Greek mystery cults and declared pagan worship a capital crime. In 380 Emperor Theodosius made the Catholic form of Christianity, as expounded in the Nicene Creed, the only legal religion in the empire and forbade all pagan cults and also prohibited the right of Christian heretics to hold office and bequeath property. Its fervent espousal by the government enhanced Christianity's prestige and esteem and made it more appealing and acceptable to the rich and aristocratic in addition to the humble and the poor. Theodosius was also the last Roman Emporer to rule both the east and the west divisions. After his death in 395 the empire was formally and finally divided into two independent states—the western Roman or Latin realm and the eastern Greek-oriented or Byzantine empire. Thenceforth the western emperors were just puppets who reigned but did not exercise any power; German military chieftains or generals set them up and were the real powers behind the throne. The last such puppet was Romulus, which was probably a derisive nickname because the first legendary king of Rome, back in 753 B.C., was also named Romulus. In 476 A.D. the second Romulus, the last Roman sovereign, was removed from his office and a German chieftain by the name of Odoacer took over the throne. Henceforth in the western half of the Roman empire the government remained in the hands of the German barbarians who crudely and roughly employed the traditional system of administration, its national and local political institutions. But they were unable to retain the unity of the various provinces. The empire became dismembered into several independent kingdoms conquered by various Teutonic tribes. The Ostrogoths occupied Italy and the lands on the eastern side of the Adriatic Sea, the Visigoths took over Spain, the Vandals dominated north Africa, the Franks subdued Gaul or modern France, and the Anglo-Saxons invaded and ruled over England.

The eastern Roman or Byzantine empire which had become independent in 395 never suffered the barbarization that the western world experienced. They too had been attacked by ferocious uncivilized hordes of German, Slavic and Asiatic tribes but all these barbarians had been driven away. The city of Constantinople was in those days virtually impregnable and so the Byzantine armies were able to repulse the barbarians and force them to move westward toward the path of less resistance. When the eastern Romans adopted the name Byzantine they let it be known that they were basically Greek rather than Roman. They rejected the Nicene Creed of Christianity and by the eleventh century they removed all forms of statuary or idols as they called them, from their churches, modified a few customs in their religious practices and severed their affiliation with the Roman Catholic organization. The Byzantines converted most of the Slavs, including the Russians, and their faith came to be known as the Greek Orthodox Church.

Until 565 the eastern emperors used Latin as the official language of the government though most of the people spoke Greek. Their political techniques were Roman and they used the laws of the Romans; in fact, their Emperor Justinian in the sixth century formulated the most definitive code of Roman law, which has influenced most of the legal systems of the western world. The empire lost part of its territory in the seventh century when Syria and Egypt broke away and were subsequently annexed by the then united Arabs. During most of its history the Byzantine empire comprised Greece, Macedonia and Asia Minor and its capital remained the gorgeous city of Constantinople. They didn't become decadent as Rome did because they had a strong economy; they enjoyed a thriving business—commercial, industrial and agricultural; they always had schools and culture; they also studied military tactics, the construction of fortifications and the art of war; they had a solid centralized government with a highly trained bureaucracy, not without corruption but always efficient, and an effective tax system. Assimilating eastern immigrants with a civilized background was easier than absorbing wild barbarians bent on plunder, a situation that confronted the west. Furthermore economic prosperity and competent government tend to promote high morale, loyalty and patriotism among the people. Unlike the west where the church only was looked up to for inspiration and guidance and where there were no secular schools, among the Byzantines, the emperor was in complete control of the church and the government and he encouraged education, art, literature and scholarship. These relatively happy people held out against furious barbarian attacks for a thousand years after the fall of Rome but they too finally succumbed in 1453 when the truculent Turks captured the famous entrepot and splendid metropolis, Constantinople or Istanbul, as they call it today.

In the western part of the empire decline and decay began to appear in the third century, after an active civilization of over eight hundred years. The government was weakened by constant civil strife between different armies seeking to put their favorite general on the throne. The bureaucracy was marked too often by inefficiency, venality and corruption, provincial governors were inept and rapacious and municipal government was helpless, being unable to collect taxes—hopelessly in debt and unable to govern. Dilapidated houses, public buildings, and institutions could not be maintained or renovated and new ones could not be built for lack of funds; there were too few prosperous business men left with sufficient money, incentive or civic pride. Streets and roads were in disrepair, crime was rampant on land and sea, and the officials were powerless while the army, composed of barbarians, was unconcerned about law and order and was much more devoted to wages and primitive pleasures. Extending from Scotland to Mesopotamia in the Middle East the empire was too large a political structure, too complex and ethnically heterogeneous to rule with the simple, elemental technology and rudimentary facilities of communication and transportation. The distant provinces were managed by appointed governors who were too often of limited intelligence and deficient in moral principles, or by subordinate, local monarchs who were perennially in revolt, desirous of seceding from the union. Many rural areas in the European territory were being controlled by great landowners who set up their own self-sufficient estates and became practically free—a new agrarian plutocracy. They provided protection and sustenance in return for farm labor, simple shop work and domestic service, thus anticipating the feudal and economic system of the Middle Ages. Some small farmers failed because their soil became exhausted or the climate in their particular region changed or perhaps they were ignorant of crop rotation or the scientific use of fertilizer or maybe they could not afford the improved methods of agriculture. Whatever the reason they fled to the city and when the middle class, the business men, abandoned the city they nearly all became workers, serfs or semi-slaves on the large estates of the lords.

The number of people in the empire or the rate of increase was declining as frequent war and plagues decimated the population. The old Roman stock, the middle and upper classes were seldom progenitively fruitful; the most prolific producers of offspring were of course the proletarians, but in times of economic depression they were unwanted by the government and the taxpayers. However, to encourage increased reproduction among literates and the well-to-do, Emperor Julian offered the *curiales* complete freedom if any one of them became the father of thirteen children. According to some historians the original strain of Romans had been obliterated and the majority of the Roman people (some say as much as eighty per cent) were descendants of slaves and immigrants—Greeks, Syrians, Jews, Egyptians, North Africans, Spaniards, Gauls, Britons and a few early

German arrivals. The Romans of the fifth century therefore were said to be devoid of qualities that had once been their greatest assets—love of country, a brave and aggressive spirit and great military skill. Even though there were many millions of Romans and only several hundred thousand German barbarians the Romans were unable to prevent the fall of their empire. Still the cities of the Byzantine Romans were also replete with immigrants of various ethnic background and yet they succeeded in driving away the barbarians and continued to thrive and live happily in an advanced cultured country for another thousand years.

One of the main causes for the decline and collapse of the Roman empire was probably the impoverishment of the mass of the people. Their patriotism had virtually disappeared because their morale was low, they were indifferent and apathetic and this psychological condition was produced by the perpetual economic slump. Why should they fight for a country where the government manipulated them, made them toil for dishonest bureaucrats, unscrupulous generals and privileged arrogant landowners. The exploited, destitute people of Rome concluded that only God could help them now, so they turned to the Christian church who would at least mitigate the misery and injustice of this life and grant them hope and charity and a promise of eternal happiness in a future world. To many converts other worldly mystical tendencies and transcendental meditation offered compensation or an avenue of escape. It led to the belief in asceticism as an ideal virtue—the cultivation of self-denial and self abnegation, that abstinence is good for the soul. This became an effective religious rationalization for the starving poor. The church did teach people to be peaceful and kind but if the masses had had something worthy to fight for the church certainly would not have stood in their way. In modern times a people's revolution would have been an inevitable salutary procedure but revolutions never succeed without aid from the army and the Roman soldiers were then also barbarians, ignorant relatives of the rulers and loyal only to their paymaster. Over the years the Romans had absorbed and assimilated a motley of ethnic groups from Greece, the middle east and north Africa. These people were already civilized and in many cases superior to the Romans, but now they were beset by barbarians and not just immigrants but armies of fierce conquerors, ignorant and ruthless, who seized the governments. It would take several hundred years to Romanize and civilize these newcomers as they were still in a very low state of development, on a par perhaps with the Aztecs and the Incas of Latin America. The first offspring of the Roman empire in the west that began to ripen and mature were those that had been provinces for a long time and had adopted and absorbed Roman customs—the Latin language, Roman law, political institutions and the Christian religion. These were Italy, France, Spain, Portugal and Romania. The Britons were a little less assimilated as they used their own legal system but the English language became more than half Latin thanks to the influence of the Catholic church and the French Normans who conquered England in the eleventh century.

The Romans also had overextended themselves. If they had not gone to the east to meddle in Greek, Egyptian and Asian politics and had concentrated instead on uniting the west back in the days of Julius Caesar, they might have created a large powerful state comprising almost all of western Europe with a fairly homogeneous population under one government, speaking the same language and following the same customs and mores. Over the centuries the Romans must have lost hundreds of thousands of their finest soldiers, many potentially cultured young men in their wars in the east. Greek and Oriental enlightenment would have filtered into the western world through commerce and travel much more effectively and less expensively than by war.

Although weak and enfeebled western Europe was taken over by virile, ferocious primitives, Roman civilization did not revert to complete barbarism. Owing to the well organized, disciplined church the uncouth German heathens were converted to Christianity, which not only curbed and restrained some of their truculence, it also educated and cultivated a few and made it possible to keep some of the Greco-Roman civilization alive. Although they were thoroughly steeped in mysticism and supernaturalism, the clergy, particularly the monks, respected the cultural achievements of the ancient scholars and authors, and therefore copied and preserved many of their great works. Also there were still a few literate Roman laymen of the old stock, among the great landlords and the few city dwellers who cooperated with the clergy. But secular schools were virtually non-existent, having been officially abolished by the authorities in the sixth century because the German rulers found no need for them. As the government fell into the hands of a semi-civilized untutored civil service staff it deteriorated and became unreliable, while the church with its strong and wealthy organization, modeled after traditional Roman law and political customs, commanded great deference and allegiance from the poeple.

Thus western civilization did not collapse completely—it entered a period known as the dark ages which would last for several hundred years. During this period the people were mostly uneducated, superstitious and benighted, and political disintegration was accompanied by social and intellectual decay. Creative ability in literature and the fine arts was absent. A bit of enlightenment, however, did appear in the eighth century and much more in the twelfth when a few individuals began to comprehend the meaning of the old classical ideas, but not until the sixteenth century did Western Europe catch up with the ancient Greeks, Romans, the Semites, the Hindus and the Chinese. And not until the advent of the scientific and technological revolutions did the western world surpass all previous civilizations. This superiority pertains to science, medicine and technology, to the present abundance of desirable goods, greater creature comforts and the increase in man's life span. But human nature remains the same in spite of countless centuries of religious and moral education, exhortation and the inculcation of ethical and spiritual idealism by religionists, theologians and philosophers. Men are just as selfish, corrupt, covetous and avaricious as ever. Poverty and crime still prevail, wars and massacres are more horrible and deadly than they were in antiquity and most people are still primarily interested in the pursuit of power and pleasure just as they were in the ancient world.

BIBLIOGRAPHY

I General Ancient History

Albright, W.F., From the Stone Age to Christianity
Breasted, J.H., Ancient Times
Caldwell, W.E., The Ancient World
Cambridge Ancient History
Muller, H.J., The Uses of the Past
Roebuck, C., The World of Ancient Times
Rostovtzeff, M.I., History of the Ancient World
Scramuzza, V., and Mackendrick, P., The Ancient World
Starr, C., A History of the Ancient World
Swain, J.W., The Ancient World
Trever, A.A., History of Ancient Civilization
Van Sickle, C.E., A Political and Cultural History of the Ancient World

II Prehistoric Man

Boas, Franz, The Mind of Primitive Man
Burkitt, M.C., Our Early Ancestors
Ceram, C., Gods, Graves and Scholars
Clark, Grahame, World Prehistory
Hooten, E.A., Up from the Ape
Levy-Bruhl, Lucien, How Natives Think
Linton, Ralph, The Tree of Culture
Lowie, R.M., Primitive Society
Radin, Paul, Primitive Religion
Renard, G.F., Life and Work in Prehistoric Times

III Egypt and Southwestern Asia

Baikie, James, A History of Egypt
Baron, S.W., History of the Jews
Breasted, J.H., A History of Egypt
Erman, Adolf, Life in Ancient Egypt
Contenau, G., Everyday Life in Babylonia and Assyria
Hall, H.R., Ancient History of the Near East
Frankfort, Henry, Birth of Civilization in the Near East
Jastrow, Morris, The Civilization of Babylonia and Assyria
Olmstead, A.T., History of the Persian Empire
Orlinsky, H.M., Ancient Israel
Rogers, R.W., History of Ancient Persia
Woolley, C.L., The Sumerians

IV India and China

Eberhard, Wolfram, A History of China
Fitzgerald, C.P., China, A Short Cultural History
Gowen, H.H., and Hall, J.W., An Outline History of China
Goodrich, L.C., A Short History of the Chinese People
Grousset, René, The Rise and Splendor of the Chinese Empire
Grousset, René, The Civilization of India
Hopkins, E.W., The Religions of India
Latourette, K.S., The Chinese, Their History and Culture
Mookerji, R.K., The History and Culture of the Indian People
Macdonnell, A.A., India's Past
Moore, C.A., The Story of Chinese Philosophy
Rawlinson, H.G., India, A Short Cultural History
Rice, Stanley, Hindu Customs and their Origin
Wilhelm, Richard, A Short History of Chinese Civilization

V Greece

Botsford, G.W., and Robinson, C.A., Hellenic History
Bury, J.B., History of Greece
Cary, M., and Haarhoff, T.J., Life and Thought in the Greek and Roman World
Couch, H.N., Classical Civilization

Dickinson, G.L., The Greek View of Life
Ehrenberg, Victor, The Greek State
Hamilton, Edith, The Greek Way
Jaeger, W., The Ideas of Greek Culture
Kitto, H.D.F., The Greeks
Laistner, M.L.W., Greek History
Mahaffy, J.P., What Have the Greeks Done for Modern Civilization
Robin, Leon, Greek Thought and the Origin of the Scientific Spirit
Robinson, C.E., Everyday Life in Ancient Greece
Sarton, George, A History of Science
Tarn, W.W., Hellenistic Civilization
Toynbee, A.J., Greek Civilization and Character
Warbeke, J.M., The Searching Mind of Greece
Zeller, Edward, Outlines of Greek Philosophy
Zimmern, A.E., The Greek Commonwealth

VI Rome

Abbott, F.F., Common People of Ancient Rome
Barrow, R.H., The Romans
Boak, A.E.R., and Sinnigen, W.G., A History of Rome
Bury, J.B., History of the Later Roman Empire
Carcopino, J., Daily Life in Ancient Rome
Carter, J.B., Religious Life in Ancient Rome
Cary, Max, A History of Rome
Chambers, Mortimer, The Fall of Rome
Charlesworth, M.P., The Roman Empire
Davis, W.S., A Day in Old Rome
Dudley, D.R., Civilization of Rome
Enslin, M.S., Christian Beginnings
Frank, Tenney, The Economic History of Rome
—— Life and Literature in the Roman Republic
—— Roman Imperialism
Geer, R.N., Classical Civilization: Rome
Grant, Michael, The World of Rome
Hamilton, Edith, The Roman Way
Hexter, J.H., The Judaeo-Christian Tradition
Katz, Solomon, The Decline of Rome
Lewis, Paul, Ancient Rome at Work

Lot, Ferdinand, The End of the Ancient World
Rostovtzeff, M.I., Social and Economic History of the Roman Empire
Showerman, G., Eternal Rome
Taylor, H.O., The Emergence of Christian Culture in the West
Walbank, F.W., The Decline of the Roman Empire

INDEX

Actium, 197
Aegeans, 107
Aeschylus, 147
Aesculapius, 161
Aesop, 137, 150
Akbar, 61, 62, 63
Alexander the Great, 126, 127, 128, 129
Alexander Severus, 272
Alexandria, 169, 170, 171, 210
Alphabet, 17, 18, 42, 110
Anaximander, 153
Antioch, 169
Antoninus Pius, 207
Antony, Marc, 196, 197
Aramaeans, 40
Architecture, Egyptian, 16; Indian, 75; Mesopotamian, 35; Chinese, 94, 95; Greek, 143, 144; Roman, 232, 233
Aristarchus, 152
Aristophanes, 148
Aristotle, 154, 164, 165
Art, Prehistoric, 5, 6; Egyptian, 17; Mesopotamian, 35; Indian, 75; Chinese, 94, 95; Greek, 143, 144, 145, 171; Roman, 232, 233

Asoka, 60
Assurbanipal, 34
Assyrians, 25, 26
Astrology, 33
Athens, 117 ff.
Augustus, 199 ff.
Aurangzeb, 64
Aurelius, Marcus, 207, 241, 242

Babur, 62
Babylonia, see Mesopotamia,
Book of the Dead, 15
Brahmans, 58, 59
Buddhism, 60, 72, 73, 83, 103, 104
Bulban, 61
Byzantine Empire, 280

Caesar, Julius, 191-196, 227, 234, 236, 237
Calendar, 18, 234
Caligula, 200, 201, 226
Cambyses, 51
Cannae, Battle of, 182
Cannibalism, 5, 7
Caracalla, 270, 271
Carthage, 179, 180
Caste system, 58, 59

Catullus, 228
Celsus, 237
Chaeronea, Battle of, 126
Chaldeans, 26
Cheops, see Khufu
Chin dynasty, 78
Chou dynasty, 78
Christianity, 256, 260 ff.
Cicero, 196, 227, 242
Claudius, 200, 201
Cleisthenes, 120, 121
Cleopatra, 194-198
Coloni, 276
Commodus, 268
Confucius, 100, 101, 102
Constantine, 267, 268 ff.
Constantinople, 279
Crete, 107, 108
Croesus, 40
Curiales, 277
Cybelian religion, the, 38, 39, 250, 251
Cynics, 167
Cyrenaics, 167
Cyrus, 51

Darius, 54
David, 44
Delphic oracle, 139
Democritus, 152
Demosthenes, 150
Diocletian, 274 ff.
Diogenes, 167, 168
Domitian, 205, 206
Draco, 118
Dravidians, 58
Economic life, Egypt, 10, 11; Mesopotamia, 23, 24; China, 84, 85, 91, 92; Greece, 110, 117, 118, 130, 131; Rome, 211, 212, 215, 216
Edict of Milan, 278
Education; Egypt, 18; Chinese, 96, 97; Jewish, 50, 51; Persian, 53; Greek, 137; Roman, 224, 225
Empedocles, 153
Epictetus, 241
Epicureanism, 168, 227, 239
Eratosthenes, 153
Essenes, 255, 257
Etruscans, 173, 176
Euclid, 151
Euripides, 147

Family, Prehistoric, 6, 7; China, 93, 94; Rome, 218, 219

Gaius, 200
Galen, 237, 238
Galerius, 267
Gauls, 176, 183
Genghiz Khan, 88
Gladiatorial contests, 221 ff.
Gracchi, 188, 189
Great Wall of China, 79
Gupta dynasty, 60

Hadrian, 206, 207, 210
Hammurabi, 28
Han dynasty, 80, 82
Hebrews, 42 ff.
Hellenistic civilization, 169-171
Heraclitus, 158
Herodotus, 149
Heron, 152

Hesiod, 146
Hinduism, 61, 68-71
Hippocrates, 156
Hittites, 37
Homer, 145
Horace, 228, 239
Hyksos, 13

Ikhnaton, 16
Imhotep, 19
Isis and Osiris, 250

Jahan, 64
Jahangir, 63
Jainism, 71, 72
Jenghiz Khan, 88
Jesus, 256 ff.
Jews, 42 ff., 253 ff.
Josephus, 229
Judaism, 48-49; 253 ff.
Julian, 279, 280, 282
Justinian, 213
Juvenal, 230

Khufu, 16
Kublai Khan, 88

Lao-tse, 102, 103
Latifundia, 185
Law, Egyptian, 19;
    Mesopotamian, 26, 27; Jewish,
    49, 50; Persian, 51, 53; Indian,
    65, 66; Chinese, 92; Greek,
    114, 116, 120-122; Roman,
    175, 213, 214
Legalists, 104
Leucippus, 152
Literature, Egyptian, 17, 18;

Mesopotamian, 34; Jewish, 50;
    Indian, 74, 75; Chinese, 95;
    Greek, 145-149; 171; Roman,
    225-230
Livy, 228
Lucretius, 227, 239, 240
Lydians, 39, 40

Manchus, 90
Mandarins, 84, 92, 97
Marathon, Battle of, 123
Marcus Aurelius, 241, 242
Marius, 190
Mauryan dynasty, 60
Medicine, Prehistoric, 4;
    Egyptian, 18, 19;
    Mesopotamian, 32-34; Persian,
    54; Indian, 74; Chinese, 97;
    Greek, 154, 157; Roman, 236
    ff.
Mencius, 104
Milan, Edict of, 278
Ming dynasty, 90
Ming Huang, 85
Mithraism, 251-253, 262
Mithradates, 191
Mogul dynasty, 61
Mohists, 104
Mongols, 88
Moses, 43
Mo Ti, 104
Music, Indian, 76; Chinese, 95;
    Greek, 144, 145; Roman, 231
Nebuchadnezzar, 36
Nero, 200-205, 269
Nerva, 206
Nicaea, Council of, 278
Nicene Creed, 278, 280

Nirvana, 69

Octavian, 197, 198
Olympic games, 140, 141
Ovid, 228

Parthenon, 143, 144
Patricians, 175
Paul, 260, 265
Peloponnesian War, 124, 125
Pericles, 121, 122, 124, 137
Persia, 51 ff.
Pheidippides, 123
Phidias, 144
Philip of Macedonia, 125, 126
Philosophy, Chinese, 100-105;
  Greek, 157-169; Roman,
  239-242
Phoenicians, 41; economic life,
  41; religion, 41, 42; alphabet,
  42
Phrygians, 38
Pindar, 146
Pisistratus, 120
Plautus, 226
Plato, 163, 164
Plebeians, 176
Pliny, the Elder, 230, 235, 236,
  238, 239
Plutarch, 229
Polybius, 227
Pompeii, 210, 211
Pompey, 191, 192
Praetorian Guard, 201
Ptolemy, the astronomer, 152
Punic Wars, 180, 181, 182,
  184
Pythagoras, 153, 158

Religion, Prehistoric, 2, 3, 4;
  Egyptian, 13-16;
  Mesopotamian, 29-31;
  Phoenician, 41, 42; Jewish,
  43-49, 253-257; Persian, 54,
  55; Phrygian, 38; Indian, 68,
  70-73; Chinese, 85, 98-104;
  Greek, 137-143; Roman,
  244-251; Christian, 256-285
Romulus, 280

Salamis, Battle of, 123
Sallust, 227
Sappho, 137, 146
Science and Mathematics,
  Egyptian, 18; Mesopotamian,
  32-34; Indian, 73, 74; Chinese,
  97, 98; Greek, 150-154;
  Roman, 233, 234
Scipio Africanus, 182
Scythians, 40
Seneca, 201, 203, 224, 235, 241
Shang dynasty, 78
Shi Huang Ti, 78, 79
Socrates, 161, 162, 163
Solomon, 44, 45
Solon, 119, 120
Sophists, 160
Sophocles, 147
Sparta, 112 ff.
Spartacus, 218
Sports and Amusements, Greeks,
  140, 141; Romans, 221-223
Stoicism, 168, 169, 240
Strabo, 234, 235
Suetonius, 280
Sulla, 190
Suis, 83

Sung dynasty, 87

Tacitus, 229
Taj Mahal, 64
Tai Tsung, 84
Tamerlane, 61
Tang dynasty, 83
Taoism, 102-104
Terence, 226
Thales, 150, 157
Theater and Drama, Chinese, 95; Greek, 146-149; Roman, 226
Themistocles, 123
Theodosius, 280
Thermopylae, Battle of, 123
Thucydides, 150
Thutmose, III, 13
Tiberius, 200
Titus, 205
Trajan, 206, 210
Untouchables, 59
Upanishads, 68, 74
Ur, 42

Vedas, 68, 74

Vergil, 228, 239
Vespasian, 205

Wang An Shih, 87
Wang Mang, 81, 82
Women, Prehistoric 2, 4, 6; Egypt, 20; Mesopotamia, 28, 29, 32; Israel, 50; Persia, 53; Scythian, 40; India, 65, 67, 68; China, 85, 93, 94; Greece, 108, 109, 115, 116, 134-137; Rome, 218-221
Wu Ti, 81

Xenophanes, 157
Xenophon, 150
Xerxes, 53, 124

Yang Ti, 83
Yang and Yin, 77, 93
Yoga, 69

Zama, Battle of, 182
Zeno, 168, 240, 241
Ziggurat, 35